GW01164032

CHINESE HEALTH TEA

Dang Yi, Wang Huizhu, Peng Yong

NEW WORLD PRESS

First Edition 1999
Edited by Ren Lingjuan
Book Design by Fang Wei
Cover Design by He Yuting

Copyright by New World Press, Beijing, China. All rights reserved. No part of this book may be reproduced in any form or by any means without permission in writing from the publisher.

ISBN-7-80005-554-X/G • 187

Published by
NEW WORLD PRESS
24 Baiwanzhuang Road, Beijing 100037, China

Distributed by
CHINA INTERNATIONAL BOOK TRADING CORPORATION
35 Chegongzhuang Xilu, Beijing 100044, China
P. O. Box 399, Beijing, China

Printed in the People's Republic of China

CONTENTS

Preface   i

保健篇 The Tea for Maintaining Health   1

01 益智健脑 For Promoting Intelligence   1
01.01 人参茶 Renshen Cha
01.02 人参大枣茶 Renshen Dazao Cha
01.03 脑清茶 Naoqing Cha
01.04 龙眼洋参饮 Longyan Yangshen Yin
01.05 灵芝薄荷饮 Lingzhi Bohe Yin

02 健美减肥 For Reducing Weight   3
02.01 三花减肥茶 Sanhua Jianfei Cha
02.02 山楂根茶 Shanzhagen Cha
02.03 山楂银菊茶 Shanzha Yin Ju Cha
02.04 牛奶茶 Niunai Cha
02.05 桑枝茶 Sangzhi Cha
02.06 荷叶茶 Heye Cha
02.07 荷叶减肥茶 Heye Jianfei Cha
02.08 减肥茶 I Jianfei Cha I
02.09 减肥茶 II Jianfei Cha II
02.10 罗布麻减肥茶 Luobuma Jianfeicha

03 明目增视 For Improving Vision   7
03.01 玉竹薄荷饮 Yuzhu Bohe Yin
03.02 决明子茶 Juemingzi Cha
03.03 杞菊茶 Qi Ju Cha
03.04 谷精菊花饮 Gujing Juhua Yin
03.05 明目茶 I Mingmu Cha I
03.06 明目茶 II Mingmu Cha II
03.07 枸杞茶 Gouqi Cha
03.08 桑银茶 Sang Yin Cha

I

03.09 草决明茶 Caojueming Cha
03.10 羚羊菊花茶 Lingyang Juhua Cha
03.11 黄芩茶 Huangqin Cha
03.12 黄花菜马齿苋饮 Huanghuacai Machixian Yin

04 美容美发 For Beautifying the Hair　　　　　　　　　　11
04.01 何首乌茶 Heshouwu Cha
04.02 芝麻枸杞饮 Zhima Gouqi Yin
04.03 嫩肤饮 Nenfu Yin

05 补虚益寿 For Invigorating Qi and Blood and Prolonging Life　　12
05.01 八仙茶 Baxian Cha
05.02 人参核桃饮 Renshen Hetao Yin
05.03 山楂核桃茶 Shanzha Hetao Cha
05.04 太子奶饮 Taizinai Yin
05.05 西洋参茶 Xiyangshen Cha
05.06 杞叶长寿茶 Qiye Changshou Cha
05.07 沙苑子茶 Shayuanzi Cha
05.08 刺五加茶 Ciwujia Cha
05.09 枸杞五味子茶 Gouqi Wuweizi Cha
05.10 红枣茶 I　Hongzao Cha I
05.11 黄精茶 Huangjing Cha
05.12 当归补血饮 Danggui Buxue Yin
05.13 擂茶 I　Lei Cha I
05.14 擂茶 II　Lei Cha II
05.15 复盆子茶 Fupenzi Cha
05.16 党参黄米茶 Dangshen Huangmi Cha
05.17 灵芝茶 Lingzhi Cha

06 益气养心 For Benefiting Qi and Nourishing the Heart　　20
06.01 人参汤 Renshen Tang
06.02 人参枣仁汤 Renshen Zaoren Tang
06.03 牛乳饮 Niuru Yin
06.04 花生红枣茶 Huasheng Hongzao Cha
06.05 参芪精 Shen Qi Jing
06.06 菖蒲茶 Changpu Cha
06.07 龙眼茶 Longyan Cha
06.08 龙眼枣仁饮 Longyan Zaoren Yin

07 镇静安神 For Tranquilizing   23

07.01 安神茶 Anshen Cha
07.02 柏子仁茶 Baiziren Cha
07.03 参味茶 Shen Wei Cha
07.04 丝瓜饮 I Sigua Yin I
07.05 灯心竹叶茶 Dengxin Zhuye Cha
07.06 党参红枣茶 Dangshen Hongzao Cha

08 利咽爽音 For Clearing Heat and Treating Sore Throat   26

08.01 二绿玉冰茶 Erlu Yu Bing Cha
08.02 西青果茶 Xiqingguo Cha
08.03 百合茶 Baihe Cha
08.04 胖大海冰糖茶 Pangdahai Bingtang Cha
08.05 茶榄海蜜饮 Cha Lan Hai Mi Yin
08.06 清咽饮 I Qingyan Yin I
08.07 清喉茶 Qinghou Cha
08.08 参叶青果茶 Shenye Qingguo Cha
08.09 丝瓜饮 II Sigua Yin II
08.10 银麦甘桔饮 Yin Mai Gan Jie Yin
08.11 绿茶合欢饮 Lucha Hehuan Yin
08.12 点地梅茶 Diandimei Cha
08.13 罗汉果速溶饮 Luohanguo Surongyin
08.14 苏叶茶 Suye Cha

09 生津止渴 For Promoting the Production of Body Fluid and Relieving Thirst   31

09.01 人参乌梅茶 Renshen Wumei Cha
09.02 三汁饮 Sanzhi Yin
09.03 三鲜茶 I Sanxian Cha I
09.04 五味子饮 Wuweizi Yin
09.05 玉竹茶 Yuzhu Cha
09.06 玉竹乌梅饮 Yuzhu Wumei Yin
09.07 甘蔗茶 Ganzhe Cha
09.08 石斛冰糖茶 Shihu Bingtang Cha
09.09 石斛甘蔗饮 Shihu Ganzhe Yin
09.10 生津茶 Shengjin Cha
09.11 花粉茶 Huafen Cha
09.12 苦竹叶速溶饮 Kuzhuye Surongyin

09.13 丝瓜茶 Sigua Cha
09.14 双花饮 Shuanghua Yin

10 温中暖胃 For Warming the Stomach and Strengthening the Middle *Jiao*   37
10.01 一味生姜饮 Yiwei Shengjiang Yin
10.02 丁香茶 Dingxiang Cha
10.03 刀豆饮 Daodou Yin
10.04 刀豆茶 I Daodou Cha I
10.05 艾叶茶 Aiye Cha
10.06 桂皮山楂饮 Guipi Shanzha Yin
10.07 干姜饮 Ganjiang Yin
10.08 益胃茶 I Yiwei Cha I
10.09 健胃茶 I Jianwei Cha I
10.10 健胃茶 II Jianwei Cha II
10.11 暖胃茶 Nuanwei Cha
10.12 葱姜饮 I Cong Jiang Yin I
10.13 葱椒饮 Cong Jiao Yin
10.14 橘花茶 Juhua Cha
10.15 糖糟茶 Tangzao Cha
10.16 薏苡叶茶 Yiyiye Cha

11 补肾聪耳 For Invigorating the Kidney and Clear Hearing   43
11.01 人参枸杞饮 Renshen Gouqi Yin
11.02 丹皮京菖茶 Danpi Jingchang Cha
11.03 平肝清热茶 Pinggan Qingre Cha
11.04 参须京菖茶 Shenxu Jingchang Cha
11.05 菟丝子茶 Tusizi Cha
11.06 槐菊茶 Huai Ju Cha

12 理气悦心 For Regulating *Qi* and Alleviating Mental Depression   45
12.01 二花参麦茶 Erhua Shen Mai Cha
12.02 二花桔萸茶 Erhua Ju Yu Cha
12.03 二绿合欢茶 Erlu Hehuan Cha
12.04 二绿女贞茶 Erlu Nuzhen Cha
12.05 佛手茶 Foshou Cha
12.06 佛手枣汤 Foshou Zao Tang
12.07 玫瑰花茶 Meiguihua Cha

12.08 青皮麦芽饮 Qingpi Maiya Yin
12.09 厚朴花茶 Houpuhua Cha
12.10 胃乐茶 Weile Cha
12.11 绿萼梅茶 Luemei Cha
12.12 橘朴茶 Ju Pu Cha
12.13 橘叶饮 Juye Yin
12.14 夏枯瓜络饮 Xiaku Gualuo Yin

13 开胃消食 For Increasing Appetite and Relieving Dyspepsia 51
13.01 二根麦萝茶 Ergen Mai Luo Cha
13.02 山楂茶 Shanzha Cha
13.03 山楂橘皮茶 Shanzha Jupi Cha
13.04 山楂神曲汤 Shanzha Shenqu Tang
13.05 小儿七星茶 Xiaoer Qixing Cha
13.06 甘露茶 Ganlu Cha
13.07 白蔻茶 Baikou Cha
13.08 谷芽露茶 Guyalu Cha
13.09 佩香茶 Pei Xiang Cha
13.10 金橘茶 Jinju Cha
13.11 玳玳花茶 Daidaihua Cha
13.12 砂仁甘草茶 Sharen Gancao Cha
13.13 消滞茶 Xiaozhi Cha
13.14 消食茶 Xiaoshi Cha
13.15 神曲饮 Shenqu Yin
13.16 陈茗饮 Chenming Yin
13.17 莱菔子饮 Laifuzi Yin
13.18 陈仓米柿饼霜茶 Chencangmi Shibingshuang Cha
13.19 麦芽茶 Maiya Cha
13.20 麦芽山楂饮 Maiya shanzha Yin
13.21 棉壳茶 Mianke Cha
13.22 隔山消白糖饮 Geshanxiao Baitang Yin
13.23 橘枣饮 Ju Zao Yin
13.24 橙子蜂蜜饮 Chengzi Fengmi Yin
13.25 蔷薇根茶 Qiangweigen Cha
13.26 槟榔饮 Binglang Yin
13.27 芦根饮 I Lugen Yin I
13.28 芦根饮 II Lugen Yin II
13.29 萝卜叶茶 I Luoboye Cha I

13.30 萝卜叶鸡蛋饮 Luoboye Jidan Yin

防治篇 For Treatment 62

14 风寒感冒 For Wind-Cold 62
14.01 刀豆茶 II Daodou Cha II
14.02 川芎糖茶 Chuanxiong Tang Cha
14.03 天中茶 Tianzhong Cha
14.04 五神汤 Wushen Tang
14.05 午时茶 Wushi Cha
14.06 白菜绿豆芽饮 Baicai Ludouya Yin
14.07 芫荽茶 Yuansui Cha
14.08 姜糖饮 I Jiang Tang Yin I
14.09 姜糖茶 I Jiang Tang Cha I
14.10 姜糖苏叶饮 Jiang Tang Suye Yin
14.11 桔姜茶 Ju Jiang Cha
14.12 紫苏叶茶 Zisuye Cha
14.13 葱姜饮 II Cong Jiang Yin II
14.14 葱豉茶 I Cong Chi Cha I
14.15 葱豉茶 II Cong Chi Cha II
14.16 葱豉饮 Cong Chi Yin
14.17 薏米防风饮 Yimi Fangfeng Yin
14.18 苏杏汤 Su Xing Tang
14.19 苏羌茶 Su Qiang Cha
14.20 藿香白蔻饮 Huoxiang Baikou Yin

15 风热感冒 For Wind-Heat 72
15.01 三鲜茶 II Sanxian Cha II
15.02 牛蒡子茶 Niubangzi Cha
15.03 六叶茶（感冒茶）Liuye Cha (Ganmao Cha)
15.04 加味菊花茶 Jiawei Juhua Cha
15.05 防风甘草茶 Fangfeng Gancao Cha
15.06 芥菜茶 Jiecai Cha
15.07 桑叶茶 Sangye Cha
15.08 桑菊茶 I Sang Ju Cha I
15.09 桑菊豆豉饮 Sang Ju Douchi Yin
15.10 桑菊薄竹饮 Sang Ju Bo Zhu Yin

15.11 苍耳子茶　Cangerzi Cha
15.12 薄荷茶 I　Bohe Cha I
15.13 薄荷茶 II　Bohe Cha II
15.14 薄荷芦根饮　Bohe Lugen Yin
15.15 薄荷砂糖饮　Bohe Shatang Yin

16　流行性感冒　For Influenza　　　　　　　　　　　　79

16.01 大青叶茶　Daqingye Cha
16.02 生姜茶　Shengjiang Cha
16.03 白菜根饮　Baicaigen Yin
16.04 白杨树皮茶　Baiyangshupi Cha
16.05 板蓝根茶　Banlangen Cha
16.06 盲肠草茶　Mangchangcao Cha
16.07 夏菊茶　Xia Ju Cha
16.08 贯仲茶　Guanzhong Cha
16.09 复方贯仲茶　Fufang Guanzhong Cha
16.10 苍术贯仲茶　Cangzhu Guanzhong Cha

17　其他类型感冒　For Colds of Other Types　　　　　　82

17.01 三鲜茶 III　Sanxian Cha III
17.02 水翁花茶　Shuiwenghua Cha
17.03 加减石膏饮　Jiajian Shigao Yin
17.04 加减香薷饮　Jiajian Xiangru Yin
17.05 车前子茶　Cheqianzi Cha
17.06 芳香化浊饮　Fangxiang Huazhuo Yin
17.07 苡仁竹叶饮　Yiren Zhuye Yin
17.08 香薷饮　Xiangru Yin
17.09 桑菊香豉梨皮饮　Sang Ju Xiangchi Lipi Yin
17.10 桑薄花蜜饮　Sang Bo Hua Mi Yin
17.11 黄瓜叶速溶饮　Huangguaye Surongyin
17.12 都梁茶　Duliang Cha
17.13 慈豉芦根饮　Cong Chi Lugen Yin
17.14 鸡苏饮　Jisu Yin
17.15 藿香饮　Huoxiang Yin
17.16 藿香芦根饮　Huoxiang Lugen Yin
17.17 芦根苡仁饮　Lugen Yiren Yin
17.18 芦根冰糖饮　Lugen Bingtang Yin
17.19 盐柠檬茶　Yan Ningmeng Cha

17.20 盐茶 Yan Cha

18 中暑 For Sun-Stroke 92

18.01 二鲜三花饮 Erxian Sanhua Cha
18.02 丁香酸梅汤 Dingxiang Suanmei Tang
18.03 七鲜汤 Qixian Tang
18.04 七鲜茶 Qixian Cha
18.05 七叶芦根饮 Qiye Lugen Yin
18.06 三叶茶 Sanye Cha
18.07 三鲜茶 I Sanxian Cha I
18.08 山楂荷叶茶 Shanzha Heye Cha
18.09 五味枸杞饮 Wuwei Gouqi Yin
18.10 五叶芦根茶 Wuye Lugen Cha
18.11 太子乌梅饮 Taizi Wumei Yin
18.12 四味茶 Siwei Cha
18.13 生脉饮 Shengmai Yin
18.14 地榆叶茶 Diyuye Cha
18.15 百解茶 Baijie Cha
18.16 防暑茶 Fangshu Cha
18.17 金银花茶 Jinyinhua Cha
18.18 金花牡荆茶 Jinhua Mujing Cha
18.19 金鸡脚草茶 Jinjijiaocao Cha
18.20 沙母二草茶 Sha Mu Ercao Cha
18.21 苦瓜茶 Kugua Cha
18.22 苦刺花茶 Kucihua Cha
18.23 茉莉花茶 Molihua Cha
18.24 建曲茶 Jianqu Cha
18.25 桑蜜茶 Sang Mi Cha
18.26 祛暑清心茶 Qushu Qingxin Cha
18.27 乌梅清暑饮 Wumei Qingshu Yin
18.28 清络饮 Qingluo Yin
18.29 清暑茶 I Qingshu Cha I
18.30 清暑茶 II Qingshu Cha II
18.31 清暑茶 III Qingshu Cha III
18.32 清暑明目茶 Qingshu Mingmu Cha
18.33 清暑解毒茶 Qingshu Jiedu Cha
18.34 清暑益气饮 Qingshu Yiqi Yin
18.35 淡盐糖水 Danyan Tangshui

VIII

18.36 野秋根茶 Yeshugen Cha
18.37 雪梨饮 Xueli Yin
18.38 焦大麦茶 Jiaodamai Cha
18.39 绿豆酸梅茶 Ludou Suanmei Cha
18.40 绿豆蜂蜜饮 Ludou Fengmi Yin
18.41 酸梅茶 Suanmei Cha
18.42 蔗菊茶 Zhe Ju Cha
18.43 积雪草茶 Jixuecao Cha
18.44 柠檬速溶饮 Ningmeng Surongyin
18.45 鸡骨草茶 Jigucao Cha
18.46 鸡蛋花茶 Jidanhua Cha
18.47 双皮茶 Shuangpi Cha
18.48 药王茶 Yaowangcha
18.49 藿香夏枯草茶 Huoxiang Xiakucao Cha
18.50 苏叶薄荷茶 Suye Bohe Cha

19 暑疖 For the Furuncle Due to Summer Heat   112

19.01 忍冬藤茶 Rendongteng Cha
19.02 银花露茶 Yinhualu Cha
19.03 银花绿豆茶 Yinhua Ludou Cha

20 咽喉炎、扁桃腺炎 For Pharyngotonsillitis   113

20.01 大海茶 I Dahai Cha I
20.02 大海瓜子茶 Dahai Guazi Cha
20.03 土牛膝茶 Tuniuxi Cha
20.04 甘桔速溶饮 Gan Jie Surongyin
20.05 玄参青果茶 Xuanshen Qingguo Cha
20.06 玄麦甘桔汤 Xuanmai Gan Jie Tang
20.07 加减清燥润肺饮 Jiajian Qingzao Runfei Yin
20.08 百两金茶 Bailiangjin Cha
20.09 冰糖木蝴蝶饮 Bingtang Muhudie Yin
20.10 利咽茶 Liyan Cha
20.11 防疫清咽茶 Fangyi Qingyan Cha
20.12 金锁茶 Jinsuo Cha
20.13 威灵仙茶 Weilingxian Cha
20.14 咽喉茶 Yanhou Cha
20.15 消炎茶 Xiaoyan Cha
20.16 清咽饮 II Qingyan Yin II

IX

20.17 清咽四味茶 Qingyan Siwei Cha
20.18 丝瓜速溶饮 Sigua Surongyin
20.19 诃玉茶 He Yu Cha
20.20 蜂蜜茶 I Fengmi Cha I
20.21 绿茶梅花饮 Lucha Meihua Yin
20.22 绿合海糖茶 Lu He Hai Tang Cha
20.23 酸浆草茶 Suanjiangcao Cha
20.24 凤衣冬蜜饮 Fengyi Dong Mi Yin
20.25 莲花茶叶茶 Lianhua Chaye Cha
20.26 蝶菊茶蜜饮 Die Ju Cha Mi Yin
20.27 橄榄冰糖饮 Ganlan Bingtang Yin
20.28 橄榄白萝卜茶 Ganlan Bailuobo Cha
20.29 萝卜糖姜饮 Luobo Tang Jiang Yin

21 咳嗽、哮喘 For Coughs and Asthma 125
21.01 人参双花茶 Renshen Shuanghua Cha
21.02 三子饮 Sanzi Yin
21.03 三分茶 Sanfen Cha
21.04 三白茶 Sanbai Cha
21.05 大蒜冰糖茶 Dasuan Bingtang Cha
21.06 小麦大枣饮 Xiaomai Dazao Yin
21.07 川贝莱菔茶 Chuanbei Laifu Cha
21.08 川贝杏仁饮 Chuanbei Xingren Yin
21.09 止咳茶 Zhike Cha
21.10 毛山茶(香风茶) Maoshancha (Xiangfengcha)
21.11 玉米须桔皮茶 Yumixu Jupi Cha
21.12 甘草醋茶 Gancao Cu Cha
21.13 甘草生姜汤 Gancao Shengjiang Tang
21.14 冬瓜麦冬饮 Donggua Maidong Yin
21.15 百药煎茶 Baiyaojian Cha
21.16 百部四味饮 Baibu Siwei Yin
21.17 杏梨饮 Xing Li Yin
21.18 杏仁冰糖饮 Xingren Bingtang Yin
21.19 杏仁奶茶 Xingren Nai Cha
21.20 皂荚芽茶 Zaojiaya Cha
21.21 沙参百合饮 Shashen Baihe Yin
21.22 沙参梨皮饮 Shashen Lipi Yin
21.23 沙参麦冬饮 Shashen Maidong Yin

X

21.24 车前根茶 Cheqiangen Cha
21.25 芹菜根陈皮茶 Qincaigen Chenpi Cha
21.26 定嗽定喘饮 Dingsou Dingchuan Yin
21.27 柚子壳荷叶饮 Youzike Heye Yin
21.28 柿蒂茶 Shidi Cha
21.29 胡萝卜大枣饮 Huluobo Dazao Yin
21.30 宣肺饮 Xuanfei Yin
21.31 姜枣饮 I Jiang Zao Yin I
21.32 姜糖饮 II Jiang Tang Yin II
21.33 扁柏叶茶 Bianbaiye Cha
21.34 桑叶枇杷茶 Sangye Pipa Cha
21.35 桑杏饮 Sang Xing Yin
21.36 桑杏豆豉饮 Sang Xing Douchi Yin
21.37 桑菊杏仁饮 Sang Ju Xingren Cha
21.38 化橘红茶 Huajuhong Cha
21.39 桔梗甘草茶 Jiegeng Gancao Cha
21.40 骨碎补茶 Gusuibu Cha
21.41 清心止嗽茶 Qingxin Zhisou Cha
21.42 清燥润肺饮 I Qingzao Runfei Yin I
21.43 清燥润肺饮 II Qingzao Runfei Yin II
21.44 雪羹汤 Xuegeng Tang
21.45 陈皮饮 Chenpi Yin
21.46 鱼腥草饮 Yuxingcao Yin
21.47 款冬花茶 Kuandonghua Cha
21.48 丝瓜花蜜饮 Siguahua Mi Yin
21.49 黑芝麻茶 Heizhima Cha
21.50 无花果茶 Wuhuaguo Cha
21.51 滋胃和中茶 Ziwei Hezhong Cha
21.52 榆皮车前茶 Yupi Cheqian Cha
21.53 葫芦茶冰糖饮 Hulucha Bingtang Yin
21.54 酸石榴饮 Suanshiliu Yin
21.55 银花芦根饮 Yinhua Lugen Cha
21.56 润肺止咳茶 Runfei Zhike Cha
21.57 橘皮饮 Jupi Yin
21.58 橘皮茶 I Jupi Cha I
21.59 橘红茶 Juhong Cha
21.60 双花杏蜜饮 Shuanghua Xing Mi Yin
21.61 罗布麻平喘茶 Luobuma Pingchuancha

XI

21.62 罗汉果柿饼饮 Luohanguo Shibing Yin
21.63 萝卜茶 I　Luobo Cha I
21.64 萝卜饴糖饮 Luobo Yitang Yin

22 肺脓疡 For Pulmonary Suppuration　　　　　　150

22.01 冬瓜藤饮 Dongguateng Yin
22.02 冬瓜子芦根饮 Dongguazi Lugen Yin
22.03 瓜蒌茶 Gualou Cha

23 高血压 For Hypertension　　　　　　151

23.01 三子茶 Sanzi Cha
23.02 三宝茶 Sanbao Cha
23.03 三七花茶 Sanqihua Cha
23.04 山楂叶(花)茶 Shanzhaye(hua) Cha
23.05 山楂决明茶 Shanzha Jueming Cha
23.06 天麻菊花饮 Tianma Juhua Yin
23.07 西瓜决明茶 Xigua Jueming Cha
23.08 西瓜翠衣茶 Xiguacuiyi Cha
23.09 向日葵叶饮 Xiangrikuiye Yin
23.10 决明菊花茶 Jueming Juhua Cha
23.11 旱芹车前茶 Hanqin Cheqian Cha
23.12 杜仲茶 Duzhong Cha
23.13 芹菜根茶 Qincaigen Cha
23.14 花生全草茶 Huashengquancao Cha
23.15 胡桐叶茶 Hutongye Cha
23.16 苦丁茶 Kuding Cha
23.17 降压茶 I　Jiangya Cha I
23.18 降压茶 II　Jiangya Cha II
23.19 香蕉根茶 Xiangjiaogen Cha
23.20 桑树根茶 Sangshugen Cha
23.21 桑根白皮茶 Sanggenbaipi Cha
23.22 桑菊枸杞饮 Sang Ju Gouqi Yin
23.23 夏枯草茶 Xiakucao Cha
23.24 夏枯草荷叶茶 Xiakucao Heye Cha
23.25 侧柏叶茶 Cebaiye Cha
23.26 梧桐茶 Wutong Cha
23.27 清热理气茶 Qingre Liqi Cha
23.28 望江南茶 Wangjiangnan Cha

23.29 菊花钩藤饮 I Juhua Gouteng Yin I
23.30 菊花钩藤饮 II Juhua Gouteng Yin II
23.31 菊槐绿茶饮 Ju Huai Lucha Yin
23.32 菊藤茶 Ju Teng Cha
23.33 黄瓜藤茶 Huangguateng Cha
23.34 钩藤茶 Gouteng Cha
23.35 葛根槐花茶 Gegen Huaihua Cha
23.36 槐花茶 Huaihua Cha
23.37 银菊茶 Yin Ju Cha
23.38 豨莶草茶 Xixiancao Cha
23.39 橘红茯苓饮 Juhong Fuling Yin
23.40 橘杏丝瓜饮 Ju Xing Sigua Yin
23.41 猪毛菜茶 Zhumaocai Cha
23.42 萝芙木根茶 Luofumugen Cha
23.43 荠菜茶 Jicai Cha
23.44 罗布麻降压茶 Luobuma Jiangyacha
23.45 罗布麻速溶饮 Luobuma Surongyin
23.46 罗布麻叶茶 Luobumaye Cha
23.47 蚕豆花茶 Candouhua Cha

24 头痛 For a Headache   167
24.01 巴豆茶 Badou Cha
24.02 杏菊饮 I Xing Ju Yin I
24.03 杏菊饮 II Xing Ju Yin II
24.04 辛夷花茶 Xinyihua Cha
24.05 青葙子速溶饮 Qingxiangzi Surongyin
24.06 香附川芎茶 Xiangfu Chuanxiong Cha
24.07 菊花茶 Juhua Cha
24.08 菊花龙井茶 Juhua Longjing Cha
24.09 棕榈槐花茶 Zonglu Huaihua Cha
24.10 葛根茶 Gegen Cha
24.11 橘皮茶 II Jupi Cha II

25 冠心病 For Coronary Atherosclerotic Heart Disease   172
25.01 丹参茶 Danshen Cha
25.02 玉竹速溶饮 Yuzhu Surongyin
25.03 柿叶降脂茶 Shiye Jiangzhi Cha
25.04 降脂茶 Jiangzhi Cha

XIII

25.05 菊楂决明饮 Ju Zha Jueming Yin
25.06 银杏叶茶 Yinxingye Cha

26 糖尿病 For Diabetes Mellitus 174

26.01 山药茶 Shanyao Cha
26.02 止消渴速溶饮 Zhixiaoke Surongyin
26.03 田螺茶 Tianluo Cha
26.04 冬瓜瓤汤 Dongguarang Tang
26.05 生地石膏茶 Shengdi Shigao Cha
26.06 加减三花饮 Jiajian Sanhua Yin
26.07 消渴茶 Xiaoke Cha
26.08 皋芦叶茶 Gaoluye Cha
26.09 益胃茶 II Yiwei Cha II
26.10 淮山药茶 Huaishanyao Cha
26.11 麦冬乌梅饮 Maidong Wumei Yin
26.12 菝葜叶茶 Baqiaye Cha
26.13 蚕茧茶 Canjian Cha
26.14 糯米草茶 Nuomicao Cha
26.15 糯稻杆茶 Nuodaogan Cha

27 肝炎、黄疸 For Hepatitis 180

27.01 石花茶 Shihua Cha
27.02 金鸡饮 Jin Ji Yin
27.03 消黄茶 Xiaohuang Cha
27.04 柴甘茅根茶 Chai Gan Maogen Cha
27.05 茵陈茶 Yinchen Cha
27.06 茵陈香芦茶 Yinchen Xiang Lu Cha
27.07 茵陈陈皮茶 Yinchen Chenpi Cha
27.08 茵陈红糖饮 Yinchen Hongtang Yin
27.09 茵陈银花饮 Yinchen Yinhua Yin
27.10 退黄饮 Tuihuang Yin
27.11 马鞭草茶 Mabiancao Cha
27.12 清肝利黄茶 Qinggan Lihuang Cha
27.13 荸荠茶 Biqi Cha
27.14 硝磺茶 Xiao Huang Cha
27.15 雄花茶 Xionghua Cha
27.16 无花果叶茶 Wuhuaguoye Cha
27.17 菟丝草茶 Tusicao Cha

27.18 滑石红糖茶 Huashi Hongtang Cha
27.19 榕树叶茶 Rongshuye Cha
27.20 螃蟹饮 Pangxie Yin

28 胃炎 For Gastritis　　　　　　　　　　　　　　　　187

28.01 石斛茶 Shihu Cha
28.02 加减人参乌梅汤 Jiajian Renshen Wumei Tang
28.03 竹茹芦根茶 Zhuru Lugen Cha
28.04 羊乳饮 Yangru Yin
28.05 枇杷饮 Pipa Yin
28.06 柚子鸡蛋饮 Youzi Jidan Yin
28.07 香橼茶 Xiangyuan Cha
28.08 扁豆益胃饮 Biandou Yiwei Yin
28.09 高粱叶茶 Gaoliangye Cha
28.10 健胃茶Ⅲ Jianwei Cha III
28.11 健胃茶Ⅳ Jianwei Cha IV
28.12 黄连食醋白糖山楂饮 Huanglian Shicu Baitang Shanzha Yin
28.13 醋浸生姜饮 Cuqin Shengjiang Yin
28.14 绿豆饮 Ludou Yin

29 消化道溃疡 For Digestive Tract Peptic　　　　　　　192

29.01 白糖茶 Baitang Cha
29.02 胃溃疡茶 Weikuiyang Cha
29.03 糖蜜红茶饮 Tang Mi Hongcha Yin

30 泄泻、肠炎、痢疾 For Diarrhea, Enteritis and Dysentery　　193

30.01 一味薯蓣饮 Yiwei Shuyu Yin
30.02 山楂红白糖茶 Shanzha Hongbaitang Cha
30.03 止泻茶Ⅰ Zhixie Cha I
30.04 止泻茶Ⅱ Zhixie Cha II
30.05 木槿花速溶饮 Mujinhua Surongyin
30.06 六和茶 Liuhe Cha
30.07 石榴叶茶 Shiliuye Cha
30.08 石榴皮茶 Shiliupi Cha
30.09 冬瓜叶饮 Dongguaye Yin
30.10 地锦草茶 Dijincao Cha
30.11 芝麻茶 Zhima Cha
30.12 车前蜂蜜饮 Cheqian Fengmi Yin

30.13 柚皮茶 I　Youpi Cha I
30.14 苦瓜根茶　Kuguagen Cha
30.15 马齿苋绿豆汤　Machixian Ludou Tang
30.16 马齿苋槟榔茶　Machixian Binglang Cha
30.17 苋菜茶　Xiancai Cha
30.18 陈醋茶　Chencu Cha
30.19 健脾饮　Jianpi Yin
30.20 无花果糖饮　Wuhuaguo Tang Yin
30.21 棕榈花茶　Zongluhua Cha
30.22 绿茶蜜饮　Lucha Mi Yin
30.23 姜枣饮 II　Jiang Zao Yin II
30.24 姜糖茶 II　Jiang Tang Cha II
30.25 姜茶饮　Jiang Cha Yin
30.26 姜茶速溶饮　Jiang Cha Surongyin
30.27 姜茶乌梅饮　Jiang Cha Wumei Yin
30.28 萝卜茶 II　Luobo Cha II
30.29 萝卜姜蜜茶　Luobo Jiang Mi Cha

31 眩晕头重　For Dizziness and Heaviness of Head　　205
31.01 生姜蔻仁汤　Shengjiang Kouren Tang
31.02 清眩饮　Qingxuan Yin
31.03 藿香苡仁饮　Huoxiang Yiren Yin

32 鼻衄　For Epistaxis　　206
32.01 三鲜饮　Sanxian Yin
32.02 玉米花茶　Yumihua Cha
32.03 白茅花茶　Baimaohua Cha
32.04 白茅根茶　Baimaogen Cha
32.05 地骨皮茶　Digupi Cha
32.06 鸡蛋清白糖饮　Jidanqing Baitang Yin
32.07 萝卜叶茶 II　Luoboye Cha II

33 咳血、吐血　For Hemoptysis and Spitting Blood　　208
33.01 小蓟根茶　Xiaojigen Cha
33.02 五君子饮　Wujunzi Yin
33.03 止血茶　Zhixue Cha
33.04 玉米须冰糖茶　Yumixu Bingtang Cha
33.05 四花饮　Sihua Yin

33.06 加味三七饮 Jiawei Sanqi Yin
33.07 仙鹤草茶 Xianhecao Cha
33.08 荷叶饮 I Heye Yin I
33.09 麦冬茅根饮 Maidong Maogen Yin
33.10 黄花菜饮 Huanghuacai Yin
33.11 双荷汤 Shuanghe Tang
33.12 藕节茶 Oujie Cha
33.13 藕节茅根茶 Oujie Maogen Cha
33.14 蚕豆花冰糖茶 Candouhua Bingtang Cha

34 便血 For Hematochezia 214
34.01 木耳芝麻茶 Muer Zhima Cha
34.02 加味槐花饮 Jiawei Huaihua Yin
34.03 旱莲草红枣汤 Hanliancao Hongzao Tang
34.04 秋梨椿根皮茶 Qiuli Chungenpi Cha
34.05 黄花菜红糖饮 Huanghuacai Hongtang Yin
34.06 蜂蜜木瓜饮 Fengmi Mugua Yin
34.07 槐花饮 Huaihua Yin
34.08 槐叶茶 Huaiye Cha
34.09 槐角茶 Huaijiao Cha
34.10 槐芽茶 Huaiya Cha
34.11 绿豆芽白皮饮 Ludouya Baipi Yin

35 血尿、泌尿系感染 For Hematuria and Urinary System Infection 218
35.01 二鲜饮 Erxian Yin
35.02 二花茶 Erhua Cha
35.03 人字草茶 Renzicao Cha
35.04 大小蓟速溶饮 Daxiaoji Surongyin
35.05 甘竹茶 Gan Zhu Cha
35.06 白果冬瓜子饮 Baiguo Dongguazi Yin
35.07 半边钱茶 Banbianqian Cha
35.08 加减小蓟饮 Jiajian Xiaoji Yin
35.09 竹茅饮 Zhu Mao Yin
35.10 向日葵根茶 Xiangrikuigen Cha
35.11 豆豉茶 Douchi Cha
35.12 旱莲草茶 Hanliancao Cha
35.13 尿利清茶 Niaoliqing Cha
35.14 车前海金饮 Cheqian Haijin Yin

XVII

35.15 玫瑰花灯心茶 Meiguihua Dengxin Cha
35.16 茅根车前饮 Maogen Cheqian Yin
35.17 茅根竹蔗饮 Maogen Zhuzhe Yin
35.18 马齿苋饮 Machixian Yin
35.19 马齿苋红糖茶 Machixian Hongtang Cha
35.20 茵地茶 Yin di Cha
35.21 清淋茶 Qinglin Cha
35.22 清明柳叶速溶饮 Qingming Liuye Surongyin
35.23 淡竹叶灯心茶 Danzhuye Dengxin Cha
35.24 扁蓄茶 Bianxu Cha
35.25 满天星茶 Mantianxing Cha
35.26 蒲公英茶 Pugongying Cha
35.27 凤眼草茶 Fengyancao Cha
35.28 绿豆芽白糖饮 Ludouya Baitang Yin
35.29 灯心柿饼汤 Dengxin Shibing Tang
35.30 糠壳老茶 Kangkelao Cha
35.31 糯稻根须饮 Nuodaogenxu Yin

36 泌尿系结石 For Urinary System Calculi   229

36.01 三金茶 Sanjin Cha
36.02 玉米根叶茶 Yumigenye Cha
36.03 石苇车前茶 Shiwei Cheqian Cha
36.04 佛耳草茶 Foercao Cha
36.05 谷皮藤茶 Gupiteng Cha
36.06 金钱草茶 Jinqiancao Cha
36.07 荸荠内金饮 Biqi Neijin Yin
36.08 葱白琥珀饮 Congbai Hupo Yin
36.09 薏苡仁汤 Yiyiren Tang

37 肾炎、水肿 For Nephritis and Edema   232

37.01 二陈竹叶茶 Erchen Zhuye Cha
37.02 大麦秸茶 Damaijie Cha
37.03 山扁豆草茶 Shanbiandoucao Cha
37.04 五皮饮 Wupi Yin
37.05 玉米芯茶 Yumixin Cha
37.06 玉米须茶 Yumixu Cha
37.07 玉米须速溶饮 Yumixu Surongyin
37.08 向日葵花茶 Xiangrikuihua Cha

37.09 车前草茶　Cheqiancao Cha
37.10 尿感茶　Niaogan Cha
37.11 茅根菠萝速溶饮　Maogen Boluo Surongyin
37.12 海金砂草茶　Haijinshacao Cha
37.13 菩提树根茶　Putishugen Cha
37.14 萱草根茶　Xuancaogen Cha
37.15 粳稻根饮　Jingdaogen Yin
37.16 蓄兰茶　Xu Lan Cha
37.17 蚕豆饮　Candou Yin
37.18 蚕豆壳茶　Candouke Cha

38 自汗、盗汗　For Spontaneous Sweating and Night Sweat　239

38.01 止汗饮　Zhihan Yin
38.02 毛桃干茶　Maotaogan Cha
38.03 白术叶茶　Baizhuye Cha
38.04 沙参蔗汁饮　Shashen Zhezhi Yin
38.05 浮麦麻根茶　Fumai Magen Cha
38.06 葡萄茶　Putao Cha
38.07 糯稻根茶　Nuodaogen Cha

39 便秘　For Constipation　241

39.01 生军茶　Shengjun Cha
39.02 芝麻核桃茶　Zhima Hetao Cha
39.03 决明苁蓉茶　Jueming Congrong Cha
39.04 连翘茶　Lianqiao Cha
39.05 黄豆皮饮　Huangdoupi Yin
39.06 番泻叶茶　Fanxieye Cha
39.07 蜂蜜茶 II　Fengmi Cha II
39.08 蜂蜜饮　Fengmi Yin
39.09 熟军苦丁茶　Shujun Kuding Cha

40 甲状腺肿大　For Thyroid Enlargement　244

40.01 五鲜茶　Wuxian Cha
40.02 海藻茶　Haizao Cha
40.03 海带茶　Haidai Cha

41 癌症　For Cancer　245

41.01 二菱茶　Erling Cha

XIX

41.02 玄参麦冬茶 Xunshen Maidong Cha
41.03 健胃防癌茶 Jianwei Fangai Cha
41.04 麦冬地黄饮 Maidong Dihuang Yin
41.05 葵髓茶 Kuisui Cha
41.06 藕橘饮 Ouju Yin

42 疝气 For Hernia 248
42.01 青果石榴茶 Qingguo Shiliu Cha
42.02 茴香茶 Huixiang Cha
42.03 荔橄茶 Li Gan Cha
42.04 双核饮 Shuanghe Yin

43 寄生虫病 For Parasitosis 249
43.01 南瓜籽茶 Nanguazi Cha
43.02 乌梅饮 Wumei Yin
43.03 椒梅茶 Jiao Mei Cha
43.04 榧子茶 Feizi Cha
43.05 绿豆大蒜饮 Ludou Dasuan Yin
43.06 祛钩虫茶 Qugouchong Cha

44 口腔疾患 For the Diseases in Oral Cavity 251
44.01 竹叶茶 I Zhuye Cha I
44.02 灶心土竹叶茶 Zaoxintu Zhuye Cha
44.03 青刺尖茶 Qingcijian Cha
44.04 茶树根茶 Chashugen Cha
44.05 绿茶 Lucha
44.06 银花柿霜饮 Yinhua Shishuang Yin

45 流脑、乙脑 For Epidemic Encephalitis and Encephalitis B 253
45.01 牛筋草茶 Niujincao Cha
45.02 生石膏荸荠汤 Shengshigao Biqi Tang
45.03 贯仲板蓝根茶 Guanzhong Banlangen Cha
45.04 银花甘草茶 Yinhua Gancao Cha

46 流行性腮腺炎 For Epidemic Parotitis 255
46.01 玄参三花饮 Xuanshen Sanhua Yin
46.02 忍冬夏枯草茶 Rendong Xiakucao Cha

46.03 板蓝根花茶 Banlangenhua Cha
46.04 荸藕茅根饮 Bi Ou Maogen Yin
46.05 绿豆菜心饮 Ludou Caixin Yin
46.06 银花薄黄饮 Yinhua Bo Huang Yin

47 麻疹、水痘 For Measles and Chickenpox　　　　　　　　257

47.01 二根茶 Ergen Cha
47.02 牛蒡子芦根茶 Niubangzi Lugen Cha
47.03 生地青果茶 Shengdi Qingguo Cha
47.04 白头翁茶 Baitouweng Cha
47.05 西河柳饮 Xiheliu Yin
47.06 赤柽柳茶 Chichengliu Cha
47.07 车杏枇杷茶 Che Xing Pipa Cha
47.08 青果芦根饮 Qingguo Lugen Cha
47.09 杏仁麦冬饮 Xingren Maidong Yin
47.10 胡萝卜饮 Huluobo Yin
47.11 胡萝卜芫荽饮 Huluobo Yuansui Yin
47.12 茅根荠菜茶 Maogen Jicai Cha
47.13 浮萍茶 Fuping Cha
47.14 柴芦茶 Chai Lu Cha
47.15 荸荠茅根茶 Biqi Maogen Cha
47.16 甜菜茶 Tiancai Cha
47.17 梨皮茶 Lipi Cha
47.18 紫草根茶 Zicaogen Cha
47.19 莲芯茶 Lianxin Cha
47.20 麦冬梅枝茶 Maidong Meizhi Cha
47.21 贯仲丝瓜络茶 Guanzhong Sigualuo Cha
47.22 银蝉饮 Yin Chan Yin
47.23 鲜生地饮 Xianshengdi Yin
47.24 鲜萝卜饮 Xianluobo Yin
47.25 腊梅绿豆饮 Lamei Ludou Yin
47.26 芦根茶 Lugen Cha
47.27 芦菊茶 Lu Ju Cha
47.28 盐梅茶 Yan Mei Cha

48 疟疾 For Malaria　　　　　　　　266

48.01 水蜈蚣茶 Shuiwugong Cha
48.02 虎杖叶茶 Huzhangye Cha

XXI

48.03 马兰糖饮 Malan Tang Yin
48.04 葵花茶 Kuihua Cha
48.05 杨桃速溶饮 Yangtao Surongyin

49 小儿夜啼、夜尿 For Night Crying of Infants, Enuresis Nocturna in Children 268
49.01 竹叶茶 II Zhuye Cha II
49.02 红枣茶 II Hongzao Cha II
49.03 灯心草茶 Dengxincao Cha
49.04 苏连茶 Su Lian Cha

50 缺乳、回乳 For Lack of Lactation and Delactation 270
50.01 山楂麦芽茶 Shanzha Maiya Cha
50.02 赤小豆饮 Chixiaodou Yin
50.03 丝瓜芝麻核桃饮 Sigua Zhima Hetao Yin

51 月经不调 For Irregular Menses 271
51.01 山楂向日葵饮 Shanzha Xiangrikui Yin
51.02 月季花汤 Yuejihua Tang
51.03 四炭止漏茶 Sitan Zhilou Cha
51.04 苎麻根饮 Zhumagen Yin
51.05 卷柏茶 Juanbai Cha
51.06 芹菜大戟饮 Qincai Daji Yin
51.07 松树皮茶 Songshupi Cha
51.08 青蒿丹皮茶 Qinghao Danpi Cha
51.09 刺玫根茶 Cimeigen Cha
51.10 柿霜桑椹饮 Shishuang Sangshen Yin
51.11 红高粱花茶 Honggaolianghua Cha
51.12 红糖姜枣茶 Hongtang Jiang Zao Cha
51.13 香附茶 Xiangfu Cha
51.14 姜艾红糖饮 Jiang Ai Hongtang Yin
51.15 桑叶苦丁茶 Sangye Kuding Cha
51.16 桂姜红糖饮 Gui Jiang Hongtang Cha
51.17 清心止血饮 Qingxin Zhixue Yin
51.18 黑白茶 Hei Bai Cha
51.19 黑豆红花饮 Heidou Honghua Yin
51.20 枣树根皮茶 Zaoshugenpi Cha
51.21 莲蓬茶 Lianpeng Cha

51.22 橘叶荔梗茶　Juye Ligeng Cha
51.23 薏苡根饮　Yiyigen Yin

52 阴道炎、带下　For Vaginitis and Abnormal Leukorrhagia　279
52.01 向日葵茎饮　Xiangrikuijing Yin
52.02 扁豆山药茶　Biandou Shanyao Cha
52.03 马兰茶　Malan Cha
52.04 鸡冠花茶　Jiguanhua Cha
52.05 鸡冠花藕汁速溶饮　Jiguanhua Ouzhi Surongyin

53 乳腺炎　For Mastitis　281
53.01 牛蒡叶茶　Niubangye Cha
53.02 野菊花茶　Yejuhua Cha
53.03 银花地丁茶　Yinhua Diding Cha

54 妊娠期疾患　For Diseases in the Duration of Pregnancy　282
54.01 止呕茶　Zhiou Cha
54.02 玉米嫩衣茶　Yuminenyi Cha
54.03 玉米须赤小豆饮　Yumixu Chixiaodou Yin
54.04 竹沥茶　Zhuli Cha
54.05 灶心土茶　Zaoxintu Cha
54.06 阿胶奶饮　Ejiao Nai Yin
54.07 南瓜蒂茶　Nanguadi Cha
54.08 红茶叶茶　Hongchaye Cha
54.09 建兰茶　Jianlan Cha
54.10 桑菊茶 II　Sang Ju Cha II
54.11 荷叶饮 II　Heye Yin II
54.12 紫苏姜橘饮　Zisu Jiang Ju Yin
54.13 葡萄须饮　Putaoxu Yin
54.14 橘皮竹茹茶　Jupi Zhuru Cha
54.15 苏叶生姜茶　Suye Shengjiang Cha

55 产后疾患　For the Diseases of Post Partum　287
55.01 四乳饮　Siru Yin
55.02 红糖胡椒茶　Hongtang Hujiao Cha
55.03 柚皮茶 II　Youpi Cha II
55.04 胡萝卜缨饮　Huluoboying Yin
55.05 南瓜须茶　Nanguaxu Cha

55.06 益母糖茶 Yimu Tang Cha
55.07 菊花根茶 Juhuagen Cha
55.08 黄瓜花茶 Huangguahua Cha

Index (Chinese)   291

Index (Pinyin)   319

Preface

Wherever and whenever you mention the history of tea, most people will think of China as the home of tea. Tea originated from China, the first country to produce and drink it. Chinese historical legends describe a person called Shennong who tasted a great variety of plants and told people which were edible or not. He was poisoned 70 times a day and was always detoxicated by tea. This shows the long history of tea for health care and disease treatment in China.

According to the taste, property and meridian classifications in traditional Chinese medicine, tea is bitter or sweet in taste and cool in nature and acts on the heart, lung and stomach meridians. The chapter "Food Therapy" of *Essentially Treasured Prescriptions for Emergencies* says, "Tea makes people energetic and pleased." The description given by Mr. Gu Yuanqing of the Ming Dynasty in his book *Tea Manual* teaches, "Drinking tea helps quench thirst, digest food, dissolve phlegm, refresh the mind, produce diuresis, promote vision, relieve irritability and remove greasiness. One cannot go without tea even for a single day." Recent studies on tea have produced scientific evidence and a greater understanding of the benefits of tea. Scientific research proves that tea can remove greasiness, refresh the mind, lower blood pressure, activate qi and blood, kill bacteria, treat inflammation, protect viscera, alleviate exposure to radioactivity, replenish vitamins, protect teeth, prevent diarrhea and cancer, and eliminate foul breath, etc. Tea is most advantageous to health. No wonder the Father of Tea, Mr. Lu Yu of the Tang Dynasty, said, "I would rather drink no wine for my entire life than drink no tea every day."

Everyone knows about tea but most people know little about health tea. The origin of health tea dates back again to the age of Shennong, when people searched for edible and medical plants. With accumulated experience in treating diseases, health teas increased in number, formulae and extent of application. Basically, there are four types of health tea: tea for health care, tea for prevention, tea for treatment and tea for rehabilitation. Tea for health care can tonify, e.g., refresh mind, improve looks, reduce body weight, promote hearing and vision, blacken hair, reinforce kidney, strengthen teeth, increase endurance, strengthen reproductive ability, and pro-long life. Tea for prevention can be used to prevent diseases such as common cold, sunstroke, pharyngitis, hoarse voice and cancers, etc. Tea for treatment can lower blood pressure, relieve diabetes, cure indigestion and so on. Tea for rehabili-tation can strengthen the body's constitution after a prolong-ed disease, quicken recovery after an operation or delivery, and improve the intelligence of mentally retarded children. From the viewpoint of the cost and benefits in promoting health, health tea is even more effective than many medicines.

Some people might think that health tea is just a kind of medicated tea. This view is not true. Health tea is not medicine. It is used as a kind of dietotherapy, which is in turn a kind of natural therapy. Natural therapy uses no medicine.

The health teas selected in this book have the following characteristics:

Good taste and smell. The teas have a good smell and no bitter taste.

Safe and effective. The teas are neutral, mild, and non-toxic in nature and flavor.

Easy to make. Anybody can make the tea at home.

Potential for product development. Packaged sport drinks and health drinks are increasingly popular. Chinese health teas selected in this book have a great potential for further development into such commercial products because of their value for money in health care and pleasant taste.

The features of the present book comprise:

Broad coverage. The present collection of health teas in this book covers a wide range of teas beneficial to health from head to feet (i.e., from blackening hair to treating diseases caused by parasites in streams and brooks) and from the exterior to the interior (e.g., improving the skin to protecting viscera). This book is useful to the general reader as well as a reference for practitioners.

Easy reference. At the end of the book health teas are indexed according to their pinyin names and the number of strokes of Chinese characters.

High standard. To make sure that correct and appropriate terms were used, we spent much time in consulting and comparing dozens of reference books, including *The Chinese Materia Medica, Pharmacology of Traditional Chinese Medical Formulae,* and dictionaries of Chinese medicine, Western medicine and pharmacology in Chinese, English and Latin, etc.

It would have been impossible to publish this book without the support and help given by so many people around us. Our special thanks to Professor Xiao Peigen, member of the Division of Medicine and Health Engineering of the Chinese Academy of Engineering, and Professor Yeung Hinwing, Director of the Institute for the Advancement of Chinese Medicine (IACM), Hong Kong Baptist University, for their enlightened advice and kind help.

In revising this book, we received generous support and assistance of Mr. Josef Siuwai Leung, and Madame Margaret Plant. We are grateful to them for their comments on the manuscripts.

We also thank our colleagues from Beijing University of Chinese Medicine and Pharmacology, WHO Collaborating Center for Traditional Medicine, the Acupuncture Institute of the China Academy of Traditional Chinese Medicine and the Institute for the Advancement of Chinese Medicine (IACM) at Hong Kong Baptist University for their encouragement during the process of writing this book.

Why not try some health tea now for your health? We invite you to try the health teas presented in this book. It will be one of the best books to your health.

Dang Yi

Wang Huizhu

Peng Yong

August 19, 1998
Beijing

保 健 篇
The Tea for Maintaining Health

01 益智健脑 For Promoting Intelligence

01.01 人参茶 Renshen Cha
Ingredients:
人参 Renshen, Ginseng (Radix Ginseng) 5g
Directions: Make as tea with boiling water. Cover the cup and let sit for 30 minutes before drinking.
Functions: To strengthen the immune system, activate the nervous system, reduce blood sugar, promote synthesis of protein and nucleic acid, enhance heart contraction, inhibit cancer cells.

It is regarded as above average medicine in Shen Nong's Herbal Classic. Provided the correct amount is prescribed, it is safe for long-term use to prolong life.
Source:《经验方》

01.02 人参大枣茶 Renshen Dazao Cha
Ingredients:
人参 Renshen, Ginseng (Radix Ginseng) 10g
大枣 Dazao, Chinese Date (Fructus Jujubae), 10 pieces
Directions: Make as tea with boiling water, cover the cup and let sit for 15 minutes before drinking.
Functions: To tonify the *yuan*-primary *qi*, calm the mind.
Indications: Deficient syndromes, coronary sclerosis and angina pectoris.
Source:《祝您健康》6:38, 1988

01.03 脑清茶 Naoqing Cha

Ingredients:

炒决明子 Chao Jueming Zi, parched Cassia Seed (Semen Cassiae) 250g
甘菊 Ganju, Chrysanthemum (Flos Chrysanthemi) 30g
夏枯草 Xiakucao, Common Selfheal Fruit-Spike (Spica Prunellae) 20g
橘饼 Jubing, Prepared Tangerine (Fructus Citri Praeparata) 30g
首乌 Shouwu, Fleece Flower Root (Radix Polygoni Multiflori) 30g
五味子 Wuweizi, Chinese Magnoliavine Fruit (Fructus Schisandrae) 30g
麦冬 Maidong, Dwarf Lilyturf Tuber (Radix Ophiopogonis) 60g
枸杞 Gouqi, Barbary Wolfberry Fruit (Fructus Lycii) 60g
桂圆肉 Guiyuanrou, Longan Aril (Arillus Longan) 60g
桑椹 Sangshen, Mulberry Fruit (Fructus Mori) 120g

Directions: Pestle into coarse powder. Use 15g each time, make as tea with boiling water. Take two times a day.

Functions: To clear liver fire, promote vision, nourish the brain and refresh the mind.

Indications: Insomnia and neurasthenia due to the *yin* deficiency of the heart, liver and kidney and hyperactivity of fire.

Source:《山东中医杂志》6:1984

01.04 龙眼洋参饮 Longyan Yangshen Yin

Ingredients:

龙眼肉 Longyanrou, Longan Aril (Arillus Longan) 30g
西洋参 Xiyangshen, American Ginseng (Radix Panacis Quinquefolii) 6g
白糖 Baitang, White Sugar, desired amount

Directions: Put all materials and a little water into a bowl. Steam for 40-50 minutes. Take the steamed mixture.

Functions: To calm the mind, improve memory, replenish *qi* and nourish the heart.

Indications: Progeria with poor memory, senile dementia, palpitation,

anxiety and neurasthenia.
Source:《食物与治病》

01.05 灵芝薄荷饮 Lingzhi Bohe Yin

Ingredients:
灵芝 Lingzhi, Lucid Ganoderma (Ganoderma Lucidum seu Japonicum) 2g
薄荷 Bohe, Peppermint (Herba Menthae) 5g
谷芽 Guya, Rice Sprout (Fructus Oryzae Germinatus) 5g

Directions: Slice Lucid ganoderma, cut peppermint, toast rice sprout. Decoct Lucid and rice sprout and add white sugar to taste. Put peppermint into the decoction and continue decocting for 10 minutes. Drink.
Functions: To replenish brain essence and refresh the mind.
Indications: Irritability in summer, fatigue and irritability due to *qi* deficiency.
Source:《中国药膳大全》

02 健美减肥 For Reducing Weight

02.01 三花减肥茶 Sanhua Jianfei Cha

Ingredients:
玫瑰花 Meigui Hua, Rose (Flos Roasae Rugosae)
茉莉花 Moli Hua, Arabian Jasmine Flower (Flos Jasmini Sambac)
玳玳花 Daidaihua, Daidaihua (Flos Citri Aurantii)
川芎 Chuanxiong, Sichun Lovage Rhizome (Rhizoma Chuanxiong)
荷叶 Heye, Lotus Leaf (Folium Nelumbinis), etc.

Directions: It is prepackaged tea. Use one bag each evening.
Functions: To reduce blood fat to lose weight.
Indications: Obesity and hyperlipemia.
Source:《中成药研究》

02.02 山楂根茶 Shanzhagen Cha

Ingredients:
山楂根 Shanzha Gen, Hawthorn Root (Radix Crataegi) 10g
茶树根 Chashu Gen, Tea Tree Root (Radix Camelliae Sinensis) 10g
荠菜花 Jicai Hua, Shepherds Purse Flower (Flos Capsellae) 10g
玉米须 Yumi Xu, Corn Stigma (Stigma Maydis) 10g

Directions: Pestle hawthorn root and tea tree root. Decoct all ingredients and drink the decoction.

Functions: To reduce blood fat, dissolve damp and induce diuresis.

Indications: Hyperlipemia and obesity.

Source:《上海中医药杂志》6:1979

02.03 山楂银菊茶 Shanzha Yin Ju Cha

Ingredients:
山楂 Shanzha, Hawthorn Fruit (Fructus Crataegi) 10g
金银花 Jinyinhua, Honeysuckle Flower (Flos Lonicerae) 10g
菊花 Juhua, Chrysanthemum Flower (Flos Chrysanthemi) 10g

Directions: Decoct and drink the decoction.

Functions: To dissolve stasis, reduce blood fat and lower blood pressure.

Indications: Obesity, hyperlipemia and hypertension.

Source:《上海中医药杂志》6:1979

02.04 牛奶茶 Niunai Cha

Ingredients:
奶粉 Naifen, Milk Powder
茶叶 Chaye, Tea Leaf (Folium Camelliae Sinensis)

Directions: Mix in a ratio of one spoon of milk powder to two spoons of tea. Make as tea with boiling water.

Functions: To reduce fat, refresh the mind, improve vision, strengthen the spleen and promote digestion.

Indications: Obesity, tiredness and indigestion.
Source: 《烟酒茶俗》

02.05 桑枝茶 Sangzhi Cha

Ingredients:
嫩桑枝　Nen Sangzhi, Young Mulberry Twigs (Ramulus Mori) 20g
Directions: Cut into thin slices. Make as tea with boiling water. Use daily for two to three months.
Functions: To eliminate wind and damp, promote water circulation.
Indications: Obesity.
Source:《医部全录》

02.06 荷叶茶 Heye Cha

Ingredients:
鲜荷叶　Xian Heye, Fresh Lotus Leaf (Folium Nelumbinis) 100g
白糖　Baitang, White Sugar, desired amount
Directions: Decoct and drink. Or use dry lotus leaves to make as tea with boiling water.
Functions: To clear heat, relax chest and quench thirst.
Indications: Sunstroke manifested as dizziness, fullness in chest, and diarrhea. Obesity (long-term use required for weight loss).
Source:《祝您健康》 5:46, 1988

02.07 荷叶减肥茶 Heye Jianfei Cha

Ingredients:
鲜荷叶　Xian Heye, Fresh Lotus Leaf (Folium Nelumbinis) 5g
山楂　Shanzha, Hawthorn Fruit (Fructus Crataegi) 5g
生薏仁　Sheng Yi Ren, Coix Seed (Semen Coicis) 3g
Directions: Make as tea with boiling water.
Functions: To expel wind, treat exterior syndrome, remove food

retention and lower blood lipids.
Indications: Headache and poor appetite of common cold, indigestion and obesity.
Source:《开卷有益》4:35, 1988

02.08 减肥茶 I Jianfei Cha I
Ingredients:
陈葫芦 Chen Hulu, Dried Bottle Gourd Peel (Pericarpium Lagenariae)15g
茶叶 Chaye, Tea Leaf (Folium Camelliae Sinensis) 3g
Directions: Pestle. Make as tea with boiling water.
Functions: To induce diuresis and reduce blood-lipids.
Indications: Obesity and hyperlipemia.
Source:《民间验方》

02.09 减肥茶 II Jianfei Cha II
Ingredients:
干荷叶 Gan Heye, Dried Lotus Leaf (Folium Nelumbinis) 60g
山楂 Shanzha, Hawthorn Fruit (Fructus Crataegi) 10g
生米仁 Sheng Mi Ren, Peanut (Arachidis) 10g
橘皮 Jupi, Dried Tangerine Peel (Pericarpium Citri Reticulatae) 5g
Directions: Grind into fine powder, make as tea with boiling water. Use daily for 100 days.
Functions: To regulate *qi*, promote water metabolism, reduce blood-lipids and dissolve turbidity.
Indications: Simple obesity and hyperlipemia.
Source:《祝您健康》5:46, 1988

02.10 罗布麻减肥茶 Luobuma Jianfeicha
Ingredients:
罗布麻叶 Luobuma Ye, Dogbane Leaf (Folium Apocyni Veneti) 10g

山楂 Shanzha, Hawthorn Fruit (Fructus Crataegi) 10g
Directions: Make as tea with boiling water.
Functions: To nourish the heart, calm the mind, pacify the liver, remove stasis and promote digestion.
Indications: Cardiovascular disease, obesity, hyperlipemia.
Source:《开卷有益》4:35, 1988

03 明目增视 For Improving Vision

03.01 玉竹薄荷饮 Yuzhu Bohe Yin
Ingredients:
玉竹 Yuzhu, Fragrant Solomonseal Rhizome (Rhizoma Polygonati Odorati) 3g
薄荷叶 Bohe Ye, Peppermint Leaf (Folium Menthae) 2 leaves
生姜 Shengjiang, Fresh Ginger (Rhizoma Zingiberis Recens), 1 slice
蜂蜜 Fengmi, Honey, desired amount
Directions: Decoct and drink in the evening before sleeping.
Functions: To nourish *yin*, promote vision, clear heat and remove toxin.
Indications: Red and painful eyes and blurred vision.
Source:《中国药膳学》

03.02 决明子茶 Juemingzi Cha
Ingredients:
决明子 Jueming Zi, Cassia Seed (Semen Cassiae) 30g
山楂 Shanzha, Hawthorn Fruit (Fructus Crataegi) 40g
白糖 Baitang, White Sugar 15g
Directions: Toast cassia seed and grind. Decoct cassia seed and hawthorn fruit, add white sugar before drinking.
Functions: To promote vision, subdue liver *yang*, reinforce kidney and expel wind-heat.

Indications: Headache and dizziness of hypertension, redness of eyes, blurred vision. It is commonly used in treatment of eye diseases.
Source:《祝您健康》5:46, 1988

03.03 杞菊茶 Qi Ju Cha
Ingredients:
枸杞子 Gouqi Zi, Barbary Wolfberry Fruit (Fructus Lycii) 12g
菊花 Juhua, Chrysanthemum Flower (Flos Chrysanthemi) 6g
霜桑叶 Shuangsangye, Mulberry Leaf (Folium Mori) 6g
谷精草 Gujingcao, Pipewort Flower (Flos Eriocauli) 3g
Directions: Make as tea with boiling water.
Functions: To strengthen the kidney by replenishing its essence, nourish the liver to improve the vision, reinforce *yin* to moisten the lung.
Indications: Blurred vision with a dry sensation in eyes, dizziness, tinnitus and optic atrophy due to the deficiency of liver and kidney.
Source:《浙江中医药》8:289, 1979

03.04 谷精菊花饮 Gujing Juhua Yin
Ingredients:
谷精草 Gujingcao, Pipewort Flower (Flos Eriocauli) 10g
枸杞子 Gouqi Zi, Barbary Wolfberry Fruit (Fructus Lycii) 10g
菊花 Juhua, Chrysanthemum Flower (Flos Chrysanthemi) 10g
红枣 Hongzao, Chinese Date (Fructus Jujubae) 10 pieces
冰糖 Bingtang, Crystal Sugar, desired amount
Directions: Decoct and drink.
Functions: To dispel wind-heat, remove nebula to improve vision, reinforce the liver and kidney, and replenish essence.
Indications: Night blindness, xerosis corneae, keratitis, myopia and keratomalacia.
Source:《中国食品》5:37, 1985

03.05 明目茶 I Mingmu Cha I

Ingredients:
枸杞子 Gouqi Zi, Barbary Wolfberry Fruit (Fructus Lycii) 10g
桂圆肉 Guiyuanrou, Longan Aril (Arillus Longan) 10 pieces

Directions: Decoct and drink.

Functions: To promote vision.

Indications: Myopia, lacrimation, blurred vision and dry sensation in the eyes.

Source:《大众医学》9:87, 1984

03.06 明目茶 II Mingmu Cha II

Ingredients:
菊花 Juhua, Chrysanthemum Flower (Flos Chrysanthemi) 6g
桑叶 Sangye, Mulberry Leaf (Folium Mori) 6g
枸杞子 Gouqi Zi, Barbary Wolfberry Fruit (Fructus Lycii) 6g

Directions: Decoct and drink.

Functions: To reinforce liver *yin* and promote vision.

Indications: Blurred vision, dizziness, tinnitus, lacrimation, photophobia and dry sensation in the eyes.

Source:《健康文摘》3:20, 1985

03.07 枸杞茶 Gouqi Cha

Ingredients:
枸杞子 Gouqi Zi, Barbary Wolfberry Fruit (Fructus Lycii) 20g

Directions: Make as tea with boiling water.

Functions: To replenish kidney essence, nourish liver and promote vision.

Indications: Hypopsia, photophobia and night blindness.

Source:《常见病验方研究参考资料》

03.08 桑银茶 Sang Yin Cha

Ingredients:
霜桑叶 Shuangsangye, Mulberry Leaf (Folium Mori) 6g
银花 Yinhua, Honeysuckle Flower (Flos Lonicerae) 6g
车前叶 Cheqian Ye, Plantain Leaf (Folium Plantaginis) 6g

Directions: Pestle into coarse powder. Make as tea with boiling water. Take one dose daily.
Functions: To clear heat, promote detoxification and induce diuresis.
Indications: Acute conjunctivitis.
Source:《常见病验方研究参考资料》

03.09 草决明茶 Caojueming Cha

Ingredients:
草决明 Caojueming, Cassia Seed (Semen Cassiae) 5g
绿茶 Lucha, Green Tea 2g

Directions: Make as tea with boiling water.
Functions: To lower blood pressure, reduce blood-fat, promote vision.
Indications: Hypertension in elderly with constipation, blurred vision.
Source:《开卷有益》 4:35, 1988

03.10 羚羊菊花茶 Lingyang Juhua Cha

Ingredients:
羚羊角 Lingyang Jiao, Pronghorn (Cornu Saigae Tataricae) 3g
菊花 Juhua, Chrysanthemum Flower (Flos Chrysanthemi) 20g
草决明 Caojueming, Cassia Seed (Semen Cassiae) 25g
五味子 Wuweizi, Chinese Magnoliavine Fruit (Fructus Schisandrae) 15g

Directions: Pestle, decoct and drink.
Functions: To clear heat, soothe the liver and promote vision.
Indications: Simple glaucoma with headache and painful eyes.
Source:《千家妙方》

03.11 黄芩茶 Huangqin Cha

Ingredients:
黄芩 Huangqin, Baical Skullcap Root (Radix Scutellariae) 15g

Directions: Pestle, make as tea with boiling water.

Functions: To reduce fire and improve vision.

Indications: Acute conjunctivitis.

Source:《中医保健杂谈》

03.12 黄花菜马齿苋饮 Huanghuacai Machixian Yin

Ingredients:
黄花菜 Huanghuacai, Foldleaf Daylily Root (Radix Hemerocallidis Plicatae) 30g

马齿苋 Machixian, Purslane Herb (Herba Portulacae) 30g

Directions: Decoct with high heat and then low heat for 30 minutes. Drink.

Functions: To clear heat, remove toxins and improve vision.

Indications: Acute conjunctivitis.

Source:《食物与治病》

04 美容美发 For Beautifying the Hair

04.01 何首乌茶 Heshouwu Cha

Ingredients:
何首乌 Heshouwu, Fleeceflower Root (Radix Polygoni Multiflori)

Directions: Grind and use 15g each time to make as tea with boiling water.

Functions: To reinforce the liver and kidney, replenish blood and essence, lower cholesterol, prevent and treat atherosclerosis, and promote the development of nerves and blood cells.

Indications: Anemia, progeria and insomnia. The ancients regarded it as

"the tea to recover one's youthful vigor".
Source:《祝您健康》6:38, 1988

04.02 芝麻枸杞饮 Zhima Gouqi Yin

Ingredients:
黑芝麻 Heizhima, Black Sesame (Semen Sesami Nigrum) 15g
枸杞子 Gouqi Zi, Barbary Wolfberry Fruit (Fructus Lycii) 15g
何首乌 Heshouwu, Fleeceflower Root (Radix Polygoni Multiflori) 15g
杭菊花 Hangjuhua, Yellow Chrysanthemum (Flos Chrysanthemi) 9g

Directions: Decoct and drink.
Functions: To reinforce liver and kidney.
Indications: Dizziness and senility due to deficiency of liver and kidney.
Source:《中国药膳学》

04.03 嫩肤饮 Nenfu Yin

Ingredients:
薏苡仁 Yiyi Ren, Coix Seed (Semen Coicis) 250g
蜂蜜 Fengmi, Honey, desired amount

Directions: Grind coin seed into fine powder and store in a bottle. Decoct 10g each time. Add honey and drink half an hour before meal. Use daily for six months.
Functions: Improve one's physical appearance.
Source:《百病饮食自疗》

05 补虚益寿 For Invigorating *Qi* and Blood and Prolonging Life

05.01 八仙茶 Baxian Cha

Ingredients:
粳米 Jingmi, Polished Round-grained Nonglutinous Rice (Cultivarietas

Oryzae Sativae) 750g
粟米 Sumi, Foxtail Millet (Semen Setariae) 750g
黄豆 Huangdou, Yellow Soybean (Semen Sojae) 750g
赤小豆 Chixiaodou, Rice Bean (Semen Phaseoli) 750g
绿豆 Ludou, Mung Bean (Semen Phaseoli Radiati) 750g
All baked well, respectively.
细茶 Xicha, Tea Leaf (Folium Camelliae Sinensis) 500g
脂麻 Zhima, Sesame Seed (Semen Sesami) 375g
花椒 Huajiao, Pricklyash Peel (Pericarpium Zanthoxyli) 75g
小茴香 Xiaohuixiang, Fennel (Fructus Foeniculi) 150g
泡干白姜 Pao Gan Baijiang, Soaked Dried Ginger (Rhizoma Zingiberis) 30g
炒白盐 Chao Baiyan, Baked Salt 30g
胡桃仁 Hutao Ren, English Walnut Seed (Semen Juglandis), desired amount
南枣 Nanzao, Axillary Choerospondias Fruit (Fructus Choerospondiatis), desired amount
松子仁 Songziren, Pine Seed (Semen Pini), desired amount
白砂糖 Baishatang, White Granulated Sugar, desired amount

Directions: Grind the first 11 ingredients. Mix with some flour and bake. Add the last four ingredients and store the mixture in a porcelain jar. Take three teaspoonfuls each time with boiled water.

Functions: To replenish essence, strengthen the kidney.

Indications: Progeria.

Source: 《韩氏医通》

05.02 人参核桃饮 Renshen Hetao Yin

Ingredients:
人参 Renshen, Ginseng (Radix Ginseng) 3g
核桃仁 Hetao Ren, English Walnut Seed (Semen Juglandis) 3 pieces

Directions: Decoct over low heat for one hour and drink as tea.

Functions: To replenish *qi*, tonify kidney.
Indications: Emaciation with shortness of breath, spontaneous sweating, and sallow complexion.
Source:《济生方》

05.03 山楂核桃茶 Shanzha Hetao Cha
Ingredients:
核桃仁 Hetao Ren, English Walnut Seed (Semen Juglandis) 150g
山楂 Shanzha, Hawthorn Fruit (Fructus Crataegi) 50g
白糖 Baitang, White Sugar 200g
Directions: Soak, grind the walnut pulp to fluid, add 2,000ml water to dilute. Set aside. Decoct the hawthorn fruit. Take the fruit out and save the decoction. Dissolve the white sugar into the decoction. Mix with the diluted walnut fluid. Decoct again for one minute. Cool the mixture and drink it as tea.
Functions: To reinforce the kidney, moisten the lung, soothe the intestine and promote digestion.
Indications: Deficiency of the body fluid, thirst and dry throat.
Source:《成都惠安堂滋补餐厅》

05.04 太子奶饮 Taizinai Yin
Ingredients:
灵芝 Lingzhi, Lucid Ganoderma (Ganoderma Lucidum seu Japonicum) 1.5g
荜茇 Bibo, Long Pepper (Fructus Piperis Longi) 0.1g
Directions: Decoct with 250ml milk, add white sugar 25g, continue to decoct for 10 minutes, and drink the decoction.
Functions: To replenish blood, tonify the body and nourish the stomach.
Indications: Gastric pain and poor appetite caused by weakness due to prolonged illness.
Source:《中国药膳大全》

05.05 西洋参茶 Xiyangshen Cha

Ingredients:
西洋参 Xiyangshen, American Ginseng (Radix Panacis Quinquefolii) 1-2g

Directions: Make as tea with warm boiled water.

Functions: To reinforce *qi*, produce body fluid, moisten the lung, clear heat.

Indications: *Qi* deficiency, lassitude, dry throat, irritability and thirst.

Source:《中国药膳学》

05.06 杞叶长寿茶 Qiye Changshou Cha

Ingredients:
枸杞叶 Gouqi Ye, Barbary Wolfberry Leaf (Folium Lycii)

Directions: Collect in May or June. Dry in the shade. Decoct over low heat and drink as tea.

It is rich in vitamins, protein, rutin, and chlorophyll. Good for reinforcing the kidney to prevent aging. The tea is dark green in color, fragrant in smell, mentally refreshing, regarded as "the syrup for prolonging life".

Source:《开卷有益》 4:35, 1988

05.07 沙苑子茶 Shayuanzi Cha

Ingredients:
沙苑子 Shayuanzi, Flatstem Milkvetch Seed (Semen Astragali Complanati) 10g

Directions: Pestle, make as tea with boiling water.

Functions: To tonify kidney and prolong life.

Notes to Canon of Materia Medica says, "The flatstem milkvetch seed is lifting in action and tonifying in nature. It is good for treating lumbago and is an important herb for kidney deficiency. It is good for health if people use it as tea everyday." Long term use is suggested for

prolonging life.
Source:《中国药膳学》

05.08 刺五加茶 Ciwujia Cha
Ingredients:
刺五加 Ciwujia, Manyprickle Acanthopanax Root (Radix Acanthopanaacis Senticosi) 30g
Directions: Grind into powder. Make as tea with boiling water.
Functions: To promote appetite, reinforce tendons and bones, dispel wind and relieve pain.
Indications: Poor appetite.
Source:《祝您健康》6:38, 1988

05.09 枸杞五味子茶 Gouqi Wuweizi Cha
Ingredients:
枸杞子 Gouqi Zi, Barbary Wolfberry Fruit (Fructus Lycii) 6g
五味子 Wuweizi, Chinese Magnoliavine Fruit (Fructus Schisandrae) 6g
冰糖 Bingtang, Crystal Sugar, desired amount
Directions: Make as tea with boiling water.
Functions: To strengthen body resistance.
Indications: Fever, irritability, thirst, spontaneous sweating, fullness in chest, poor appetite, weakness of the body and summer weight loss.
Source:《中国药膳学》

05.10 红枣茶 I Hongzao Cha I
Ingredients:
红枣 Hongzao, Chinese Date (Fructus Jujubae), 3-5 pieces
Directions: Make as tea with boiling water.
Functions: To strengthen spleen and stomach, replenish liver blood, reinforce *qi* and prolong life.

Indications: Weakness of spleen and stomach, *qi* and blood deficiency during pregnancy and post partum and weakness after an illness.
Source:《中国医药报》第 318 期

05.11 黄精茶 Huangjing Cha
Ingredients:
黄精 Huangjing, Solomonseal Rhizome (Rhizoma Polygonati) 60g
Directions: Slice, soak in warm boiled water for 10 minutes, filter, and drink the fluid.
Functions: To strengthen memory, blacken the hair. Modern research proves that Huangjing (Solomonseal Rhizome) can prolong life.
Indications: Tiredness, sluggish action and listlessness in old people.
Source:《祝您健康》6:38, 1988

05.12 当归补血饮 Danggui Buxue Yin
Ingredients:
黄芪 Huangqi, Milkvetch Root (Radix Astragali) 30g
当归 Danggui, Chinese Angelica (Radix Angelicae Sinensis) 6g
莲子 Lianzi, Lotus Seed (Semen Nelumbinis), 10 seeds (plumule removed)
Directions: Decoct first two, filter, save the fluid. Soak lotus seeds in a bowl, add 20g crystal sugar and steam for one hour. Remove steamed fluid from the bowl. Mix the two fluids. Take the mixture two or three times a day.
Functions: To replenish *qi* and clear heat.
Indications: Fever due to *qi* deficiency, aggravated on exertion, and accompanied by dizziness, lassitude, spontaneous sweating, shortness of breath, lack of desire to talk, poor appetite, loose stools, pale tongue with white thin coating and a soft and slow pulse.
Source:《内外伤辨惑论》

05.13 擂茶 I　Lei Cha I

Ingredients:

生米　Raw Rice, desired amount

生姜　Sheng Jiang, Fresh Ginger (Rhizoma Zingiberis Recens), desired amount

生茶　Fresh Tea, desired amount

Directions: Pestle, make as tea with boiling water.

Functions: To clear heat, promote detoxification, remove obstruction of meridians and regulate lung.

Indications: Febrile disease.

History: Leicha is also named as Sanshengtang. It originated in the Taohua River Area, and tradition has it that, during the period of the Three Kingdoms, (Wei, Shuhan and Wu), Liu Bei, the king of Shuhan, led his soldiers south to fight. Unfortunately, many soldiers became ill on the way. Forced to encamp in the Taohua River Area. Liu Bei ordered his men to search for medicine. Many were offered, none were effective. One day, an old man passed by. Deeply moved by the highly disciplined but helpless army, he presented his secret prescription Sanshengtang handed down from his ancestors. The common people nearby helped to pestle the medicines which were infused as tea with boiling water. After drinking this tea, the ill soldiers recovered quickly. Those who had not yet became ill didn't succumb after using the medicine. Since then, the people in the Taohua River Area use Sanshengtang for health promotion. In the prescription, Shengmi moistens the lungs to clear lung fire, Shengjiang promotes the function of spleen and dispels exterior syndromes, and Shengcha refreshes the mind to activate energy.

Source:《健康报》第 2703 期

05.14 擂茶 II　Lei Cha II

Ingredients:

芝麻　Zhima, Sesame Seed (Semen Sesami), desired amount

花生 Huasheng, Peanut (Arachidis), desired amount
茉莉花茶 Molihuacha, Tea Leaf and Jasmine Flower (Folium Camelliae Sinensis cum Flos Jasmini Sambac), desired amount
白砂糖 Baishatang, White Granulated Sugar, desired amount

Directions: Toast sesame seeds and peanuts well. Mix with tea leaf and jasmine flower. Pestle into powder and make as tea with boiling water. It looks like milk, tastes sweet and fragrant, and is good for health promotion.

Source:《健康报》第 2703 期

05.15 复盆子茶 Fupenzi Cha

Ingredients:
复盆子 Fupenzi, Palmleaf Raspberry Fruit (Fructus Rubi) and
绿茶 Lucha, Green Tea in the ratio of 2 to 1.

Directions: Make as tea with boiling water.

Functions: To reinforce the kidney to control essence, strengthen *yang* to promote vision and prevent aging.

Indications: Frequent urination, seminal emission, impotence, poor memory, decline of vision, poor appetite. Helps to improve summer heat endurance to prevent sunstroke.

Source:《祝您健康》 5:46, 1988

05.16 党参黄米茶 Dangshen Huangmi Cha

Ingredients:
党参 Dangshen, Pilose Asiabell Root (Radix Codonopsis Pilosulae)15-30g
炒黄米 Chao Huangmi, Parched Foxtail Millet (Semen Setariae) 30g

Directions: Decoct and drink. Take once every other day.

Functions: To strengthen spleen, reinforce *yang*.

Indications: Poor appetite, fatigue, cold extremities, loose stools, borborygmus, abdominal pain, thin leukorrhagia, pale tongue with white

coating and weak deep slow pulse due to spleen *yang* deficiency.
Source: 《饮食疗法》

05.17 灵芝茶 Lingzhi Cha

Ingredients:
灵芝草 Lingzhicao, Lucid Ganoderma (Ganoderma Lucidum seu Japonicum) 10g

Directions: Slice, make as tea with boiling water.
Functions: To reinforce middle *jiao*, replenish *qi* and prolong life. To prevent and treat hyperlipemia.
Source: 《中国医药报》第 318 期

06 益气养心 For Benefiting *Qi* and Nourishing the Heart

06.01 人参汤 Renshen Tang

Ingredients:
人参 Renshen, Ginseng (Radix Ginseng) 3-5g
橘皮 Jupi, Dried Tangerine Peel (Pericarpium Citri Reticulatae) 10g

Directions: Decoct and add granulated sugar to taste before drinking.
Functions: To reinforce *qi*, nourish the heart and calm the mind.
Indications: Palpitations and dream disturbed sleep.
Source: 《饮膳正要》

06.02 人参枣仁汤 Renshen Zaoren Tang

Ingredients:
人参 Renshen, Ginseng (Radix Ginseng) 5g
茯神 Fushen, Poria with Hostwood (Poria cum Ligno Hospite) 15g
酸枣仁 Suanzao Ren, Spina Date Seed (Semen Ziziphi Spinosae) 10g

Directions: Decoct and add granulated sugar to taste before drinking.

(Renshen is wrapped in a gauze bag and can be reused three times.)
Functions: To reinforce *qi*, nourish the heart, calm the mind and relieve palpitation.
Indications: Anxiety, irritability and palpitations.
Source:《百病饮食自疗》

06.03 牛乳饮 Niuru Yin

Ingredients:
牛奶 Niunai, Milk 250g

Directions: Boil the milk, add white sugar to taste, and boil again.
Functions: To reinforce *qi*, nourish heart, tonify whole body.
Indications: Weakness caused by prolonged illness.
Source:《温病条辨》

06.04 花生红枣茶 Huasheng Hongzao Cha

Ingredients:
花生米 Huasheng Mi, Peanut (Arachidis)
红枣 Hongzao, Chinese Date (Fructus Jujubae) in equal amounts

Directions: Decoct and drink.
Functions: To reinforce heart and spleen, regulate *qi* and induce diuresis.
Indications: Edema due to the deficiency of heart and spleen.
Source:《常见病验方研究参考资料》

06.05 参芪精 Shen Qi Jing

Ingredients:
党参 Dangshen, Pilose Asiabell Root (Radix Codonopsis Pilosulae) 250g
黄芪 Huangqi, Milkvetch Root (Radix Astragali) 250g

Directions: Soak in water. Decoct three times for half an hour each time. Filter, save the decoctions and mix together. Enrich the mixed decoction to a thick paste. Remove from heat, cool, add 500g white sugar. Dry, crush, and store in a bottle. Use 10g each time and make as tea with boiling water. Take two doses a day.

Functions: To reinforce *qi*, strengthen spleen.

Indications: Irritability, shortness of breath, poor appetite, loose stools, visceroptosis, edema, asthmatic breathing, and dizziness due to *qi* deficiency.

Source:《民间验方》

06.06 菖蒲茶 Changpu Cha

Ingredients:
九节菖蒲 Jiujiechangpu, Irkutsk Anemone Rhizome (Rhizoma Anemones Altaicae) 1.5g
酸梅肉 Suanmeirou, Smoked Plum (Fructus Mume), 2 pieces
大枣 Dazao, Chinese Date (Fructus Jujubae), 2 pieces
赤砂糖 Chishatang, Brown Granulated Sugar, desired amount

Directions: Tear smoked plum into small pieces. Make as tea with boiling water.

Functions: To restore consciousness after collapse and remove mental stress.

Indications: Insomnia with dream-disturbed sleep and irritability.

Source:《气功药饵疗法与救治偏差手术》

06.07 龙眼茶 Longyan Cha

Ingredients:
龙眼肉 Longyanrou, Longan Aril (Arillus Longan), 5-10 fruits

Directions: Put into a bowl and steam. Transfer to a cup and infuse as tea with boiling water. Drink the tea.

Functions: To reinforce heart and spleen, produce *qi* and blood and calm mind.

Indications: Neurasthenia, blood deficiency, palpitation, forgetfulness

and insomnia. Long term use may prolong life.
Source:《经验方》

06.08 龙眼枣仁饮 Longyan Zaoren Yin

Ingredients:
龙眼肉 Longyanrou, Longan Aril (Arillus Longan) 10g
炒枣仁 Chao Zao Ren, Parched Spine Date Seed (Semen Ziziphi Spinosae) 10g
芡实 Qianshi, Gordon Euryale Seed (Semen Euryales) 12g

Directions: Decoct over high heat and then simmer for 20 minutes. Drink the fluid as tea.
Functions: To replenish blood, calm the mind, reinforce the kidney, control essence.
Indications: Palpitation, anxiety, insomnia, forgetfulness, headache, dizziness, listlessness, and seminal emission due to *yin* and blood deficiency of heart and flaring-up of *xu*-fire (*xu* means deficiency).
Source:《食物与治病》

07 镇静安神 For Tranquilizing

07.01 安神茶 Anshen Cha

Ingredients:
煅龙齿 Duan Longchi, Calcined Dragon's Teeth (Dens Draconis) 9g (ground)
石菖蒲 Shichangpu, Grassleaf Sweetflag Rhizome (Rhizoma Acori Tatarinowi) 3g

Directions: Decoct and drink.
Functions: To calm the heart and ease the mind.
Indications: Insomnia with dream-disturbed sleep, palpitation, dizziness and blurred vision.

Source:《慈禧光绪医方选议》

07.02 柏子仁茶 Baiziren Cha
Ingredients:
柏子仁 Baiziren, Chinese Arbrvitae Kernel (Semen Platycladi) 10-15g
Directions: Pestle and make as tea with boiling water.
Functions: To replenish heart blood, ease the mind and moisten bowels to promote purgation.
Indications: Insomnia with dream-disturbed sleep due to heart blood deficiency, constipation caused by intestinal dryness and blood deficiency in old age and post partum.
Source:《气功药饵疗法与救治偏差手术》

07.03 参味茶 Shen Wei Cha
Ingredients:
党参 Dangshen, Pilose Asiabell Root (Radix Codonopsis Pilosulae) 20g
五味子 Wuweizi, Chinese Magnoliavine Fruit (Fructus Schisandrae) 10g
Directions: Decoct and drink one hour before sleep in the evening. Decoct the residue of the herbs again next day in the morning and drink. Use every day for seven or ten days as one course of treatment.
Functions: To replenish *qi* and blood, produce body fluid, treatment for a collapse, reinforce kidney to control nocturnal emission, calm mind and normalize liver.
Indications: Neurasthenia manifested as insomnia, dizziness and profuse sweating.
Source:《祝您健康》5:47, 1988

07.04 丝瓜饮 I Sigua Yin I
Ingredients:
经霜丝瓜 Jingshuang Sigua, Frosted Towel Gourd (Luffae Cylindricae), 1 piece

芡实 Qianshi, Gordon Euryale Seed (Semen Euryales) 10g
Directions: Cut towel gourd into small pieces and soak in the boiled water. Decoct Gordon Euryale seeds, filter and mix the decoction into the water used for soaking. Take the mixture.
Functions: To replenish *yin*, ease mind, control emission.
Indications: Nocturnal emission with dream-disturbed sleep, irritability, dizziness, listlessness, scant and dark yellow urine, red tongue, thready rapid pulse.
Source: 《食物与治病》

07.05 灯心竹叶茶 Dengxin Zhuye Cha
Ingredients:
灯心草 Dengxincao, Common Rush (Medulla Junci) 5g
鲜竹叶 Xian Zhuye, Fresh Bamboo Leaf (Folium Phyllostachys Nigra) 30g
Directions: Pestle into coarse powder, decoct and drink.
Functions: To clear heart fire and calm the mind.
Indications: Neurosis and neurasthenia.
Source: 《常见病验方研究参考资料》

07.06 党参红枣茶 Dangshen Hongzao Cha
Ingredients:
党参 Dangshen, Pilose Asiabell Root (Radix Codonopsis Pilosulae) 15-30g
红枣 Hongzao, Chinese Date (Fructus Jujubae), 5-10 jujubes
陈皮 Chenpi, Dried Tangerine Peel (Pericarpium Citri Reticulatae) 2-3g
Directions: Decoct and drink. Use daily.
Functions: To replenish heart blood and calm the mind.
Indications: Palpitation, forgetfulness, insomnia, dream-disturbed sleep, pale complexion, pale tongue, thready pulse or pulse missing a beat due to heart blood deficiency.
Source: 《百病饮食自疗》

08 利咽爽音 For Clearing Heat and Treating Sore Throat

08.01 二绿玉冰茶 Erlu Yu Bing Cha

Ingredients:
绿茶 Lucha, Green Tea 3g
绿萼梅 Luemei, White Mume Flower (Flos Mume Albus) 3g
玉蝴蝶 Yuhudie, Oroxylum Seed (Semen Oroxyli) 3g
冰糖 Bingtang, Crystal Sugar, desired amount
Directions: Make as tea with boiling water.
Functions: To clear toxic heat and relieve sore throat.
Indications: Hoarse voice.
Source:《新中医》3:1985

08.02 西青果茶 Xiqingguo Cha

Ingredients:
西青果 Xiqingguo, Immature Terminalia Chebula (Fructus Chebulae Immaturus) 6 pieces
Directions: Pestle and make as tea with boiling water.
Functions: To clear heat, produce body fluid, relieve hoarse voice and treat incontinence of stool.
Indications: Chronic pharyngitis and laryngitis.
Source:《常见病验方研究参考资料》

08.03 百合茶 Baihe Cha

Ingredients:
鲜百合汁 Xian Baihe Zhi, Fresh Juice of Lily Bulb (Succus Lilii)
Directions: Make as tea with warm boiled water.
Functions: To clear lung heat and ease the mind.
Indications: Thirst, sore throat, and hemoptysis due to *xu*-heat.
Source:《卫生简易方》

08.04 胖大海冰糖茶 Pangdahai Bingtang Cha

Ingredients:

胖大海 Pangdahai, Boat-Fruited Sterculia Seed (Semen Sterculiae Lychnophorae), 4-6 pieces

冰糖 Bingtang, Crystal Sugar, desired amount

Directions: Make as tea with boiling water. Take two doses a day.
Functions: To clear heat and dissolve phlegm.
Indications: Loss of voice, sore throat, cough with thick yellow phlegm, red tongue with a yellow sticky coating, rolling and rapid pulse due to invasion of wind-heat.
Source: 《饮食疗法》

08.05 茶榄海蜜饮 Cha Lan Hai Mi Yin

Ingredients:
绿茶 Lucha, Green Tea 6g
橄榄 Ganlan, Olive (Fructus Canarii) 6g
胖大海 Pangdahai, Boat-Fruited Sterculia Seed (Semen Sterculiae Lychnophorae), 3 pieces
蜂蜜 Fengmi, Honey, one teaspoonful

Directions: Decoct olive for a short time. Use the decoction to make green tea and boat-fruited Sterculia seeds as tea, add honey before drinking.
Functions: To replenish *yin* and clear fire.
Indications: Chronic laryngitis with hoarseness and sore throat.
Source: 《中国食品》 4:37, 1985

08.06 清咽饮 I   Qingyan Yin I

Ingredients:
银花 Yinhua, Honeysuckle Flower (Flos Lonicerae) 9g
玄参 Xuanshen, Figwort Root (Radix Scrophulariae) 9g
青果 Qingguo, Chinese White Olive (Fructus Canarii) 9g

Directions: Decoct and drink.
Functions: To clear heat, remove toxins and treat a sore throat.
Indications: Chronic pharyngitis.
Source:《百病中医自我疗养丛书·咽喉炎·扁桃体炎》

08.07 清喉茶 Qinghou Cha

Ingredients:
胖大海 Pangdahai, Boat-Fruited Sterculia Seed (Semen Sterculiae Lychnophorae) 10g
金灯 Jindeng, Groundcherry Calyx and Fruit (Calyx et Fructus Physalis) 2g
蝉蜕 Chantui, Cicada Slough (Periostracum Cicadae) 2g
麦冬 Maidong, Dwarf Lilyturf Tuber (Radix Ophiopogonis) 5g
冰糖 Bingtang, Crystal Sugar, desired amount
Directions: Decoct and add crystal sugar before drinking.
Functions: To clear heat and treat sore throat.
Indications: Dry and sore throat and hoarseness.
Source:《健康文摘》 3:20, 1985

08.08 参叶青果茶 Shenye Qingguo Cha

Ingredients:
人参叶 Renshen Ye, Ginseng Leaf (Folium Ginseng) 9g
青果 Qingguo, Chinese White Olive (Fructus Canarii) 30g
Directions: Make as tea with boiling water.
Functions: To clear heat, produce body fluid and moisten dryness.
Indications: Chronic pharyngitis.
Source:《百病中医自我疗养丛书·咽喉炎》

08.09 丝瓜饮 II Sigua Yin II

Ingredients:
丝瓜汁 Sigua Zhi, Towel Gourd Juice (Succus Luffae Cylindricae), 1 cup

冰糖 Bingtang, Crystal Sugar, desired amount

Directions: Boil and add crystal sugar before drinking.
Functions: To replenish *yin*, treat throat diseases.
Indications: Chronic laryngitis with hoarseness and sore throat.
Source:《中国食品》4:37, 1985

08.10 银麦甘桔饮 Yin Mai Gan Jie Yin
Ingredients:
银花 Yinhua, Honeysuckle Flower (Flos Lonicerae) 9g
麦冬 Maidong, Dwarf Lilyturf Tuber (Radix Ophiopogonis) 9g
桔梗 Jiegeng, Platycodon Root (Radix Platycodi) 6g
生甘草 Sheng Gancao, Liquorice Root (Radix Glycyrrhizae) 6g

Directions: Make as tea with boiling water.
Functions: To nourish *yin*, clear lung heat, treat throat diseases.
Indications: Sore throat, dry mouth and thirst.
Source:《中国药膳学》

08.11 绿茶合欢饮 Lucha Hehuan Yin
Ingredients:
绿茶 Lucha, Green Tea 3g
合欢花 Hehuan Hua, Albizzia Flower (Flos Albizziae) 3g
胖大海 Pangdahai, Boat-Fruited Sterculia Seed (Semen Sterculiae Lychnophorae), 2 pieces
冰糖 Bingtang, Crystal Sugar, desired amount

Directions: Make as tea with boiling water.
Functions: To clear heat, moisten throat.
Indications: Acute and chronic pharygolaryngitis and loss of voice due to flaring of fire and dryness of lung.
Source:《新中医》3:42, 1985

08.12 点地梅茶 Diandimei Cha

Ingredients:
点地梅 Diandimei, Rockjasmine (Herba Androsacis) 10g

Directions: Make as tea with boiling water.

Functions: To clear heat, promote detoxification, treat throat and relieve swelling.

Indications: Sore throat.

Source: 《百病中医自我疗养丛书·咽喉炎》

08.13 罗汉果速溶饮 Luohanguo Surongyin

Ingredients:
罗汉果 Luohanguo, Chinese Momordica Fruit (Fructus Momordicae) 250g

Directions: Decoct, collecting the decocted fluid every 30 minutes. Add water to decoct three times. Mix all the decocted fluid and continue boiling until very thick. Remove from heat, cool, and add 500g white sugar. Stir, dry, crush, and store in a bottle. Use 10g each time and make as tea with boiling water.

Functions: To replenish *yin*, treat throat.

Indications: Pharyngolaryngitis.

Source: 《广西中药志》

08.14 苏叶茶 Suye Cha

Ingredients:
炒苏叶 Chao Su Ye, parched Perilla Leaf (Folium Perillae) 3g
炒盐 Chao Yan, Baked Salt 6g

Directions: Decoct and drink.

Functions: To dispel wind heat, replenish *yin* and treat the throat.

Indications: Loss of voice in common cold.

Source: 《云南中医验方》

09 生津止渴 For Promoting the Production of Body Fluid and Relieving Thirst

09.01 人参乌梅茶 Renshen Wumei Cha

Ingredients:

人参 Renshen, Ginseng (Radix Ginseng) 6g

乌梅 Wumei, Smoked Plum (Fructus Mume) 10g

白糖 Baitang, White Sugar, desired amount

Directions: Make as tea with boiling water.

Functions: To tonify the whole body, produce body fluid and quench thirst.

Indications: Deficient syndromes.

Source:《祝您健康》6:38, 1988

09.02 三汁饮 Sanzhi Yin

Ingredients:

麦冬 Maidong, Dwarf Lilyturf Tuber (Radix Ophiopogonis) 10g

地黄 Dihuang, Rehmannia Root (Radix Rehmanniae) 15g

藕 Ou, Lotus Rhizome (Nelumbinis Rhizomatis), proper amount

Directions: Decoct Dwarf Lilyturf tuber and Rehmannia root by bringing to a boil and then simmering for 20 minutes. Filter and save the decoction. Decoct lotus by bringing to a boil and then simmering for 30 minutes. Filter and save the decoction. Mix the two decoctions and drink the mixture.

Functions: To produce body fluid and relieve dryness.

Indications: Dry throat, regurgitation and vomiting.

Source:《民间验方》

09.03 三鲜茶 I Sanxian Cha I

Ingredients:

鲜藿香 Xian Huoxiang, Fresh Cablia Patchouli Herb (Herba

Pogostemonis) 30g
鲜荷叶　Xian Heye, Fresh Lotus Leaf (Folium Nelumbinis) 50g
鲜芦根　Xian Lugen, Fresh Reed Rhizome (Rhizoma Phragmitis) 100g

Directions: Decoct and drink the decoction.

Functions: To resolve damp and treat illness caused by summer heat.

Indications: Aestival fever with thirst and poor appetite. It can be used as an ordinary drink in summer.

Source:《中医儿科临证浅解》

09.04　五味子饮　Wuweizi Yin

Ingredients:
五味子　Wuweizi, Chinese Magnoliavine Fruit (Fructus Schisandrae) 100g
紫苏叶　Zisu Ye, Perilla Leaf (Folium Perillae) 50g
人参　Renshen, Ginseng (Radix Ginseng) 30g

Directions: Decoct and add white sugar to taste to the decoction before drinking it.

Functions: To produce body fluid, quench thirst, warm essence and reinforce *qi*.

Indications: *Qi* deficiency, seminal emission.

Source:《饮膳正要》

09.05　玉竹茶　Yuzhu Cha

Ingredients:
玉竹　Yuzhu, Fragrant Solomonseal Rhizome (Rhizoma Polygonati Odorati) 9g

Directions: Make as tea with boiling water.

Functions: To nourish *yin*, moisten dryness and produce body fluid.

Indications: Thirst and dry throat due to *yin* deficiency.

Source:《经验方》

09.06 玉竹乌梅饮 Yuzhu Wumei Yin

Ingredients:

玉竹 Yuzhu, Fragrant Solomonseal Rhizome (Rhizoma Polygonati Odorati) 9g

北沙参 Beishashen, Coastal Glehnia Root (Radix Glehniae) 9g

石斛 Shihu, Dendrobium (Herba Dendrobii) 9g

麦冬 Maidong, Dwarf Lilyturf Tuber (Radix Ophiopogonis) 9g

乌梅 Wumei, Smoked Plum (Fructus Mume), 5 pieces

冰糖 Bingtang, Crystal Sugar, desired amount

Directions: Decoct and drink.

Functions: To nourish *yin*, moisten dryness, produce body fluid and quench thirst.

Indications: Profuse sweating and thirst due to the damage of *yin* in a febrile disease.

Source:《中国药膳学》

09.07 甘蔗茶 Ganzhe Cha

Ingredients:

甘蔗 Ganzhe, Sugarcane Stem (Caulis Saccharum Sinensis) 120g

Directions: Slice, decoct, and drink.

Functions: To clear heat, remove toxins and quench thirst.

Indications: Body fluid damage due to excessive heat in measles complicated by prolonged rash.

Source:《上海常用中草药》

09.08 石斛冰糖茶 Shihu Bingtang Cha

Ingredients:

鲜石斛 Xian Shihu, Fresh Dendrobium (Herba Dendrobii) 15g

冰糖 Bingtang, Crystal Sugar, desired amount

Directions: Make as tea with boiling water.

Functions: To nourish *yin*, reinforce the stomach, clear heat and produce body fluid.
Indications: Irritability, thirst, dry throat and poor appetite.
Source:《中国药膳学》

09.09 石斛甘蔗饮 Shihu Ganzhe Yin

Ingredients:
鲜石斛 Xian Shihu, Fresh Dendrobium (Herba Dendrobii) 15g
玉竹 Yuzhu, Fragrant Solomonseal Rhizome (Rhizoma Polygonati Odorati) 12g
麦冬 Maidong, Dwarf Lilyturf Tuber (Radix Ophiopogonis) 12g
北沙参 Beishashen, Coastal Glehnia Root (Radix Glehniae) 5g
山药 Shanyao, Common Yam Rhizome (Rhizoma Dioscoreae) 10g
甘蔗汁 Ganzhe Zhi, Sugarcane Stem Juice (Succus Saccharum Sinensis Caulis) 250g

Directions: Decoct the first five. Mix the decoction with sugarcane stem juice. Drink as tea.
Functions: To reinforce *yin*, produce body fluid, harmonize the stomach, stop nausea and vomiting.
Indications: Thirst, nausea and poor appetite.
Source:《中国药膳学》

09.10 生津茶 Shengjin Cha

Ingredients:
青果 Qingguo, Chinese White Olive (Fructus Canarii), 5 pieces (ground)
石斛 Shihu, Dendrobium (Herba Dendrobii) 6g
菊花 Juhua, Chrysanthemum Flower (Flos Chrysanthemi) 6g
竹茹 Zhuru, Bamboo Shavings (Caulis Bambusae in Taeniam) 6g
麦冬 Maidong, Dwarf Lilyturf Tuber (Radix Ophiopogonis) 9g
桑叶 Sangye, Mulberry Leaf (Folium Mori) 9g

鲜藕　Xian Ou, Fresh Lotus Rhizome (Nelumbinis Rhizomatis), 10 slices
黄梨　Huangli, Pear (Fructus Pyri), 2 pears (peeled)
荸荠　Biqi, Waternut Corm (Cormus Eleocharis Dulcis), 5 pieces (peeled)
鲜芦根　Xian Lugen, Fresh Reed Rhizome (Rhizoma Phragmitis) 20g
Directions: Decoct, drink.
Functions: To produce body fluid, moisten dryness.
Indications: Thirst, irritability and cough with thick phlegm due to excessive heat in febrile disease.
Source:《慈禧光绪医方选议》

09.11 花粉茶　Huafen Cha

Ingredients:
天花粉　Tianhuafen, Snakegourd Root (Radix Trichosanthis) 125g
Directions: Grind into powder. Use 15-20g each time and make as tea with boiling water.
Functions: To clear heat, produce body fluid and quench thirst.
Indications: Diabetes, hemoptysis due to dryness in the lungs.
Source:《新中医》3:1977

09.12 苦竹叶速溶饮　Kuzhuye Surongyin

Ingredients:
鲜苦竹叶　Xian Kuzhu Ye, Fresh Bitter Bamboo Leaf (Folium Pleioblasti) 500g　**or**
干苦竹叶　Gan Kuzhu Ye, Dried Bitter Bamboo Leaf (Folium Pleioblasti) 250g
Directions: Decoct for one hour, filter and boil the decoction over low heat until thickened. Remove from heat, cool and mix the thick paste with 250g white sugar. Dry, crush, and store in a bottle. Use 10g each time to make as tea with boiling water. Take two doses a day.

Functions: To clear heat and relieve irritability.
Indications: Thirst, irritability and insomnia in febrile disease.
Source: 《圣济总录》

09.13 丝瓜茶 Sigua Cha

Ingredients:
丝瓜　Sigua, Towel Gourd (Luffae Cylindricae) 200g
茶叶　Chaye, Tea Leaf (Folium Camelliae Sinensis) 5g

Directions: Slice towel gourd, decoct with salt water. Make tea. Mix the tea with the fluid. Drink the mixture. Take twice a day.
Functions: To replenish *yin*, produce body fluid and quench thirst.
Indications: Weakness after illness and diabetes.
Source: 《烟酒茶俗》

09.14 双花饮 Shuanghua Yin

Ingredients:
金银花　Jinyinhua, Honeysuckle Flower (Flos Lonicerae) 500g
山楂　Shanzha, Hawthorn Fruit (Fructus Crataegi) 500g
菊花　Juhua, Chrysanthemum Flower (Flos Chrysanthemi) 500g
蜂蜜　Fengmi, Honey 5,000g

Directions: Decoct first three with 30kg water using low heat for 30 minutes. Filter, and save fluid. Decoct honey separately using low heat until it becomes yellowish. Mix the decocted honey fluid into the above fluid. When the honey is completely melted, filter with gauze, cool, and take the mixture.
Functions: To clear heat, promote detoxification, produce body fluid, moisten dryness, dispel wind and remove stasis.
Indications: Irritability, thirst, palpitation, dizziness, headache, and red eyes caused by summer heat.
Source: 《成都同仁堂滋补餐厅》

10 温中暖胃 For Warming the Stomach and Strengthening the Middle *Jiao*

10.01 一味生姜饮 Yiwei Shengjiang Yin

Ingredients:
生姜 Sheng Jiang, Fresh Ginger (Rhizoma Zingiberis Recens) 50g

Directions: Cut into slices. Decoct over low heat for 30 minutes. Drink three times a day.

Functions: To warm the middle *jiao*, to stop vomiting.

Indications: Vomiting, gastric ulcer, duodenal ulcer.

Source: 《贵阳中医学院学报》 4:46, 1983

10.02 丁香茶 Dingxiang Cha

Ingredients:
丁香 Dingxiang, Cloves (Flos Caryophylli), 1-2 cloves

Directions: Make as tea with boiling water.

Functions: To warm middle *jiao*, redirect *qi*, warm the kidney to reinforce its *yang*.

Indications: Hiccups, vomiting, impotence, genital coldness and damp-cold leukorrhagia.

Source: 《饮馔服食笺》

10.03 刀豆饮 Daodou Yin

Ingredients:
刀豆 Daodou, Jack Bean (Semen Canavaliae) 10g
柿蒂 Shi Di, Persimmon Calyx (Calyx Kaki), 10 pieces

Directions: Decoct and drink as tea two or three times a day.

Functions: To reinforce the spleen and stomach.

Indications: Spleen and stomach deficiency with symptoms including hiccups, shortness of breath, pale or sallow complexion, cold limbs, poor appetite,

tiredness, pale tongue with white sticky coating, thready and weak pulse.
Source:《百病饮食自疗》

10.04 刀豆茶 I Daodou Cha I
Ingredients:
刀豆 Daodou, Jack Bean (Semen Canavaliae) 15g

Directions: Crush, decoct and drink as tea.
Functions: To warm middle *jiao*, redirect *qi*.
Indications: Hiccup.
Source:《中国医药报》225:1987

10.05 艾叶茶 Aiye Cha
Ingredients:
艾叶 Aiye, Argyi Wormwood Leaf (Folium Artemisiae Argyi)

Directions: Collect the young shoots in spring. Dry them in the sun. Pestle into rough powder, and store in a dry cool place. Use 3g each time and make as tea with boiling water. Take three or four doses a day.
Functions: To warm meridian, expel cold and stop pain.
Indications: Gastric pain due to cold.
Source:《常见病验方研究参考资料》

10.06 桂皮山楂饮 Guipi Shanzha Yin
Ingredients:
桂皮 Gui Pi, Cassia Bark (Cortex Cinnamomi) 6g
山楂肉 Shanzharou, Hawthorn Fruit (Fructus Crataegi) 10g

Directions: Decoct over high heat and then low heat for 30 minutes. Filter, add 30g brown sugar before drinking.
Functions: To warm stomach, dispel cold, promote digestion and remove food retention.
Indications: Epigastric pain and distention due to overeating, poor

appetite, constipation.
Source:《食物与治病》

10.07 干姜饮 Ganjiang Yin

Ingredients:
干姜 Gan Jiang, Dried Ginger (Rhizoma Zingiberis) 3g (ground)

Directions: Mix into the cooked rice fluid and take it.

Functions: To warm middle *jiao* and stomach, send stomach *qi* downward, stop vomiting.

Indications: Gastric pain of the *xu*-cold type, vomiting.

Source:《中国药膳学》

10.08 益胃茶 I Yiwei Cha I

Ingredients:
丁香 Dingxiang, Cloves (Flos Caryophylli) 2g
神曲 Shenqu, Medicated Leaven (Massa Fermentata Medicinalis) 15g

Directions: Make as tea with boiling water.

Functions: To warm middle *jiao*, regulate *qi*, promote digestion and remove food retention.

Indications: Vomiting and indigestion caused by cold affecting the stomach.

Source:《食品周报》1984 年 10 月 5 日

10.09 健胃茶 I Jianwei Cha I

Ingredients:
徐长卿 Xuchangqing, Paniculate Swallowwort Root (Radix Cynanchi Paniculati) 4.5g
北沙参 Beishashen, Coastal Glehnia Root (Radix Glehniae) 3g
化橘红 Huajuhong, Pummelo Peel (Exocarpium Citri Grandis) 3g
白芍 Baishao, White Peony Root (Radix Paeoniae Alba) 3g
生甘草 Sheng Gancao, Liquorice Root (Radix Glycyrrhizae) 2g

玫瑰花 Meigui Hua, Rose (Flos Roasae Rugosae) 1.5g
红茶 Hongcha, Black Tea 1.5g

Directions: Pestle into coarse powder. Make as tea with boiling water. Take one dose every day for three months.

Functions: To strengthen spleen, warm middle *jiao*, soothe liver and activate blood circulation.

Indications: Superficial gastritis of *xu*-cold type with a dull pain in the epigastric region.

Source: 《新中医》 9:1981

10.10 健胃茶 II   Jianwei Cha II

Ingredients:
徐长卿 Xuchangqing, Paniculate Swallowwort Root (Radix Cynanchi Paniculati) 3g
北沙参 Beishashen, Coastal Glehnia Root (Radix Glehniae) 3g
当归 Danggui, Chinese Angelica (Radix Angelicae Sinensis) 3g
黄芪 Huangqi, Milkvetch Root (Radix Astragali) 4.5g
乌梅肉 Wumeirou, Smoked Plum (Fructus Mume) 1.5g
生甘草 Sheng Gancao, Liquorice Root (Radix Glycyrrhizae) 1.5g
红茶 Hongcha, Black Tea 1.5g

Directions: Pestle into coarse powder, make as tea with boiling water. Take one dose every day for three months.

Functions: To reinforce *qi*, strengthen spleen, harmonize middle *jiao* and nourish stomach.

Indications: Atrophic gastritis of *xu*-cold type.
Source: 《新中医》 9:1981

10.11 暖胃茶 Nuanwei Cha

Ingredients:
干姜 Gan Jiang, Dried Ginger (Rhizoma Zingiberis) 5g

紫蔻 Zikou, Round Cardamom (Fructus Amomi Cardamomi) 3g
吴茱萸 Wuzhuyu, Medicinal Evodia Fruit (Fructus Evodiae) 2g

Directions: Decoct and drink.
Functions: To warm stomach, stop vomiting.
Indications: Abdominal pain and distention, vomiting, and poor appetite due to stomach cold.
Source:《健康文摘》3:20, 1985

10.12 葱姜饮 I   Cong Jiang Yin I

Ingredients:
葱白带根 Cong Bai Daigen, Fistular Onion Stalk and Root (Bulbus cum Radix Allii Fistulosi), 3 stalks
生姜 Sheng Jiang, Fresh Ginger (Rhizoma Zingiberis Recens), 3 slices
荔枝叶 Lizhi Ye, Lychee Leaf (Folium Litchi) 3g

Directions: Decoct and drink.
Functions: To strengthen spleen and warm stomach.
Indications: Vomiting, dizziness, pallor, lassitude, preference for warm drinks, cold extremities, loose stools, pale tongue, soft and weak pulse.
Source:《百病饮食自疗》

10.13 葱椒饮 Cong Jiao Yin

Ingredients:
葱 Cong, Fistular Onion (Herba Allii Fistulosi), 3 pieces
生姜 Sheng Jiang, Fresh Ginger (Rhizoma Zingiberis Recens), 3 slices
胡椒粉 Hujiao Fen, Black Pepper Powder (Pulvis Piperis Nigri Fructus)

Directions: Make as tea with boiling water.
Functions: To dispel cold and relieve pain.
Indications: Cold pain in the epigastrium and abdomen, vomiting.
Source:《民间验方》

10.14 橘花茶 Juhua Cha

Ingredients:
橘花 Juhua, Tangerine Flower (Flos Citri Reticulatae) 3-5g
红茶 Hongcha, Black Tea 3-5g

Directions: Make tea with boiling water. Take three or four times a day.
Functions: To warm middle *jiao*, regulate *qi* and harmonize stomach.
Indications: Gastric pain due to cold in stomach, accompanied by cough with copious phlegm, and food retention.
Source:《云林堂饮食制度集》

10.15 糖糟茶 Tangzao Cha

Ingredients:
糖糟 Tangzao, Sugar Slops 500g
鲜生姜 Xian Sheng Jiang, Fresh Ginger (Rhizoma Zingiberis Recens) 120g

Directions: Grind well. Make pieces of 10-15g each, dry and store in a bottle. Use one piece each time and make as tea with boiling water.
Functions: To replenish *qi*, warm stomach, promote digestion.
Indications: Indigestion, epigastric fullness and distention.
Source:《种福堂公选良方》

10.16 薏苡叶茶 Yiyiye Cha

Ingredients:
薏苡叶 Yiyi Ye, Coix Leaf (Folium Coicis) 30g

Directions: Decoct and drink.
Functions: To warm stomach, reinforce *qi*. Use as a daily drink in summer.
Source:《中国食品》 7:22, 1985

11 补肾聪耳 For Invigorating the Kidney and Clear Hearing

11.01 人参枸杞饮 Renshen Gouqi Yin

Ingredients:
人参 Renshen, Ginseng (Radix Ginseng) 10g
枸杞子 Gouqi Zi, Barbary Wolfberry Fruit (Fructus Lycii) 30g

Directions: Decoct and drink as tea.

Functions: To warm the kidney, invigorate *yang*.

Indications: Headache, dizziness, tinnitus, lassitude and soreness of the lumbar area and lower extremities.

Source:《百病饮食自疗》

11.02 丹皮京菖茶 Danpi Jingchang Cha

Ingredients:
粉丹皮 Fendanpi, Tree Peony Bark (Cortex Moutan Radicis) 5g
川芎 Chuanxiong, Szechwan Lovage Rhizome (Rhizoma Chuanxiong) 5g
京菖 Jingchang, Irkutsk Anemone Rhizome (Rhizoma Anemones Altaicae) 3g
茶叶 Chaye, Tea Leaf (Folium Camelliae Sinensis) 3g

Directions: Make as tea with boiling water.

Functions: Cool blood, activate blood circulation, expel wind, treat ear diseases.

Indications: Otitis media catarrhalis, otitis mycotica.

Source:《经验方》

11.03 平肝清热茶 Pinggan Qingre Cha

Ingredients:
龙胆草 Longdancao, Chinese Gentian (Radix Gentianae) 1.8g
醋柴胡 Cu Chaihu, Red Thorowax Root (Radix Bupleuri) (parched with vinegar) 1.8g
川芎 Chuanxiong, Sichuan Lovage Rhizome (Rhizoma Chuanxiong) 1.8g

菊花 Juhua, Chrysanthemum Flower (Flos Chrysanthemi) 3g
生地黄 Sheng Dihuang, Dried Rehmannia Root (Radix Rehmanniae) 3g

Directions: Pestle. Decoct. Drink.
Functions: To soothe the liver, clear heat.
Indications: Otitis media catarrhalis.
Source: 《慈禧光绪医方选议》

11.04 参须京菖茶 Shenxu Jingchang Cha

Ingredients:
参须 Shenxu, Ginseng Tendril (Radix Ginseng) 3g
京菖 Jingchang, Irkutsk Anemone Rhizome (Rhizoma Anemones Altaicae) 3g
茶叶 Chaye, Tea Leaf (Folium Camelliae Sinensis) 3g

Directions: Make as tea with boiling water. One dose is for one day.
Functions: To reinforce *qi*, promote hearing.
Indications: Decline of hearing, tinnitus.
Source: 《经验方》

11.05 菟丝子茶 Tusizi Cha

Ingredients:
菟丝子 Tusizi, Dodder Seed (Semen Cuscutae) 10g
红糖 Hongtang, Brown Sugar, desired amount

Directions: Pestle dodder seeds. Make as tea with boiling water.
Functions: To reinforce kidney, replenish essence, nourish liver and improve vision.
Indications: Infertility, sterility. Long-term use may prolong life.
Source: 《江苏中医杂志》 5:1982

11.06 槐菊茶 Huai Ju Cha

Ingredients:
槐花 Huai Hua, Pagodatree Flower (Flos Sophorae) 3g

菊花　Juhua, Chrysanthemum Flower (Flos Chrysanthemi) 3g
绿茶　Lucha, Green Tea 3g

Directions: Make as tea with boiling water.
Functions: To clear liver fire.
Indications: Chronic otitis media, mild deafness.
Source: 《百病中医自我疗养丛书·化脓性中耳炎》

12 理气悦心 For Regulating *Qi* and Alleviating Mental Depression

12.01 二花参麦茶　Erhua Shen Mai Cha
Ingredients:
厚朴花　Houpu Hua, Officinal Magnolia Flower (Flos Magnoliae Officinalis) 3g
佛手花　Foshou Hua, Finger Citron Flower (Flos Citri Sarcodactylis) 3g
红茶　Hongcha, Black Tea 3g
橘络　Juluo, Tangerine Pith (Retinervus Citri Reticulatae Fructus) 2g
党参　Dangshen, Pilose Asiabell Root (Radix Codonopsis Pilosulae) 6g
炒麦芽　Chao Mai Ya, Parched Germinated Barley (Fructus Hordei Germinatus) 6g

Directions: Grind into coarse powder. Make as tea with boiling water. Drink for 20 days as one course.
Functions: To soothe the liver, regulate *qi*, strengthen the spleen, dissolve phlegm, promote digestion.
Indications: Pharyngitis due to stagnation of the liver *qi* and retention of phlegm.
Source: 《江西中医药》2:1986

12.02 二花桔英茶　Erhua Ju Yu Cha
Ingredients:
月季花　Yueji Hua, Chinese Rose Flower (Flos Rosae Chinensis) 3g
玫瑰花　Meigui Hua, Rose (Flos Roasae Rugosae) 3g

绿茶 Lucha, Green Tea 3g
桔梗 Jiegeng, Platycodon Root (Radix Platycodi) 6g
山茱萸 Shanzhuyu, Asiatic Cornelian Cherry Fruit (Fructus Corni) 6g

Directions: Grind into coarse powder. Make as tea with boiling water. Drink for 20 days as one course.

Functions: To soothe the liver, nourish *yin*, relieve sore throat.

Indications: Pharyngolaryngitis due to *qi* stagnation and blood stasis.

Source: 《江西中医药》 2:1986

12.03 二绿合欢茶 Erlu Hehuan Cha

Ingredients:
绿萼梅 Luemei, White Mume Flower (Flos Mume Albus) 3g
绿茶 Lucha, Green Tea 3g
合欢花 Hehuan Hua, Albizzia Flower (Flos Albizziae) 3g
枸杞子 Gouqi Zi, Barbary Wolfberry Fruit (Fructus Lycii) 5g

Directions: Make as tea with boiling water. Drink for 20 days one course.

Functions: To soothe the liver, regulate *qi*, nourish the heart, calm the mind.

Indications: Pharyngitis due to liver *qi* stagnation.

Source: 《江西中医药》 2:1986

12.04 二绿女贞茶 Erlu Nuzhen Cha

Ingredients:
绿萼梅 Luemei, White Mume Flower (Flos Mume Albus) 3g
绿茶 Lucha, Green Tea 3g
橘络 Juluo, Tangerine Pith (Retinervus Citri Reticulatae Fructus) 3g
女贞子 Nuzhen Zi, Glossy Privet Fruit (Fructus Ligustri Lucidi) 6g (pounded)

Directions: Make as tea with boiling water. Drink for 20 days as one course.

Functions: To soothe the liver, regulate *qi*, nourish *yin*, dissolve phlegm.

Indications: Pharyngitis due to heat combined with phlegm.
Source:《江西中医药》2:1986

12.05 佛手茶 Foshou Cha

Ingredients:
佛手 Foshou, Finger Citron (Fructus Citri Sarcodactylis) 10g
Directions: Make as tea with boiling water.
Functions: To soothe liver, regulate *qi*.
Indications: Laryngitis.
Source:《经验方》

12.06 佛手枣汤 Foshou Zao Tang

Ingredients:
佛手 Foshou, Finger Citron (Fructus Citri Sarcodactylis) 10g
生姜 Sheng Jiang, Fresh Ginger (Rhizoma Zingiberis Recens), 2 slices
红枣 Hongzao, Chinese Date (Fructus Jujubae), 10 pieces
Directions: Decoct and add white sugar to taste before drinking.
Functions: To soothe the liver, regulate *qi*, strengthen the spleen.
Indications: Melancholia due to the damage of liver by anger accompanied with fullness in chest, distending pain in hypochondrium, impotence, sticky tongue coating and wiry pulse.
Source:《食物与治病》

12.07 玫瑰花茶 Meiguihua Cha

Ingredients:
玫瑰花瓣 Meigui Huaban, Rose (Flos Roasae Rugosae) 6-10g
Directions: Make as tea with boiling water.
Functions: To soothe the liver and regulate *qi*.
Indications: Fullness and distending pain in chest and hypochondrium with poor appetite.

Source:《饮食疗法》

12.08 青皮麦芽饮 Qingpi Maiya Yin

Ingredients:
青皮 Qingpi, Green Tangerine Peel (Pericarpium Citri Reticulatae Viride) 10g
生麦芽 Sheng Mai Ya, Germinated Barley (Fructus Hordei Germinatus) 30g
Directions: Decoct by bringing to a boil and then simmer for five minutes.
Functions: To soothe liver, regulate *qi*.
Indications: Distending pain in the hypochondrium and poor appetite due to liver *qi* stagnation.
Source:《民间验方》

12.09 厚朴花茶 Houpuhua Cha

Ingredients:
厚朴花 Houpu Hua, Officinal Magnolia Flower (Flos Magnoliae Officinalis) 10g
Directions: Make as tea with boiling water.
Functions: To regulate *qi*, dissolve phlegm.
Indications: Laryngitis.
Source:《常见病验方研究参考资料》

12.10 胃乐茶 Weile Cha

Ingredients:
制香附 Zhi Xiangfu, Prepared Nutgrass Galingale Rhizome (Rhizoma Cyperi Praeparatum) 300g
焦建曲 Jiao Jianqu, Charred Medicated Leaven (Massa Fermentata Medicinalis) 180g

制金柑 Zhi Jingan, Prepared Ovar Kumquat Fruit (Fructus Fortunellae Margaritae Praeparatum) 180g
木香 Muxiang, Costusroot (Radix Aucklandiae) 90g
陈皮 Chenpi, Dried Tangerine Peel (Pericarpium Citri Reticulatae) 90g
甘草 Gancao, Liquorice Root (Radix Glycyrrhizae) 30g

Directions: Grind the last three ingredients into powder. Decoct the first three twice for one hour each. Mix the decoctions. Settle the fluid for six hours, filter and heat to concentrate to a thick paste. Add the powder, dry, sieve, and store in small bags with 12g in each. Use one bag each time and make as tea with boiling water. Take two doses a day.

Functions: To regulate *qi*, dissolve stagnation, harmonize stomach and strengthen spleen.

Indications: Indigestion with fullness in chest and epigastric region due to *qi* stagnation and retention of food.

Source:《中草药制剂方法》

12.11 绿萼梅茶 Luemei Cha

Ingredients:
绿萼梅 Luemei, White Mume Flower (Flos Mume Albus) 5g
冰糖 Bingtang, Crystal Sugar, desired amount

Directions: Make as tea with boiling water.

Functions: To soothe liver, harmonize stomach, dissolve phlegm.

Indications: Laryngitis.

Source:《河北中药手册》

12.12 橘朴茶 Ju Pu Cha

Ingredients:
橘络 Juluo, Tangerine Pith (Retinervus Citri Reticulatae Fructus) 3g
厚朴 Houpu, Officinal Magnolia Bark (Cortex Magnoliae Officinalis) 3g
红茶 Hongcha, Black Tea 3g

党参 Dangshen, Pilose Asiabell Root (Radix Codonopsis Pilosulae) 6g
Directions: Pestle into coarse powder. Make as tea with boiling water.
Functions: To soothe liver, regulate liver *qi*, dissolve phlegm.
Indications: Laryngitis due to *qi* stagnation and phlegm-damp.
Source:《江西中医药》2:1986

12.13 橘叶饮 Juye Yin
Ingredients:
橘叶 Juye, Tangerine Leaf (Folium Citri Reticulatae) 30g
Directions: Decoct and drink.
Functions: To regulate *qi*, relieve pain.
Indications: Gastric pain and hypochondriac pain due to an attack on the stomach by the liver *qi*, accompanied by belching, regurgitation, non-smooth discharge of stools, white thin tongue coating and wiry pulse.
Source:《百病饮食自疗》

12.14 夏枯瓜络饮 Xiaku Gualuo Yin
Ingredients:
夏枯草 Xiakucao, Common Selfheal Fruit-spike (Spica Prunellae) 10g
丝瓜络 Sigua Luo, Luffa Vegetable Sponge (Retinervus Luffae Fructus) 10g
Directions: Decoct, filter, mix the decoction with melted crystal sugar to taste. Boil again for a short time. Take two or three times a day.
Functions: To regulate *qi*, clear heat.
Indications: Feverish sensation, irritability, quick temper, fullness and distention in chest and hypochondrium, bitter taste in mouth, reddish tongue with yellow coating, wiry and rapid pulse due to *qi* stagnation.
Source:《百病饮食自疗》

13 开胃消食 For Increasing Appetite and Relieving Dyspepsia

13.01 二根麦萝茶 Ergen Mai Luo Cha
Ingredients:
铁扫帚根 Tiesaozhou Gen, Cuneata Bush Clover Root (Radix Lespedeza Cuneatae) 500g
胡颓子 Hutuizi, Elaeagnus Fruit (Fructus Elaeagni) 500g (stir-fried with honey)
麦芽 Mai Ya, Germinated Barley (Fructus Hordei Germinatus) 10g
枯萝卜 Ku Luobo, Withered Radish (Raphanus Sativus) 10g
Directions: Grind into coarse powder. Decoct and drink the decoction.
Functions: To clear heat, strengthen the spleen and relieve distention.
Indications: Infantile indigestion.
Source:《全国中草药汇编》

13.02 山楂茶 Shanzha Cha
Ingredients:
炒山楂 Chao Shanzha, Parched Hawthorn Fruit (Fructus Crataegi) 15g
Directions: Decoct and drink the decoction.
Functions: To promote digestion, remove food retention, dispel blood stasis and expel tapeworm.
Indications: Food retention (especially meat), abdominal pain and dysentery.
Source:《食品周报》1984 年 10 月 5 日

13.03 山楂橘皮茶 Shanzha Jupi Cha
Ingredients:
山楂 Shanzha, Hawthorn Fruit (Fructus Crataegi) 20g
橘皮 Jupi, Dried Tangerine Peel (Pericarpium Citri Reticulatae) 5g
Directions: Decoct the fruit over low heat until it becomes yellow.

Remove the fruit and save. Cut the peel. Put the decocted fruit and the sliced peel in a cup. Make as tea with boiling water.

Functions: To promote digestion, regulate *qi* and harmonize the stomach.

Indications: Poor appetite, food retention.

Source:《经验方》

13.04 山楂神曲汤 Shanzha Shenqu Tang

Ingredients:

山楂 Shanzha, Hawthorn Fruit (Fructus Crataegi) 15g
神曲 Shenqu, Medicated Leaven (Massa Fermentata Medicinalis) 15g

Directions: Decoct and drink the decoction.

Functions: To promote digestion, remove food retention, harmonize the stomach and redirect *qi*.

Indications: Food retention, vomiting, epigastric and abdominal distention, diarrhea with undigested food in the stool.

Source:《百病饮食自疗》

13.05 小儿七星茶 Xiaoer Qixing Cha

Ingredients:

钩藤 Gouteng, Gambir Plant (Ramulus Uncariae cum Uncis) 10g
山楂 Shanzha, Hawthorn Fruit (Fructus Crataegi) 10g
淡竹叶 Danzhuye, Lophatherum Herb (Herba Lophatheri) 10g
薏苡仁 Yiyi Ren, Coix Seed (Semen Coicis) 15g
麦芽 Mai Ya, Germinated Barley (Fructus Hordei Germinatus) 15g
蝉蜕 Chantui, Cicada Slough (Periostracum Cicadae) 4g
甘草 Gancao, Liquorice Root (Radix Glycyrrhizae) 4g

Directions: Pestle, decoct and drink the decoction.

Functions: To expel wind, clear heat, promote digestion, remove food retention, relieve anxiety and calm the mind.

Indications: Infantile malnutrition.

Source:《家庭医生》6:1986

13.06 甘露茶 Ganlu Cha

Ingredients:
橘皮 Jupi, Dried Tangerine Peel (Pericarpium Citri Reticulatae) 200g
乌药 Wuyao, Combined Spicebush Root (Radix Linderae) 50g
炒山楂 Chao Shanzha, Parched Hawthorn Fruit (Fructus Crataegi) 50g
川朴 Chuanpu, Officinal Magnolia Bark (Cortex Magnoliae Officinalis) 50g (stir-baked with ginger juice)
枳壳 Zhiqiao, Orange Fruit (Fructus Aurantii) 50g (parched with wheat bran)
炒谷芽 Chao Guya, Parched Rice Sprout (Fructus Oryzae Germinatus) 60g
神曲 Shenqu, Medicated Leaven (Massa Fermentata Medicinalis) 100g (parched with wheat bran)
茶叶 Chaye, Tea Leaf (Folium Camelliae Sinensis) 150g

Directions: Soak dried tangerine peel in salt solution and toast. Pestle all the herbs, mix them, sift, and store in bags with 20g in each. Use one bag each time together with one slice of fresh ginger and make as tea with boiling water.

Functions: To promote digestion, normalize the stomach.

Indications: Fullness and distention in the epigastric region due to retention of food, poor appetite and/or diarrhea associated with a new living environment.

Source:《家用中成药》

13.07 白蔻茶 Baikou Cha

Ingredients:
白豆蔻 Baidoukou, Round Cardamom Fruit (Fructus Amomi Rotundus) 3g

Directions: Make as tea with boiling water.
Functions: To regulate *qi,* dissolve damp, warm the stomach and remove food retention.
Indications: Food retention due to overeating cold food or fruit.
Source:《食品周报》1984 年 10 月 5 日

13.08 谷芽露茶 Guyalu Cha

Ingredients:
谷芽 Guya, Rice Sprout (Fructus Oryzae Germinatus) 1,000g
Directions: Soak in water, distil twice. Take the distilled fluid as tea.
Functions: To strengthen spleen, promote digestion and harmonize the stomach.
Indications: Poor appetite and indigestion due to weakness of spleen after illness.
Source:《中国医学大辞典》

13.09 佩香茶 Pei Xiang Cha

Ingredients:
佩兰 Peilan, Fortune Eupatorium Herb (Herba Eupatorii) 6g
藿香 Huoxiang, Cablia Patchouli Herb (Herba Pogostemonis) 3g
薄荷 Bohe, Peppermint (Herba Menthae) 4.5g
白蔻仁 Baikouren, Round Cardamom Fruit (Fructus Amomi Rotundus) 1.5g
Directions: Make as tea with boiling water.
Functions: To reinforce spleen, remove food retention.
Indications: Poor appetite, foul breath and indigestion.
Source:《浙江中医药》8:289, 1979

13.10 金橘茶 Jinju Cha

Ingredients:
金橘 Jinju, Ovar Kumquat Fruit (Fructus Fortunellae Margaritae), 3 pieces

Directions: Press flat. Make as tea with boiling water.
Functions: To regulate *qi*, promote digestion and harmonize the stomach.
Indications: Poor appetite, nausea and vomiting due to food retention.
Source: 《中医大辞典·中药分册》

13.11 玳玳花茶 Daidaihua Cha

Ingredients:
玳玳花 Daidaihua, Daidaihua (Flos Citri Aurantii) 1.5-3g

Directions: Make as tea with boiling water.
Functions: To regulate *qi*, promote appetite.
Indications: Fullness in chest, nausea, distending pain in abdomen.
Source: 《中医大辞典·中药分册》

13.12 砂仁甘草茶 Sharen Gancao Cha

Ingredients:
砂仁 Sharen, Villous Amomum Fruit (Fructus Amomi), 3-5 pieces
甘草 Gancao, Liquorice Root (Radix Glycyrrhizae) 6g

Directions: Make as tea with boiling water.
Functions: To remove stagnation, relieve swelling.
Indications: Laryngitis due to the stagnation of stomach *qi* in the throat.
Source: 《饮馔服食笺》

13.13 消滞茶 Xiaozhi Cha

Ingredients:
山楂 Shanzha, Hawthorn Fruit (Fructus Crataegi) 1,000g
麦芽 Mai Ya, Germinated Barley (Fructus Hordei Germinatus) 1,000g
白梅花 Bai Meihua, White Mume Flower (Flos Mume Albus) 1,500g
布渣叶 Buzhaye, Paniculate Microcos Leaf (Folium Microcotis) 1,500g

Directions: Pestle first two ingredients into coarse powder. Decoct the last two for one hour, filter and add water to decoct a second time for half an hour. Filter, mix the decoctions and boil to enrich to 1,000 ml. Mix the powder into the enriched paste. Dry, crush, and store in paper bags with 20g in each. Use one bag each time, make as tea with boiling water. Take two doses a day.

Functions: To promote digestion, remove food retention.

Indications: Indigestion, diarrhea, loose stools, infantile diarrhea in summer, poor appetite.

Source:《农村中草药制剂技术》

13.14 消食茶 Xiaoshi Cha

Ingredients:

佩兰　Peilan, Fortune Eupatorium Herb (Herba Eupatorii) 5g
白蔻　Baikou, Round Cardamom Fruit (Fructus Amomi Rotundus) 3g
山楂　Shanzha, Hawthorn Fruit (Fructus Crataegi) 15g

Directions: Decoct and drink.

Functions: To replenish *yin*, clear heat, quench thirst.

Indications: Dry throat, thirst.

Source:《健康文摘》 3:20, 1985

13.15 神曲饮 Shenqu Yin

Ingredients:

神曲　Shenqu, Medicated Leaven (Massa Fermentata Medicinalis) 30g

Directions: Make as tea with boiling water.

Functions: To promote digestion, remove food retention.

Indications: Egg food retention.

Source:《食品周报》 1984 年 10 月 5 日

13.16 陈茗饮 Chenming Yin

Ingredients:

粳米　Jingmi, Polished Round-grained Nonglutinous Rice (Cultivarietas

Oryzae Sativae) 50-100g
陈茶叶 Chenchaye, Tea Leaf (Folium Camelliae Sinensis) 5-10g

Directions: Decoct the rice, use the decocted rice fluid to infuse the tea.

Functions: To promote digestion, remove food retention.

Indications: Food retention due to overeating resulting in a distending epigastric pain, regurgitation, vomiting, non-smooth discharge of stools, thick sticky tongue coating, rolling pulse.

Source:《食疗本草》

13.17 莱菔子饮 Laifuzi Yin

Ingredients:

炒莱菔子 Chao Laifuzi, Parched Radish Seed (Semen Raphani) 2g

Directions: Pestle, decoct and drink.

Functions: To promote digestion.

Indications: Wheat food retention.

Source:《食品周报》1984 年 10 月 5 日

13.18 陈仓米柿饼霜茶 Chencangmi Shibingshuang Cha

Ingredients:

陈仓米 Chencangmi, Old Millet (Semen Oryzae seu Setariae) 60g
柿霜 Shishuang, Persimmon Sugar (Mannosum Kaki) 30g

Directions: Toast the millet on low heat, decoct, pour into a bowl. Melt the sugar into the bowl. Let settle. Drink when clear.

Functions: To promote appetite, strengthen the spleen.

Indications: Indigestion due to spleen and stomach deficiency.

Source:《气功药饵疗法与救治偏差手术》

13.19 麦芽茶 Maiya Cha

Ingredients:

炒麦芽 Chao Mai Ya, Parched Germinated Barley (Fructus Hordei

Germinatus) 20g
Directions: Decoct and drink.
Functions: To promote digestion, remove food retention.
Indications: Wheat food retention.
Source:《食品周报》1984 年 10 月 5 日

13.20 麦芽山楂饮 Maiya shanzha Yin
Ingredients:
炒麦芽 Chao Mai Ya, Parched Germinated Barley (Fructus Hordei Germinatus) 10g
炒山楂 Chao Shanzha, Parched Hawthorn Fruit (Fructus Crataegi) 3g
红糖 Hongtang, Brown Sugar, desired amount
Directions: Make as tea with boiling water.
Functions: To promote digestion, remove food retention.
Indications: Food retention causing vomiting, regurgitation, distention in epigastrium, belching, abdominal pain aggravated by pressure, foul smelling stools, thick sticky tongue coating, rolling forceful pulse.
Source:《民间验方》

13.21 棉壳茶 Mianke Cha
Ingredients:
棉花壳 Mianhua Ke, Levant Cotton Exocarp (Exocarpium Gossypii) 30g
Directions: Pestle, decoct and drink.
Functions: To regulate *qi*, stop vomiting, reduce phlegm.
Indications: Hiccuping, nausea, vomiting.
Source:《中医大辞典·中药分册》

13.22 隔山消白糖饮 Geshanxiao Baitang Yin
Ingredients:
隔山消 Geshanxiao, Auriculate Swallowwort Root (Radix Cynanchi

Auriculati) 30g
Directions: Decoct and add white sugar to taste before drinking. Take three to five times a day.
Functions: To remove food retention, promote digestion.
Indications: Pediatric food retention.
Source: 《中国药膳学》

13.23 橘枣饮 Ju Zao Yin
Ingredients:
红枣 Hongzao, Chinese Date (Fructus Jujubae), 10 dates
鲜橘皮 Xian Jupi, Fresh Tangerine Peel (Pericarpium Citri Reticulatae) 10g **or**
干橘皮 Gan Jupi, Dried Tangerine Peel (Pericarpium Citri Reticulatae) 3g
Directions: Toast dates to dark brown. Make as tea with two ingredients in boiling water, cover and let sit for 10 minutes. Drink the tea before and after meals.
Functions: To activate appetite, help digestion.
Indications: Poor appetite, indigestion.
Source: 《民间验方》

13.24 橙子蜂蜜饮 Chengzi Fengmi Yin
Ingredients:
橙子 Chengzi, Fragrant Citrus (Fructus Citri Junoris), 1 fruit
蜂蜜 Fengmi, Honey 50g
Directions: Soak citrus, cut into four pieces, decoct together with honey over high heat and then simmer for 20-25 minutes. Filter, and take the fluid.
Functions: To promote digestion and remove food retention.
Indications: Food retention, epigastric fullness and poor appetite.
Source: 《民间验方》

13.25 蔷薇根茶 Qiangweigen Cha

Ingredients:
蔷薇根 Qiangwei Gen, Rose Root (Radix Rosae Multiflorae) 30g
Directions: Pestle into coarse powder, decoct and drink.
Functions: To clear heat, dissolve damp, activate blood and remove toxins.
Indications: Infantile indigestion.
Source:《备急千金要方》

13.26 槟榔饮 Binglang Yin

Ingredients:
槟榔 Binglang, Areca Seed (Semen Arecae) 10g (crushed)
莱菔子 Laifuzi, Radish Seed (Semen Raphani) 10g (toasted)
橘皮 Jupi, Dried Tangerine Peel (Pericarpium Citri Reticulatae)
Directions: Decoct and add white sugar to taste before drinking the decoction.
Functions: To remove food retention, relieve pain.
Indications: Distending pain in epigastrium, belching, regurgitation, poor appetite, non-smooth discharge of stools, thick sticky tongue coating and rolling pulse caused by food retention.
Source:《民间验方》

13.27 芦根饮 I Lugen Yin I

Ingredients:
生芦根 Sheng Lugen, Reed Rhizome (Rhizoma Phragmitis) 30g
青竹茹 Qingzhuru, Bamboo Shavings (Caulis Bambusae in Taeniam) 30g
生姜 Sheng Jiang, Fresh Ginger (Rhizoma Zingiberis Recens) 10g
粳米 Jingmi, Polished Round-Grained Nonglutinous Rice (Cultivarietas Oryzae Sativae)
Directions: Decoct rice, save fluid. Decoct first three ingredients, reserve fluid. Combine both fluids and take the mixture.

Functions: To warm stomach, stop vomiting.
Indications: Vomiting caused by invasion of stomach by cold.
Source:《备急千金要方》

13.28 芦根饮 II   Lugen Yin II

Ingredients:
通草 Tongcao, Ricepaper Plant Pith (Medulla Tetrapanacis) 10g
生芦根 Sheng Lugen, Reed Rhizome (Rhizoma Phragmitis) 30g
橘皮 Jupi, Dried Tangerine Peel (Pericarpium Citri Reticulatae) 3g
粳米 Jingmi, Polished Round-Grained Nonglutinous Rice (Cultivarietas Oryzae Sativae)

Directions: Decoct rice, reserve fluid. Decoct first three ingredients, reserve fluid. Combine both fluids and take the mixture three times a day.
Functions: To warm stomach, stop nausea.
Indications: Nausea and poor appetite following invasion of stomach by cold.
Source:《备急千金要方》

13.29 萝卜叶茶 I   Luoboye Cha I

Ingredients:
干萝卜叶 Gan Luobo Ye, Dried Radish Leaf (Folium Raphani) 30-60g

Directions: Decoct and drink.
Functions: To circulate *qi*, promote digestion, dissolve stagnation and stop diarrhea.
Indications: Diarrhea due to food retention.
Source:《常见病验方研究参考资料》

13.30 萝卜叶鸡蛋饮 Luoboye Jidan Yin

Ingredients:
陈萝卜叶 Chen Luobo Ye, Dried Radish Leaf (Folium Raphani) 30g

鸡蛋 Jidan, Egg

Directions: Decoct radish leaves, break and boil the egg in it. Drink the decoction and eat the egg.

Functions: To remove food retention, harmonize middle *jiao*, clear heat, treat exterior syndromes.

Indications: Indigestion, sallow complexion and fullness in chest and abdomen.

Source:《河南省中医秘方验方汇编》

防治篇 For Treatment

14 风寒感冒 For Wind-Cold

14.01 刀豆茶 II Daodou Cha II

Ingredients:

刀豆根 Daodou Gen, Jack Bean Root (Radix Canavaliae) 30g

Directions: Decoct for 15 minutes, add black tea 3g to the decoction, and drink as tea.

Functions: To relieve exterior syndromes.

Indications: Common cold of wind-cold type with symptoms of headache, sensitivity to wind, and intolerance of cold.

Source:《食物与治病》

14.02 川芎糖茶 Chuanxiong Tang Cha

Ingredients:

川芎 Chuanxiong, Sichuan Lovage Rhizome (Rhizoma Chuanxiong) 6g

绿茶 Lucha, Green Tea 6g

红糖 Hongtang, Brown Sugar, desired amount

Directions: Decoct and drink the decoction.
Functions: To eliminate wind, dispel cold and treat exterior syndromes.
Indications: Common cold of wind-cold type with symptoms such as headache, sensitivity to wind and cold, light red tongue with white thin coating, and superficial pulse.
Source: 《饮食疗法》

14.03 天中茶 Tianzhong Cha
Ingredients:
大腹皮 Dafupi, Areca Peel (Pericarpium Arecae) 60g
荆芥 Jingjie, Fineleaf Schizonepeta Herb (Herba Schizonepetae) 60g
槟榔 Binglang, Areca Seed (Semen Arecae) 60g
香薷 Xiangru, Mosla Herb (Herba Moslae) 60g
干姜 Gan Jiang, Dried Ginger (Rhizoma Zingiberis) 60g
炒车前子 Chao Cheqian Zi, Parched Plantain Seed (Semen Plantaginis) 60g
羌活 Qianghuo, Notopterygium Root (Rhizoma et Radix Notopterygii) 60g
薄荷 Bohe, Peppermint (Herba Menthae) 60g
炒枳实 Chao Zhishi, Parched Immature Orange Fruit (Fructus Aurantii Immaturus) 60g
柴胡 Chaihu, Chinese Thorowax Root (Radix Bupleuri) 60g
炒青皮 Chao Qingpi, Parched Green Tangerine Peel (Pericarpium Citri Reticulatae Viride) 60g
炒白芥子 Chao Baijie Zi, Parched White Mustard Seed (Semen Sinapis Albae) 60g
猪苓 Zhuling, Chuling (Polyporus) 60g
防风 Fangfeng, Divaricate Saposhnikovia Root (Radix Saposhnikoviae) 60g
前胡 Qianhu, Hogfennel Root (Radix Peucedani) 60g
炒白芍 Chao Baishao, Parched White Peony Root (Radix Paeoniae Alba) 60g
独活 Duhuo, Doubleteeth Pubescent Angelica Root (Radix Angelicae pubescentis) 60g

炒苏子 Chao Suzi, Parched Perilla Fruit, (Fructus Perillae) 60g
土藿香 Tuhuoxiang, Cablia Patchouli Herb (Herba Pogostemonis) 60g
桔梗 Jiegeng, Platycodon Root (Radix Platycodi) 60g
藁本 Gaoben, Chinese Lovage (Rhizoma Ligustici) 60g
木通 Mutong, Akebia Stem (Caulis Akebiae) 60g
紫苏 Zisu, Perilla Stem (Caulis Perillae) 60g
泽泻 Zexie, Oriental Waterplantain Rhizome (Rhizoma Alismatis) 60g
炒苍术 Chao Cangzhu, Parched Swordlike Atractylodes Rhizome (Rhizoma Atractylodis) 60g
炒白术 Chao Baizhu, Parched Largehead Atractylodes Rhizome (Rhizoma Atractylodis Macrocephalae) 60g
制川朴 Zhi Chuanpu, Prepared Officinal Magnolia Bark (Cortex Magnoliae Officinalis Praeparata) 90g
制半夏 Zhi Banxia, Prepared Pinellia Tuber (Rhizoma Pinelliae Praeparata) 90g
杏仁 Xing Ren, Apricot Seed (Semen Armeniacae Amarum) 90g
炒莱菔子 Chao Laifuzi, Parched Radish Seed (Semen Raphani) 90g
陈皮 Chenpi, Dried Tangerine Peel (Pericarpium Citri Reticulatae) 90g
炒麦芽 Chao Mai Ya, Parched Germinated Barley (Fructus Hordei Germinatus) 120g
炒神曲 Chao Shenqu, Parched Medicated Leaven (Massa Fermentata Medicinalis) 120g
炒山楂 Chao Shanzha, Parched Hawthorn Fruit (Fructus Crataegi) 120g
茯苓 Fuling, Indian Bread (Poria) 120g
白芷 Baizhi, Dahurian Angelica Root (Radix Angelicae Dahuricae) 30g
甘草 Gancao, Liquorice Root (Radix Glycyrrhizae) 30g
炒草果仁 Chao Caoguoren, Parched Caoguo (Fructus Tsaoko) 30g
秦艽 Qinjiao, Largeleaf Gentian Root (Radix Gentianae Macrophyllae) 30g
川芎 Chuanxiong, Sichuan Lovage Rhizome (Rhizoma Chuanxiong) 30g
红茶 Hongcha, Black Tea 300g

Directions: Decoct areca peel. Pestle the others into coarse powder. Mix the powder with the decoction. Dry and wrap in gauze bags with 9g in each. Use one bag each time. Make as tea with boiling water. Cover the cup and let sit for 10-15 minutes before drinking. Take twice a day.

Functions: To expel wind cold, strengthen the spleen, harmonize the stomach.

Indications: Common cold of wind cold type with fever, sensitivity to cold, headache, general aching, fullness in chest, nausea and vomiting, abdominal pain, and diarrhea.

Source: 《沈氏尊生书》

14.04 五神汤 Wushen Tang

Ingredients:

荆芥　Jingjie, Fineleaf Schizonepeta Herb (Herba Schizonepetae) 6g
苏叶　Suye, Perilla Leaf (Folium Perillae) 6g
茶叶　Chaye, Tea Leaf (Folium Camelliae Sinensis) 6g
生姜　Sheng Jiang, Fresh Ginger (Rhizoma Zingiberis Recens) 2g
冰糖　Bingtang, Crystal Sugar 25g

Directions: Decoct the first four materials for five minutes and then filter and save the decoction. Add water and decoct again, filter and save the decoction. Pour the two decoctions into a bottle. Add 50ml water to the pot, continue to decoct, melt crystal sugar in it, filter and mix the sugar decoction with the decoction kept in the bottle. Drink in three divided doses a day.

Functions: To dispel wind cold, promote the dispersion of the lung and treat exterior syndromes.

Indications: common cold of wind cold type with fever, sensitivity to cold, headache, non-sweating, general aching, nasal obstruction, runny nose, itchy throat, and cough.

Source: 《惠宜堂经验方》

14.05 午时茶 Wushi Cha

Ingredients:

苍术 Cangzhu, Swordlike Atractylodes Rhizome (Rhizoma Atractylodis) 30g

柴胡 Chaihu, Chinese Thorowax Root (Radix Bupleuri) 30g

前胡 Qianhu, Hogfennel Root (Radix Peucedani) 30g

防风 Fangfeng, Divaricate Saposhnikovia Root (Radix Saposhnikoviae) 30g

羌活 Qianghuo, Notopterygium Root (Rhizoma et Radix Notopterygii) 30g

橘皮 Jupi, Dried Tangerine Peel (Pericarpium Citri Reticulatae) 30g

山楂 Shanzha, Hawthorn Fruit (Fructus Crataegi) 30g

连翘 Lianqiao, Weeping Forsythia Capsule (Fructus Forsythiae) 30g

神曲 Shenqu, Medicated Leaven (Massa Fermentata Medicinalis) 30g

藿香 Huoxiang, Cablia Patchouli Herb (Herba Pogostemonis) 30g

白芷 Baizhi, Dahurian Angelica Root (Radix Angelicae Dahuricae) 30g

枳实 Zhishi, Immature Orange Fruit (Fructus Aurantii Immaturus) 30g

川芎 Chuanxiong, Sichuan Lovage Rhizome (Rhizoma Chuanxiong) 30g

甘草 Gancao, Liquorice Root (Radix Glycyrrhizae) 30g

川朴 Chuanpu, Officinal Magnolia Bark (Cortex Magnoliae Officinalis) 45g

桔梗 Jiegeng, Platycodon Root (Radix Platycodi) 45g

麦芽 Mai Ya, Germinated Barley (Fructus Hordei Germinatus) 45g

紫苏叶 Zisu Ye, Perilla Leaf (Folium Perillae) 45g

红茶 Hongcha, Black Tea 1,000g

Directions: Pestle, mix with baked flour to make a thick paste. Dry, crush, and store in a bottle. Use 4.5g each time. Make as tea with boiling water.

Functions: To eliminate wind, expel cold, send stomach *qi* downward, warm the middle *jiao,* remove food retention. Pain relief and antiemetic.

Indications: Common cold of wind cold type accompanied by retention of food, vomiting, abdominal pain, and diarrhea. When the above herbs are decocted with ginger and jujube, the therapeutic effect will be enhanced.

Source: 《陕西中医》 7:38, 1984

14.06 白菜绿豆芽饮 Baicai Ludouya Yin

Ingredients:
白菜根 Baicai Gen, Peking Cabbage Root (Radix Brassicae Pekinensis) 1 piece (sliced)
绿豆芽 Ludou Ya, Mung Bean Sprout (Semen Phaseoli Radiati Germinatus) 30g

Directions: Decoct to a boil and then simmer for 15 minutes. Filter, cool and store the decoction in a jar. Take as tea.

Functions: To clear heat, remove toxins.

Indications: Fever, headache, nasal obstruction, dry throat, non-sweating.

Source: 《民间验方》

14.07 芫荽茶 Yuansui Cha

Ingredients:
芫荽 Yuansui, Coriander (Herba Coriandri) 10g
薄荷 Bohe, Peppermint (Herba Menthae) 6g
生姜 Sheng Jiang, Fresh Ginger (Rhizoma Zingiberis Recens) 4.5g

Directions: Make as tea with boiling water.

Functions: To dispel wind-cold.

Indications: Mild case of common cold of wind-cold type.

Source: 《上海常用中草药》

14.08 姜糖饮 I Jiang Tang Yin I

Ingredients:
生姜 Sheng Jiang, Fresh Ginger (Rhizoma Zingiberis Recens) 10g
红糖 Hongtang, Brown Sugar 15g

Directions: Make ginger as tea with boiling water, add brown sugar before drinking. Take while promoting sweating by wearing several layers of clothing or covered with blankets.

Functions: To dispel wind-cold.

Indications: Common cold of wind-cold type manifested by fever, headache, general aching, absence of sweating, poor appetite and nausea.
Source: 《民间验方》

14.09 姜糖茶 I   Jiang Tang Cha I

Ingredients:
生姜 Sheng Jiang, Fresh Ginger (Rhizoma Zingiberis Recens), 5 slices
绿茶 Lucha, Green Tea 10g
冰糖 Bingtang, Crystal Sugar 30g

Directions: Decoct for 10 minutes and drink while hot, promote sweating by covering with blankets.
Functions: To dispel wind-cold.
Indications: Common cold of wind-cold type manifested as nasal obstruction, headache and, cough with white phlegm.
Source: 《惠宜堂经验方》

14.10 姜糖苏叶饮   Jiang Tang Suye Yin

Ingredients:
生姜 Sheng Jiang, Fresh Ginger (Rhizoma Zingiberis Recens) 3g
苏叶 Suye, Perilla Leaf (Folium Perillae) 3g

Directions: Make as tea with boiling water. Add 15g brown sugar and, drink while hot. Take two or three doses a day.
Functions: To dispel wind-cold.
Indications: Common cold of wind-cold type and gastroenteric type and sea-food poisoning.
Source: 《本草汇言》

14.11 桔姜茶   Ju Jiang Cha

Ingredients:
桔皮 Jupi, Tangerine Peel (Pericarpium Citri Reticulatae) 5g

生姜 sheng Jiang, Fresh Ginger (Rhizoma Zingiberis Recens) 5g
冰糖 Bingtang, Crystal Sugar 8g

Directions: Make as tea with boiling water.

Functions: To regulate *qi*, dissolve phlegm, dispel wind-cold.

Indications: Abdominal distension, cough with phlegm, common cold of wind-cold type.

Source: 《开卷有益》 4:35, 1988

14.12 紫苏叶茶 Zisuye Cha

Ingredients:

紫苏叶 Zisu Ye, Perilla Leaf (Folium Perillae)

Directions: Dry in the sun. Roll into coarse powder. Use 16g each time, add brown sugar to taste and make as tea with boiling water.

Functions: To dispel wind-cold, regulate *qi*, harmonize *yin* system.

According to modern research, Zisu Ye (Perilla Leaf) contains a volatile oil which dilates blood vessels inducing sweating and lowering body temperature.

Indications: Early stage of common cold of wind-cold type.

Source: 《饮馔服食笺》

14.13 葱姜饮 II Cong Jiang Yin II

Ingredients:

葱白 Cong Bai, Onion (Bulbus Allii Fistulosi), 10 onions
生姜 Sheng Jiang, Fresh Ginger (Rhizoma Zingiberis Recens) 100g

Directions: Decoct and drink while hot, encourage sweating after drinking by covering with blankets.

Functions: To dispel wind-cold, treat exterior syndromes.

Indications: Common cold during pregnancy.

Source: 《备急千金要方》

14.14 葱豉茶 I Cong Chi Cha I

Ingredients:
葱白 Cong Bai, Onion (Bulbus Allii Fistulosi), 7 onions
豆豉 Douchi, Prepared Soybean (Semen Sojae Fermentatum) 10g

Directions: Make as tea with boiling water, drink while hot to encourage sweating.

Functions: To induce sweating, treat exterior syndromes.

Indications: Common cold of wind-cold type.

Source:《本草纲目》

14.15 葱豉茶 II Cong Chi Cha II

Ingredients:
葱白 Cong Bai, Onion (Bulbus Allii Fistulosi), 3 onions
淡豆豉 Dandouchi, Fermented Soybean (Semen Sojae Preparatum) 15g
荆芥 Jingjie, Fineleaf Schizonepeta Herb (Herba Schizonepetae) 5g
薄荷 Bohe, Peppermint (Herba Menthae), 30 leaves
栀子 Zhizi, Cape Jasmine Fruit (Fructus Gardeniae), 5 fruits
石膏 Shigao, Gypsum (Gypsum Fibrosum) 60g
茶叶 Chaye, Tea Leaf (Folium Camelliae Sinensis) 10g

Directions: Decoct and drink, drink while hot.

Functions: To treat exterior syndromes with its pungent and warm nature.

Indications: Common cold of wind-cold type with high fever and headache.

Source:《太平圣惠方》

14.16 葱豉饮 Cong Chi Yin

Ingredients:
葱白 Cong Bai, Onion (Bulbus Allii Fistulosi), 5-10 pieces
淡豆豉 Dandouchi, Fermented Soybean (Semen Sojae Preparatum) 10g
荔梗 Ligeng, Litchi Branch (Ramusculus Litchi) 3g **or**

陈皮 Chenpi, Dried Tangerine Peel (Pericarpium Citri Reticulatae) 3g

Directions: Decoct and add brown sugar to taste before drinking.

Functions: To dispel wind-cold, treat exterior syndromes.

Indications: Cough induced by wind-cold, running nose and nasal obstruction.

Source:《百病饮食自疗》

14.17 薏米防风饮 Yimi Fangfeng Yin

Ingredients:

生薏米 Sheng Yi Mi, Coix Seed (Semen Coicis) 30g

防风 Fangfeng, Divaricate Saposhnikovia Root (Radix Saposhnikoviae) 10g

Directions: Decoct over high heat and then simmer for 40-50 minutes. Filter, cool, and drink the fluid.

Functions: To treat exterior syndromes, dispel wind cold.

Indications: Common cold with sensitivity to cold, fever, headache, non-sweating and vomiting.

Source:《食物与食治》

14.18 苏杏汤 Su Xing Tang

Ingredients:

紫苏 Zisu, Perilla Stem (Caulis Perillae) 10g

杏仁 Xing Ren, Apricot Seed (Semen Armeniacae Amarum) 10g

生姜 Sheng Jiang, Fresh Ginger (Rhizoma Zingiberis Recens) 10g

红糖 Hongtang, Brown Sugar 10g

Directions: Pestle the first two well, decoct with ginger and add brown sugar when the decoction is ready. Drink two or three times a day.

Functions: To dispel wind cold, promote dispersing function of lung.

Indications: Common cold of wind-cold type manifested as cough, nasal obstruction and running nose.

Source:《百病饮食自疗》

14.19 苏羌茶 Su Qiang Cha

Ingredients:
紫苏叶 Zisu Ye, Perilla Leaf (Folium Perillae) 9g
羌活 Qianghuo, Notopterygium Root (Rhizoma et Radix Notopterygii) 9g
茶叶 Chaye, Tea Leaf (Folium Camelliae Sinensis) 9g

Directions: Pestle into coarse powder. Make as tea with boiling water. Take one dose every day.
Functions: To treat exterior syndromes.
Indications: Common cold of wind cold type manifested as sensitivity to cold, fever, absence of sweating.
Source:《常见病验方研究参考资料》

14.20 藿香白蔻饮 Huoxiang Baikou Yin

Ingredients:
藿香 Huoxiang, Cablia Patchouli Herb (Herba Pogostemonis) 5-10g
白蔻 Baikou, Round Cardamom Fruit (Fructus Amomi Rotundus) 3g
生姜 Sheng Jiang, Fresh Ginger (Rhizoma Zingiberis Recens), 3 slices

Directions: Decoct for 10 minutes, and drink.
Functions: Dispel cold damp, stop diarrhea, eliminate wind cold and relieve pain.
Indications: Diarrhea with borborygmus and pain, fullness in epigastrium, poor appetite, or sensitivity to cold, fever, nasal obstruction, headache, general body aching, accompanied by vomiting, white sticky tongue coating, soft and slow pulse due to invasion of cold damp or wind cold.
Source:《百病饮食自疗》

15 风热感冒 For Wind-Heat

15.01 三鲜茶 II Sanxian Cha II

Ingredients:
鲜藿香 Xian Huoxiang, Fresh Cablia Patchouli Herb (Herba Pogostemonis)

10-15g
鲜苏叶 Xian Su Ye, Fresh Perilla Leaf (Folium Perillae) 10-15g
薄荷 Bohe, Peppermint (Herba Menthae) 10-15g

Directions: Wash with boiling water first and then make as tea with boiling water.

Functions: To eliminate wind, clear heat, treat exterior syndromes.

Indications: Common cold of wind-heat type. It can be used as a daily drink to prevent common cold.

Source: 《河北中药手册》

15.02 牛蒡子茶 Niubangzi Cha

Ingredients:
牛蒡子 Niubang Zi, Great Burdock Achene (Fructus Arctii) 10g

Directions: Dry well, powder and make as tea with boiling water.

Functions: To expel wind, reduce swelling.

Indications: Common cold of wind heat type with high fever, mild chills, and sore throat.

Source: 《食疗本草》

15.03 六叶茶 (感冒茶) Liuye Cha (Ganmao Cha)

Ingredients:
大叶龙胆草 Dayelongdancao, Hedyotidous Hedyotis Twig & Leaf (Ramusculus et Folium Hedyotis Hedyotideae) 500g
甘草 Gancao, Liquorice Root (Radix Glycyrrhizae) 250g
茅根 Maogen, Lalang Grass Rhizome (Rhizoma Imperatae) 250g
菊花 Juhua, Chrysanthemum Flower (Flos Chrysanthemi) 250g
岗梅根 Gangmeigen, Scaly Holly Root (Radix Ilicis Asprellae) 500g (powdered)
如意花根 Ruyihua Gen, Common Lantana Root (Radix Lantanae Camarae) 250g (powdered)

黄皮叶粉 Huangpi Ye Fen, Clausena Leaf Powder (Pulvis Clausenae Lansii Folium) 500g
芒果叶粉 Mangguo Ye Fen, Mango Leaf Powder (Pulvis Mangiferae Indicae Folium) 500g
紫药叶粉 Ziyao Ye Fen, Leucas Ciliata Leaf Powder (Pulvis Leucas Ciliatae Folium) 500g
薄荷叶粉 Boheye Fen, Peppermint Leaf Powder (Pulvis Menthae Folium) 500g
桑叶粉 Sangye Fen, Mulberry Leaf Powder (Pulvis Mori Folium) 500g
地胆头粉 Didantou Fen, Elephantfoot Powder (Pulvis Elephantopi Herba) 500g
米粉 Mi Fen, Rice Flour (Pulvis Oryzae Sativae), proper amount

Directions: Decoct the first four herbs twice. Mix all the powders with the decoction. Dry, cut into pieces 9g each. Use one piece each time, twice a day. Make as tea with boiling water.

Functions: To clear heat, remove toxins, expel wind and relieve *qi* stagnation.

Indications: Common cold of wind-heat type accompanied with abdominal distending pain, severe fever, mild chills, sore throat, fullness in chest, nausea and vomiting.

Source:《医药科技动态》

15.04 加味菊花茶 Jiawei Juhua Cha

Ingredients:
菊花 Juhua, Chrysanthemum Flower (Flos Chrysanthemi) 5g
蝉蜕 Chantui, Cicada Slough (Periostracum Cicadae) 3g

Directions: Make chrysanthemum flower as tea with boiling water. Decoct cicada slough, filter, and mix the decoction into the tea before drinking.

Functions: To eliminate wind-heat, promote the lung in dispersing, relieve spasms.

Indications: Invasion of wind-heat manifested as loss of voice, cough with yellow and sticky sputum, dry throat, red tongue with sticky coating, rolling and rapid pulse.
Source:《百病饮食自疗》

15.05 防风甘草茶 Fangfeng Gancao Cha

Ingredients:
防风 Fangfeng, Divaricate Saposhnikovia Root (Radix Saposhnikoviae) 6g
甘草 Gancao, Liquorice Root (Radix Glycyrrhizae) 3g
Directions: Make as tea with boiling water. Take one dose a day.
Functions: To dispel wind, strengthen defensive resistance.
Indications: Prevention treatment of mild common cold in any season.
Source:《常见病验方研究参考资料》

15.06 芥菜茶 Jiecai Cha

Ingredients:
芥菜 Jiecai, India Mustard Stem and Leaf (Caulis et Folium Brassicae) 100g
Directions: Decoct, add white sugar to taste to the decoction before drinking.
Functions: To promote the lung in dispersing, dissolve phlegm, warm middle *jiao*, regulate *qi*.
Indications: Common cold and cough with phlegm due to pathogenic cold attacking lung, causing lung to fail in dispersing.
Source:《常见病验方研究参考资料》

15.07 桑叶茶 Sangye Cha

Ingredients:
霜桑叶 Shuangsangye, Mulberry Leaf (Folium Mori) 10g
蜂蜜 Fengmi, Honey or

白糖 Baitang, White Sugar, desired amount

Directions: Pestle mulberry leaves into coarse powder, add honey or white sugar, and make as tea with boiling water.

Functions: To expel exogenous pathogenic wind-heat, moisten dryness, promote detoxification, improve hearing and visual acuity, strengthen tendons and bones, subdue liver fire.

Indications: Exterior syndromes of wind-heat, cough due to dryness, headache, dizziness, redness of eye.

Source:《祝您健康》5:40, 1988

15.08 桑菊茶 I　Sang Ju Cha I

Ingredients:

桑叶 Sangye, Mulberry Leaf (Folium Mori) 1,000g

黄菊花 Huangjuhua, Yellow Chrysanthemum Flower (Flos Chrysanthemi) 500g

枇杷叶 Pipa Ye, Loquat Leaf (Folium Eriobotryae) 500g

Directions: Pestle into coarse powder, wrap in gauze bags with 10-15g in each. Use one bag each time and make as tea with boiling water.

Functions: To dispel wind-heat, treat exterior syndromes.

Indications: Common cold of wind-heat type.

Source:《中药临床手册》

15.09 桑菊豆豉饮　Sang Ju Douchi Yin

Ingredients:

桑叶 Sangye, Mulberry Leaf (Folium Mori) 10g

菊花 Juhua, Chrysanthemum Flower (Flos Chrysanthemi) 10g

豆豉 Douchi, Prepared Soybean (Semen Sojae Fermentatum) 6g

Directions: Decoct and drink.

Functions: To dispel wind-heat.

Indications: Common cold of wind-heat type with symptoms of fever,

mild sensitivity to wind, headache, cough, sore throat, and thirst.
Source:《民间验方》

15.10 桑菊薄竹饮 Sang Ju Bo Zhu Yin
Ingredients:
桑叶 Sangye, Mulberry Leaf (Folium Mori) 5g
菊花 Juhua, Chrysanthemum Flower (Flos Chrysanthemi) 5g
苦竹叶 Kuzhu Ye, Bitter Bamboo Leaves (Folium Pleioblasti) 30g
白茅根 Baimao Gen, Imperata Rhizome (Rhizoma Imperatae) 30g
薄荷 Bohe, Peppermint (Herba Menthae) 3g
Directions: Make as tea with boiling water.
Functions: To dispel wind-heat.
Indications: Common cold of wind-heat type, acute conjunctivitis and early stage measles.
Source:《广东凉茶验方》

15.11 苍耳子茶 Cangerzi Cha
Ingredients:
苍耳子 Canger Zi, Siberian Cocklebur Fruit (Fructus Xanthii) 6g
Directions: Decoct and drink.
Functions: To remove wind heat, stop pain.
Indications: Headache caused by wind heat with manifestations of splitting pain, red face and eyes, fever, sensitivity to wind, thirst, constipation, emaciation, red tongue with yellow coating, superficial and rapid pulse.
Source:《百病饮食自疗》

15.12 薄荷茶 I Bohe Cha I
Ingredients:
鲜薄荷叶 Xian Bohe Ye, Fresh Peppermint Leaf (Folium Menthae), many

茶叶 Chaye, Tea Leaf (Folium Camelliae Sinensis) 10g

Directions: Make as tea with boiling water, cover and let sit for 2-3 minutes. Drink the tea. Add ice before drinking.

Functions: To clear heat, promote stomach.

Indications: Common cold of wind-heat type, headache, red eyes, sore throat, sporadic skin eruptions of measles, distending pain in chest and hypochondrium due to liver *qi* stagnation, abdominal pain due to attack of summer heat.

Source: 《祝您健康》 5:46, 1988

15.13 薄荷茶 II Bohe Cha II

Ingredients:

薄荷叶 Bohe Ye, Peppermint Leaf (Folium Menthae), 30 leaves
生姜 Sheng Jiang, Fresh Ginger (Rhizoma Zingiberis Recens), 2 slices
人参 Renshen, Ginseng (Radix Ginseng) 5g
石膏 Shigao, Gypsum (Gypsum Fibrosum) 30g
麻黄 Mahuang, Ephedra (Herba Ephedrae) 2g

Directions: Pestle, decoct and drink.

Functions: To treat exterior syndromes.

Indications: Common cold of wind heat type in old people with a weak constitution, manifested as fever, headache, sore throat, and cough.

Source: 《普济方》

15.14 薄荷芦根饮 Bohe Lugen Yin

Ingredients:

芦根 Lugen, Reed Rhizome (Rhizoma Phragmitis) 30g
薄荷 Bohe, Peppermint (Herba Menthae) 5g

Directions: Decoct reed first and add peppermint, and continue decocting for a short time. Remove from heat, filter, and take the fluid.

Functions: To dispel wind heat, treat exterior syndromes.

Indications: Common cold of wind heat type with symptoms of fever and cough with yellow sticky phlegm.
Source:《百病饮食自疗》

15.15 薄荷砂糖饮 Bohe Shatang Yin

Ingredients:
薄荷 Bohe, Peppermint (Herba Menthae)

Directions: Make as tea with boiling water, add white granulated sugar to taste before drinking.
Functions: To dispel wind heat, treat exterior syndromes and relieve sore throat.
Indications: Common cold of wind heat type, sore throat, distending pain in epigastrium.
Source:《中国药膳学》

16 流行性感冒 For Influenza

16.01 大青叶茶 Daqingye Cha

Ingredients:
大青叶 Daqingye, Dyers Woad Leaf (Folium Isatidis) 15g

Directions: Make as tea with boiling water. Use continuously for three or five days.
Functions: To clear heat, cool blood, relieve exterior syndromes.
Indications: Influenza.
Source:《中药临床手册》

16.02 生姜茶 Shengjiang Cha

Ingredients:
茶叶 Chaye, Tea Leaf (Folium Camelliae Sinensis) 7g
生姜 Sheng Jiang, Fresh Ginger (Rhizoma Zingiberis Recens), 10 slices

Directions: Decoct, drink.
Functions: To induce sweating, relieve exterior syndromes, moisten the lung, control cough.
Indications: Influenza, common cold of wind-cold type.
Source: 《烟酒茶俗》

16.03 白菜根饮 Baicaigen Yin
Ingredients:
白菜根 Baicai Gen, Peking Cabbage Root (Radix Brassicae Pekinensis), 1 piece (sliced)
Directions: Decoct, add white sugar to taste before drinking the decoction. Take twice a day.
Functions: To clear heat, induce diuresis and remove toxins.
Indications: Influenza.
Source: 《食物疗法精萃》

16.04 白杨树皮茶 Baiyangshupi Cha
Ingredients:
白杨树皮 Baiyangshu Pi, David Poplar Bark (Cortex Populi Davidianae) 20g
Directions: Decoct, drink.
Functions: To clear heat, eliminate wind. To prevent influenza.
Source: 《常见病验方研究参考资料》

16.05 板蓝根茶 Banlangen Cha
Ingredients:
板蓝根 Banlangen, Isatis Root (Radix Isatidis) 18g
Directions: Pestle into coarse powder. Decoct and drink.
Functions: To clear heat, remove toxins and treat throat diseases.
Indications: Influenza, epidemic cerebrospinal meningitis, encephalitis B, scarlet fever.

Source:《中药临床手册》

16.06 盲肠草茶 Mangchangcao Cha

Ingredients:
盲肠草 Mangchangcao, Railway Beggarticks Herb (Herba Bidentis Pilosae) 30g
Directions: Decoct and drink.
Functions: To clear heat, remove toxins.
Indications: Influenza.
Source:《中药临床手册》

16.07 夏菊茶 Xia Ju Cha

Ingredients:
夏枯草 Xiakucao, Common Selfheal Fruit-Spike (Spica Prunellae) 15g
野菊花 Yejuhua, Wild Chrysanthemum Flower (Flos Chrysanthemi Indici) 15g
Directions: Pestle into coarse powder, decoct and drink. Use daily for three or five days.
Functions: To clear heat, remove toxins.
Indications: Influenza.
Source:《中药临床手册》

16.08 贯仲茶 Guanzhong Cha

Ingredients:
贯仲 Guanzhong, Thickrhizome Wood Fern (Rhizoma Dryopteris Crassirhizomae) 15g
Directions: Pestle and make as tea with boiling water. Use daily for three or five days.
Functions: To clear heat, remove toxins.
Indications: Influenza, febrile skin eruptions, hematemesis and epistaxis.
Source:《中药临床手册》

16.09 复方贯仲茶 Fufang Guanzhong Cha

Ingredients:
贯仲 Guanzhong, Thickrhizome Wood Fern (Rhizoma Dryopteris Crassirhizomae) 500g
金银花 Jinyinhua, Honeysuckle Flower (Flos Lonicerae) 240g
甘草 Gancao, Liquorice Root (Radix Glycyrrhizae) 120g
黄芩 Huangqin, Baical Skullcap Root (Radix Scutellariae) 500g

Directions: Pestle into coarse powder, wrap in gauze-bags 20g in each. Use one bag each time, make as tea with boiling water.

Functions: Clear heat, remove toxins and treat exterior syndromes. To prevent influenza.

Source: 《常见病验方研究参考资料》

16.10 苍术贯仲茶 Cangzhu Guanzhong Cha

Ingredients:
苍术 Cangzhu, Swordlike Atractylodes Rhizome (Rhizoma Atractylodis)
贯仲 Guanzhong, Thickrhizome Wood Fern (Rhizoma Dryopteris Crassirhizomae)

In equal amounts.

Directions: Pestle into coarse powder, wrap in cloth-bags with 30g in each. Use one bag each time, make as tea with boiling water.

Functions: To clear heat, promote detoxification, dry damp, promote spleen. To prevent influenza.

Source: 《常见病验方研究参考资料》

17 其他类型感冒 For Colds of Other Types

17.01 三鲜茶 III Sanxian Cha III

Ingredients:
鲜藿香 Xian Huoxiang, Fresh Cablia Patchouli Herb (Herba Pogostemonis) 30g

鲜佩兰 Xian Peilan, Fresh Fortune Eupatorium (Herba Eupatorii) 30g
鲜薄荷 Xian Bohe, Fresh Peppermint (Herba Menthae) 60g

Directions: Grind into coarse powder. Make as tea with boiling water.

Functions: To dissolve damp, treat illness caused by summer heat, relieve exterior syndromes. It is used to prevent influenza.

Source: 《常见病验方研究参考资料》

17.02 水翁花茶 Shuiwenghua Cha

Ingredients:

水翁花 Shuiweng Hua, Lidded Cleistocalyx Flower (Flos Cleistocalycis Operculati) 5-10g

Directions: Make as tea with boiling water.

Functions: To treat exterior syndromes caused by summer heat.

Indications: Common cold in summer with the symptoms of sensitivity to cold, fever, headache, and poor appetite.

Source: 《全国中草药汇编》

17.03 加减石膏饮 Jiajian Shigao Yin

Ingredients:

生石膏 Sheng Shigao, Gypsum (Gypsum Fibrosum) 20g
杏仁 Xing Ren, Apricot Seed (Semen Armeniacae Amarum) 10g
银花 Yinhua, Honeysuckle Flower (Flos Lonicerae) 10g
通草 Tongcao, Ricepaperplant Pith (Medulla Tetrapanacis) 6g
扁豆花 Biandou Hua, Hyacinth Bean Flower (Flos Dolichoris), 8-10 pieces
西瓜翠衣 Xigua Cuiyi, Exocarp of Watermelon (Exocarpium Citrulli) 30g

Directions: Decoct and drink.

Functions: To clear heat, dissolve damp, regulate water passage (*sanjiao*).

Indications: Fever, red face, hearing loss, fullness in the epigastric region, diarrhea, yellow and scanty urine, red tongue with yellow and sticky coat-ing caused by invasion of summer damp-heat permeating into *sanjiao*.

Source:《百病饮食自疗》

17.04 加减香薷饮 Jiajian Xiangru Yin

Ingredients:
香薷 Xiangru, Mosla Herb (Herba Moslae) 6g
滑石 Huashi, Talc (Talcum) 10g
薏仁 Yi Ren, Coix Seed (Semen Coicis) 15g
银花 Yinhua, Honeysuckle Flower (Flos Lonicerae) 10g
扁豆花 Biandou Hua, Hyacinth Bean Flower (Flos Dolichoris) 6g
丝瓜花 Sigua Hua, Towel Gourd Flower (Flos Luffae) 6g

Directions: Decoct and drink, one dose a day.

Functions: To induce sweating to relieve the exterior syndromes.

Indications: The exterior syndromes caused by summer heat with symptoms of headache, aching all over the body, non-sweating, sensitivity to cold, fever, irritability, thirst, scanty and yellow urine, sticky tongue coating and soft pulse; or fever with a slight aversion to cold, little sweating, dry throat without thirst, red tongue with little coating, superficial thready and rapid pulse.

Source:《百病饮食自疗》

17.05 车前子茶 Cheqianzi Cha

Ingredients:
车前子 Cheqian Zi, Plantain Seed (Semen Plantaginis) 15g

Directions: Decoct and drink.

Functions: To clear heat, dissolve damp, stop diarrhea.

Indications: Diarrhea with abdominal pain, burning sensation in anus, irritability, thirst, scant and dark yellow urine due to invasion of damp-

heat or summer-damp.
Source: 《百病饮食自疗》

17.06 芳香化浊饮 Fangxiang Huazhuo Yin
Ingredients:
藿香叶 Huoxiang Ye, Cablia Patchouli Leaf (Folium Pogostemonis) 5g
佩兰叶 Peilan Ye, Fortune Eupatorium Leaf (Folium Eupatorii) 5g
厚朴花 Houpu Hua, Officinal Magnolia Flower (Flos Magnoliae Officinalis) 5g
扁豆花 Biandou Hua, Hyacinth Bean Flower (Flos Dolichoris) 5g
鲜荷叶 Xian Heye, Fresh Lotus Leaf (Folium Nelumbinis), proper amount
Directions: Decoct, add watermelon juice to the decoction before drinking.
Functions: To remove damp, relieve exterior syndromes and summer heat, promote appetite, stop vomiting.
Indications: Acute filthy disease, namely, a disease occurring at the end of summer and beginning of autumn, caused by infection of filthy pathogens, and marked by fever, chest fullness, headache, irritability, sweating, or even deafness, and loss of consciousness.
Source: 《百病饮食自疗》

17.07 苡仁竹叶饮 Yiren Zhuye Yin
Ingredients:
苡仁 Yiren, Coix Seed (Semen Coicis) 20g
鲜竹叶 Xian Zhuye, Fresh Bamboo Leaf (Folium Phyllostachys Nigra) 15g
厚朴花 Houpu Hua, Officinal Magnolia Flower (Flos Magnoliae Officinalis) 6g
扁豆花 Biandou Hua, Hyacinth Bean Flower (Flos Dolichoris) 6g
丝瓜花 Sigua Hua, Towel Gourd Flower (Flos Luffae) 6g

Directions: Decoct the first two, then add the last three, and continue decocting. Drink.

Functions: To clear heat, dissolve damp, promote defensive *qi*.

Indications: Febrile disease due to damp-heat in summer marked by more damp than heat and obstruction of defensive *qi* with the manifestations of aversion to cold, little sweating, fever, heaviness in head as if wrapped in cloth, fullness in chest and epigastric region, loose stools, and turbid urine.

Source: 《百病饮食自疗》

17.08 香薷饮 Xiangru Yin

Ingredients:

香薷 Xiangru, Mosla Herb (Herba Moslae) 10g
厚朴 Houpu, Officinal Magnolia Bark (Cortex Magnoliae Officinalis) 5g
白扁豆 Baibiandou, White Hyacinth Bean (Semen Lablab Album) 5g

Directions: Toast beans until they are slightly burnt and pestle them into coarse powder. Mix the powder with the first two. Make as tea with boiling water. Take two doses a day.

Functions: To dispel wind-cold, stop pain and diarrhea.

Indications: Common cold in summer marked by fever, headache, heaviness in head, fullness in chest, tiredness, abdominal pain, vomiting, and diarrhea.

Source: 《太平惠民和剂局方》

17.09 桑菊香豉梨皮饮 Sang Ju Xiangchi Lipi Yin

Ingredients:

桑叶 Sangye, Mulberry Leaf (Folium Mori) 6g
菊花 Juhua, Chrysanthemum Flower (Flos Chrysanthemi) 6g
香豉 Xiangchi, Prepared Soybean (Semen Sojae Praeparatum) 6g
梨皮 Li Pi, Pear Pericarp (Pericarpium Pyri) 6g

Directions: Decoct and drink.

Functions: To moisten lung, dispel wind-cold.

Indications: Cough due to wind-cold with symptoms of fever, mild sensitivity to wind-cold, headache, some sweating, dry throat, thirst, red tongue with white coating, rapid pulse.

Source:《百病饮食自疗》

17.10 桑薄花蜜饮 Sang Bo Hua Mi Yin

Ingredients:
桑叶 Sangye, Mulberry Leaf (Folium Mori) 5g
杭菊 Hangju, Yellow Chrysanthemum (Flos Chrysanthemi) 5g
丝瓜花 Sigua Hua, Towel Gourd Flower (Flos Luffae) 10g
薄荷 Bohe, Peppermint (Herba Menthae) 3g
蜂蜜 Fengmi, Honey, desired amount

Directions: Decoct the first three ingredients for half an hour. Filter and add peppermint to the decoction. Boil again for a short time. Filter and add honey before drinking.

Functions: To dispel wind, treat exterior syndrome.

Indications: Common cold with fever, headache and cough.

Source:《百病饮食自疗》

17.11 黄瓜叶速溶饮 Huangguaye Surongyin

Ingredients:
鲜黄瓜叶 Xian Huanggua Ye, Fresh Cucumber Leaf (Folium Cucumeris sativi) 1,000g
白糖 Baitang, White Sugar 500g

Directions: Decoct for one hour, filter. Boil to concentrate the decoction again with low heat. When it becomes very thick, remove from heat, cool, mix white sugar into it. Dry, crush, and store in a bottle. Use 10g each time, dissolve in a little boiling water and drink. Take three doses a day.

Functions: To clear heat, relieve pain and diarrhea.
Indications: Pediatric diarrhea in common cold of gastrointestinal type with fever and abdominal pain.
Source:《重庆草药》

17.12 都梁茶 Duliang Cha
Ingredients:
白芷 Baizhi, Dahurian Angelica Root (Radix Angelicae Dahuricae) 10g
Directions: Decoct and add white sugar to taste before drinking.
Functions: Dispel wind-damp.
Indications: Headache of common cold caused by exogenous pathogenic wind damp manifested as constricted headache, tiredness and heaviness in body, fullness in chest, poor appetite, scant urine, loose stools, white sticky tongue, soft pulse.
Source:《百病饮食自疗》

17.13 葱豉芦根饮 Cong Chi Lugen Yin
Ingredients:
鲜葱白 Xian Cong Bai, Fresh Chinese Green Onion (Bulbus Allii Fistulosi), 3-5 onions
淡豆豉 Dandouchi, Fermented Soybean (Semen Sojae Preparatum) 10-15g
鲜芦根 Xian Lugen, Fresh Reed Rhizome (Rhizoma Phragmitis) 60g
薄荷 Bohe, Peppermint (Herba Menthae) 3g
鲜竹叶 Xian Zhuye, Fresh Bamboo Leaf (Folium Phyllostachys Nigra), 10-20 leaves
Directions: Decoct and drink.
Functions: To replenish *qi*, produce body fluid.
Indications: Syndrome of *qi* stage in an acute febrile disease, manifested as fever, bitter taste in mouth, thirst, irritability, scant and dark yellow urine, red tongue with yellow coating, string-taut and rapid pulse.

Source:《百病饮食自疗》

17.14 鸡苏饮 Jisu Yin

Ingredients:

六一散 Liuyisan [滑石 Huashi, Talc (Talcum) : 甘草 Gancao, Liquorice Root (Radix Glycyrrhizae) = 6:1] 10g

薄荷 Bohe, Peppermint (Herba Menthae) 3g

Directions: Decoct the first ingredient until cooked. Add peppermint and continue decocting for a short time. Remove from heat. Filter and take the decocted fluid.

Functions: To clear heat, treat exterior syndromes.

Indications: Common cold due to invasion of summer heat, manifested as fever, sensitivity to cold, no sweating, tiredness, constricted distention in the head, irritability, thirst, scant and yellow urine, red tongue with sticky coating, soft and rapid pulse.

Source:《百病饮食自疗》

17.15 藿香饮 Huoxiang Yin

Ingredients:

藿香叶 Huoxiang Ye, Cablia Patchouli Leaf (Folium Pogostemonis) 10g

Directions: Decoct and add sugar to taste before drinking.

Functions: To clear heat, dissolve damp, dispel wind.

Indications: Common cold of summer-damp type with fever, sensitivity to cold, heaviness of body, tiredness, constricted distention in the head, irritability, thirst, dark yellow urine.

Source:《百病饮食自疗》

17.16 藿香芦根饮 Huoxiang Lugen Yin

Ingredients:

鲜藿香 Xian Huoxiang, Fresh Cablia Patchouli Herb (Herba

Pogostemonis) 10g
鲜芦根 Xian Lugen, Fresh Reed Rhizome (Rhizoma Phragmitis) 100g
Directions: Decoct and drink.
Functions: To clear and dissolve damp-heat of *qi* stage in febrile disease which is damp more than heat.
Indications: Febrile disease in *qi* stage with symptoms of sensitivity to cold, little sweating, fever, constricted heaviness in the head, tiredness, fullness in the chest and epigastrium, loose stools, turbid urine, white sticky coating, soft and slow pulse.
Source:《百病饮食自疗》

17.17 芦根苡仁饮 Lugen Yiren Yin

Ingredients:
鲜芦根 Xian Lugen, Fresh Reed Rhizome (Rhizoma Phragmitis) 50g
苡仁 Yiren, Coix Seed (Semen Coicis) 30g
鲜竹叶 Xian Zhuye, Fresh Bamboo Leaf (Folium Phyllostachys Nigra), 20 leaves
白通草 Baitongcao, Ricepaperplant Pith (Medulla Tetrapanacis) 6g
厚朴花 Houpu Hua, Officinal Magnolia Flower (Flos Magnoliae Officinalis) 6g
扁豆花 Biandou Hua, Hyacinth Bean Flower (Flos Dolichoris) 6g
Directions: Decoct the first four ingredients, add the last two, filter, and drink.
Functions: To clear and dissolve damp heat.
Indications: Febrile disease due to damp heat with symptoms of fever, thirst, fullness and distention in chest and abdomen, tiredness, sore throat, dark yellow urine, yellow sticky tongue coating. Or fever, thirst without drinking, nausea, vomiting, irritability, loose stools, yellow sticky tongue coating, rolling and rapid pulse caused by retention of damp heat in middle *jiao*.

Source:《百病饮食自疗》

17.18 芦根冰糖饮 Lugen Bingtang Yin

Ingredients:
鲜芦根 Xian Lugen, Fresh Reed Rhizome (Rhizoma Phragmitis) 120g
冰糖 Bingtang, Crystal Sugar 50g

Directions: Stew in an earthenware container. Filter, and take the stewed fluid.

Functions: To dispel wind-heat of *qi* stage.

Indications: Heat in lung with symptoms of fever, sweating, irritability, thirst, cough with copious sticky phlegm, asthmatic breathing, red tongue with yellow coating, rapid pulse.

Source:《饮食疗法》

17.19 盐柠檬茶 Yan Ningmeng Cha

Ingredients:
柠檬 Ningmeng, Lemonlike Citrus (Fructus Citri Limoniae), many
食盐 Shiyan, Salt, desired amount

Directions: Boil citrus and peel. Dry in the sun. Place in a chinaware container with salt to preserve taste longer. Use one piece each time, make as tea with boiling water. Cover and let stand, then drink.

Functions: To dispel damp, relieve pain.

Indications: Diarrhea with abdominal pain, burning anal pain, irritability, thirst, scant and dark-yellow tongue coating, soft rapid pulse due to invasion of damp heat in summer.

Source:

17.20 盐茶 Yan Cha

Ingredients:
茶叶 Chaye, Tea Leaf (Folium Camelliae Sinensis) 3g

食盐 Shiyan, Salt 1g

Directions: Make tea with boiling water. Drink four or six times a day.

Functions: To promote vision, treat inflammation, dissolve phlegm and reduce fire.

Indications: Cough of common cold, acute conjunctivitis and toothache.

Source:《烟酒茶俗》

18　中暑　For Sun-Stroke

18.01　二鲜三花饮　Erxian Sanhua Cha

Ingredients:
鲜竹叶 Xian Zhuye, Fresh Bamboo Leaf (Folium Phyllostachys Nigra), 30 pieces
鲜荷梗 Xian Hegeng, Fresh Lotus Petiole (Petiolus Nelumbinis) 30g
沙参 Shashen, Ladybell Root (Radix Adenophorae) 30g
绿豆 Ludou, Mung Bean (Semen Phaseoli Radiati) 30g
丝瓜花 Sigua Hua, Towel Gourd Flower (Flos Luffae), 20 pieces
扁豆花 Biandou Hua, Hyacinth Bean Flower (Flos Dolichoris), 20 pieces
南瓜花 Nangua Hua, Pumpkin Flower (Flos Cucurbitae), 5 pieces

Directions: Decoct the first two while the beans are cooking. Add other herbs and continue boiling for 30 minutes. Drink the decoction as tea several times a day.

Functions: To clear heat, reinforce *qi*, produce body fluid.

Indications: Sunstroke with symptoms of fever, coarse breathing, irritability, yellow urine, thirst, fatigue, and weak pulse.

Source:《百病饮食自疗》

18.02　丁香酸梅汤　Dingxiang Suanmei Tang

Ingredients:
乌梅 Wumei, Smoked Plum (Fructus Mume) 2kg

山楂 Shanzha, Hawthorn Fruit (Fructus Crataegi) 20g
陈皮 Chenpi, Dried Tangerine Peel (Pericarpium Citri Reticulatae) 10g
桂皮 Gui Pi, Cassia Bark (Cortex Cinnamomi) 1g
丁香 Dingxiang, Cloves (Flos Caryophylli) 5g

Directions: Place all ingredients in a gauze bag, decoct over high heat first and then simmer for 30 minutes, remove the bag, let the decoction sit for 15 minutes, filter and add 5kg of white sugar, stir to mix well.

Functions: To produce body fluid, quench thirst, calm the mind.

Indications: Irritability, poor appetite and dry throat.

Source:《民间验方》

18.03 七鲜汤 Qixian Tang

Ingredients:
鲜藿香 Xian Huoxiang, Fresh Cablia Patchouli Herb (Herba Pogostemonis) 6g
鲜佩兰 Xian Peilan, Fresh Fortune Eupatorium (Herba Eupatorii) 6g
鲜荷叶 Xian Heye, Fresh Lotus Leaf (Folium Nelumbinis) 6g
鲜建兰叶 Xian Jianlan Ye, Swordleaf Cymbidium Leaf (Folium Cymbidium Ensifolium) 6g
鲜地黄 Xian Dihuang, Fresh Rehmannia Root (Radix Rehmanniae) 6g
鲜首乌 Xian Shouwu, Fresh Fleeceflower Root (Radix Polygoni Multiflori) 5g
鲜梨汁 Xian Lizhi, Fresh Pear Juice 10g

Directions: Decoct Rehmannia and fleeceflower roots first for 15 minutes, and then add the first four ingredients and continue to decoct for another five minutes. Filter and mix pear juice into the decoction. Add white sugar to taste before drinking.

Functions: To clear heat, produce body fluid and eliminate irritability.

Indications: Irritability and thirst in summer.

Source:《惠宜堂经验方》

18.04 七鲜茶 Qixian Cha

Ingredients:
鲜藿香 Xian Huoxiang, Fresh Cablia Patchouli Herb (Herba Pogostemonis) 10g
鲜佩兰 Xian Peilan, Fresh Fortune Eupatorium (Herba Eupatorii) 10g
鲜荷叶 Xian Heye, Fresh Lotus Leaf (Folium Nelumbinis) 10g
鲜竹叶 Xian Zhuye, Fresh Bamboo Leaf (Folium Phyllostachys Nigra) 10g
鲜薄荷 Xian Bohe, Fresh Peppermint (Herba Menthae) 10g
鲜芦根 Xian Lugen, Fresh Reed Rhizome (Rhizoma Phragmitis) 10g
鲜石斛 Xian Shihu, Fresh Dendrobium (Herba Dendrobii) 10g

Directions: Decoct and use as tea.
Functions: To resolve damp turbidity and reduce heat.
Indications: Aestival fever with thirst.
Source: 《中医儿科临证浅解》

18.05 七叶芦根饮 Qiye Lugen Yin

Ingredients:
藿香叶 Huoxiang Ye, Cablia Patchouli Leaf (Folium Pogostemonis) 5g
佩兰叶 Peilan Ye, Fortune Eupatorium Leaf (Folium Eupatorii) 5g
冬桑叶 Dongsangye, Mulberry Leaf (Folium Mori) 5g
大青叶 Daqingye, Dyers Woad Leaf (Folium Isatidis) 9g
薄荷 Bohe, Peppermint (Herba Menthae) 3g
鲜竹叶 Xian Zhuye, Fresh Bamboo Leaf (Folium Phyllostachys Nigra), 30 pieces
青箬叶 Qing Ruoye, Green Broadleaf Indocalamus Leaf (Folium Indocalamus Latifolius) 30g
鲜芦根 Xian Lugen, Fresh Reed Rhizome (Rhizoma Phragmitis) 60g

Directions: First decoct broadleaf Indocalamus leaves and reed. Use this decoction to decoct the other herbs. Add white sugar to taste before drinking. Drink three times a day.

Functions: To reduce heat, dissolve damp.
Indications: Common cold due to summer heat and damp in late summer.
Source:《中国药膳学》

18.06 三叶茶 Sanye Cha

Ingredients:
鲜荷叶 Xian Heye, Fresh Lotus Leaf (Folium Nelumbinis)
丝瓜叶 Sigua Ye, Towel Gourd Leaf (Folium Luffae)
苦瓜叶 Kugua Ye, Balsampear Leaf (Folium Momordicae Charantiae)
In equal amounts.
Directions: Decoct and drink the decoction.
Functions: To clear heat.
Indications: Aestival fever with thirst, desire to drink, and polyuria.
Source:《中医儿科学》

18.07 三鲜茶 I Sanxian Cha I

Ingredients:
鲜藿香 Xian Huoxiang, Fresh Cablia Patchouli Herb (Herba Pogostemonis) 30g
鲜荷叶 Xian Heye, Fresh Lotus Leaf (Folium Nelumbinis) 50g
鲜芦根 Xian Lugen, Fresh Reed Rhizome (Rhizoma Phragmitis) 100g
Directions: Decoct and drink the decoction.
Functions: To resolve damp, treat illness caused by summer heat.
Indications: Aestival fever with thirst and poor appetite. It can be used as an ordinary drink in summer.
Source:《中医儿科临证浅解》

18.08 山楂荷叶茶 Shanzha Heye Cha

Ingredients:
山楂 Shanzha, Hawthorn Fruit (Fructus Crataegi) 30g

鲜荷叶 Xian Heye, Fresh Lotus Leaf (Folium Nelumbinis), 1 piece

Directions: Cut, decoct and drink the decoction.

Functions: To strengthen the spleen and stomach, promote digestion, clear heat, stop nausea and vomiting.

Indications: Fever, epigastric and abdominal distention, nausea, vomiting, thirst, loose stools, cloudy urine, white and sticky tongue coating, soft pulse.

Source:《饮食疗法》

18.09 五味枸杞饮 Wuwei Gouqi Yin

Ingredients:

五味子 Wuweizi, Chinese Magnoliavine Fruit (Fructus Schisandrae) 100g (vinegar-baked)

枸杞子 Gouqi Zi, Barbary Wolfberry Fruit (Fructus Lycii) 100g

Directions: Placet in a big jar, pour 1,500ml boiling water in and cover the jar and let sit for three days. Add crystal sugar to taste before drinking.

Functions: To nourish kidney essence and liver blood, produce body fluid, stop sweating, ease the mind.

Indications: Poor appetite and emaciation in summer.

Source:《摄生众妙方》

18.10 五叶芦根茶 Wuye Lugen Cha

Ingredients:

枇杷叶 Pipa Ye, Loquat Leaf (Folium Eriobotryae) 30g

鲜芦根 Xian Lugen, Fresh Reed Rhizome (Rhizoma Phragmitis) 30g

冬瓜 Donggua, Chinese Waxgourd (Benincasae) 60g

藿香叶 Huoxiang Ye, Cablia Patchouli Leaf (Folium Pogostemonis) 3g

薄荷 Bohe, Peppermint (Herba Menthae) 3g

佩兰叶 Peilan Ye, Fortune Eupatorium Leaf (Folium Eupatorii) 3g

荷叶 Heye, Lotus Leaf (Folium Nelumbinis) 3g

Directions: Decoct the first three, filter and use the decoction as fluid to decoct the others. Filter and add white sugar to taste before drinking. Take three times a day.

Functions: To clear heat, produce body fluid, quench thirst, send stomach *qi* downward.

Indications: Sunstroke with fever, sensitivity to cold, profuse sweating, and irritability.

Source:《中国药膳学》

18.11 太子乌梅饮 Taizi Wumei Yin

Ingredients:

太子参 Taizishen, Pseudostellaria Root (Radix Pseudostellariae) 15g

乌梅 Wumei, Smoked Plum (Fructus Mume) 15g

甘草 Gancao, Liquorice Root (Radix Glycyrrhizae) 6g

Directions: Decoct and add crystal sugar to taste before drinking the decoction.

Functions: To strengthen the spleen and stomach, replenish *qi*, produce body fluid, quench thirst and ease the mind.

Indications: Sunstroke with thirst, profuse sweating, poor appetite, and fatigue.

Source:《中国药膳学》

18.12 四味茶 Siwei Cha

Ingredients:

藿香 Huoxiang, Cablia Patchouli Herb (Herba Pogostemonis) 10g

佩兰叶 Peilan Ye, Fortune Eupatorium Leaf (Folium Eupatorii) 10g

鲜竹叶 Xian Zhuye, Fresh Bamboo Leaf (Folium Phyllostachys Nigra) 10g

苡仁 Yiren, Coix Seed (Semen Coicis) 10g

Directions: Decoct, drink.
Functions: To remove damp, clear heat.
Indications: Infantile aestival heat.
Source: 《浙江中医杂志》6:1982

18.13 生脉饮 Shengmai Yin

Ingredients:
人参 Renshen, Ginseng (Radix Ginseng) 10g
麦冬 Maidong, Dwarf Lilyturf Tuber (Radix Ophiopogonis) 6g
五味子 Wuweizi, Chinese Magnoliavine Fruit (Fructus Schisandrae) 3g
Directions: Decoct with high heat and then low heat till the decoction is thick, filter, mix the decoction with watermelon juice and pear juice of a desired amount, add white sugar to taste, take the mixture.
Functions: To reinforce *qi* to treat collapse, stop sweating, cough and asthmatic breathing.
Indications: Collapse due to exhaustion of *qi* and body fluid.
Source: 《内外伤辨惑论》

18.14 地榆叶茶 Diyuye Cha

Ingredients:
地榆叶 Diyu Ye, Garden Burnet Leaf (Folium Sanguisorbae) 10g
Directions: Make as tea with boiling water.
Functions: To clear heat, cool blood.
Indications: Summer heat syndrome.
Source: 《普济方》

18.15 百解茶 Baijie Cha

Ingredients:
百解 Baijie, Roughhaired Holly Root (Radix Ilicis Asprellae) 60g
Directions: Decoct and drink.

Functions: To clear heat, remove toxins, produce body fluid and quench thirst. To prevent sunstroke.
Source:《简易中医疗法》

18.16 防暑茶 Fangshu Cha
Ingredients:
绿豆皮 Ludou Pi, Seed-Coat of Mung Bean (Testa Phaseoli Radiati) 6g
六一散 Liuyisan [滑石 Huashi, Talc (Talcum) : 甘草 Gancao, Liquorice Root (Radix Glycyrrhizae) = 6:1] 7g
薄荷 Bohe, Peppermint (Herba Menthae) 3g
白糖 Baitang, White Sugar, desired amount
盐 Yan, Salt, a little

Directions: Decoct and drink.
Functions: To clear heat, cure illness caused by summer heat, induce diuresis.
Indications: Fever, thirst, fullness in chest, irritability and little sweating, scanty urine.
Source:《健康文摘》 3:20, 1985

18.17 金银花茶 Jinyinhua Cha
Ingredients:
金银花 Jinyinhua, Honeysuckle Flower (Flos Lonicerae) 15g
白糖 Baitang, White Sugar 15g

Directions: Make as tea with boiling water.
Functions: To clear heat, dispel wind and remove toxins.
Indications: Tinnitus, headache, dizziness, fever, skin eruption, sore throat, dysentery. Also for the prevention of coronary heart disease, hypertension and arteriosclerosis.
Source:《祝您健康》 5:46, 1988

18.18 金花牡荆茶 Jinhua Mujing Cha

Ingredients:
玉叶金花藤 Yuyejinhua Teng, Buddha's Lamp Twig (Ramulus Mussaendae Pubescentis) 20-30g
牡荆叶 Mujing Ye, Hempleaf Negundo Chastetree Leaf (Folium Viticis Negundo) 20-30g
薄荷 Bohe, Peppermint (Herba Menthae), a little

Directions: Make as tea with boiling water.
Functions: To prevent sunstroke.
Source:《全国中草药汇编》

18.19 金鸡脚草茶 Jinjijiaocao Cha

Ingredients:
金鸡脚草 Jinjijiao Cao, Lemonfragrant Angelica Herb (Herba Angelicae Citriodorae) 10g

Directions: Pestle into coarse powder. Make as tea with boiling water.
Functions: To promote *qi* circulation, dissolve damp, clear heat, remove toxins.
Indications: Diseases caused by the summer heat.
Source:《常用中草药》

18.20 沙母二草茶 Sha Mu Ercao Cha

Ingredients:
海金沙藤 Haijinsha Teng, Japanese Fern Herb (Herba Lygodii) 20g
火炭母草 Huotanmucao, Chinese Knotweed Herb (Herba Polygoni Chinensis) 20g
地胆草 Didancao, Scabrous Elephantfoot Herb (Herba Elephantopi) 20g
甘草 Gancao, Liquorice Root (Radix Glycyrrhizae) 20g

Directions: Pestle into coarse powder, decoct and drink.
Functions: To clear heat, remove toxins and treat summer diseases.

Indications: Diseases caused by summer heat.
Source:《全国中草药汇编》

18.21 苦瓜茶 Kugua Cha

Ingredients:

鲜苦瓜 Xian Kugua, Fresh Momordica Charantia Fruit (Fructus Momordicae Charantiae), 1 fruit

绿茶 Lucha, Green Tea, desired amount

Directions: Cut the top off the fruit, put the tea into it. Hang in a well-ventilated place to dry. Pestle. Use 10g each time to make as tea with boiling water.

Functions: To clear heat, relieve irritability and induce diuresis.

Indications: Irritability with thirst and oliguria caused by summer heat.

Source:《福建中草药》

18.22 苦刺花茶 Kucihua Cha

Ingredients:

苦刺花 Kucihua, Vetchleaf Sophora Root (Radix Sophorae Viciifoliae) 5g

Directions: Make as tea with boiling water.

Functions: To clear heat.

Indications: Diseases caused by summer heat.

Source:《全国中草药汇编》

18.23 茉莉花茶 Molihua Cha

Ingredients:

茉莉花 Moli Hua, Arabian Jasmine Flower (Flos Jasmini Sambac), 10-20 flowers

Directions: Make as tea with boiling water.

Functions: To regulate *qi*, harmonize middle *jiao*, dissolve damp.

Source:《常见病验方研究参考资料》

18.24 建曲茶 Jianqu Cha

Ingredients:
藿香 Huoxiang, Cablia Patchouli Herb (Herba Pogostemonis) 120g
苏叶 Suye, Perilla Leaf (Folium Perillae) 120g
香附 Xiangfu, Nutgrass Galingale Rhizome (Rhizoma Cyperi) 120g
苍术 Cangzhu, Swordlike Atractylodes Rhizome (Rhizoma Atractylodis) 120g
陈皮 Chenpi, Dried Tangerine Peel (Pericarpium Citri Reticulatae) 120g
川朴 Chuanpu, Officinal Magnolia Bark (Cortex Magnoliae Officinalis) 60g
白芷 Baizhi, Dahurian Angelica Root (Radix Angelicae Dahuricae) 60g
白蔻衣 Baikou Yi, Peel of Round Cardamom (Pericarpium Amomi Rotundus) 60g
法半夏 Fa Banxia, Prepared Pinellia (Rhizoma Pinelliae Praeparata) 60g
茯苓 Fuling, Indian Bread (Poria) 60g
砂仁 Sharen, Villous Amomum Fruit (Fructus Amomi) 45g
桔梗 Jiegeng, Platycodon Root (Radix Platycodi) 90g
槟榔 Binglang, Areca Seed (Semen Arecae) 90g
麦芽 Mai Ya, Germinated Barley (Fructus Hordei Germinatus) 240g
山楂 Shanzha, Hawthorn Fruit (Fructus Crataegi) 180g
甘草 Gancao, Liquorice Root (Radix Glycyrrhizae) 30g
陈曲 Chenqu, Medicated Leaven (Massa Fermentata Medicinalis) 3,250g
榆叶粉 Yuye Fen, Powder of Siberian Elm Leaf (Pulvis Ulmi Pumilae Folium) 425g

Directions: Grind the first 17 materials into fine powder, mix in the last material. Use water to make the mixture into square pieces of 20g each. Use one piece each time and make as tea with boiling water.
Functions: To dissolve damp, strengthen spleen and harmonize stomach.
Indications: Diseases due to summer heat.
Source:《本草纲目拾遗》

18.25 桑蜜茶 Sang Mi Cha

Ingredients:
桑叶 Sangye, Mulberry Leaf (Folium Mori) 10g

蜂蜜 Fengmi, Honey, desired amount

Directions: Spread honey onto leaves. Stretch the leaves and dry in the shade. Cut the leaves into threadlike pieces and make as tea with boiling water.

Functions: To clear lung heat.

Indications: Infantile aestival heat with thirst.

Source:《本草纲目》

18.26 祛暑清心茶 Qushu Qingxin Cha

Ingredients:

鲜竹叶心 Xian Zhuyexin, Fresh Bamboo Leaf (Folium Phyllostachys Nigra) 6g

麦冬 Maidong, Dwarf Lilyturf Tuber (Radix Ophiopogonis) 6g

莲子心 Lianzi Xin, Lotus Plumule (Plumula Nelumbinis) 6g

鲜佩兰 Xian Peilan, Fresh Fortune Eupatorium (Herba Eupatorii) 6g

Directions: Decoct and drink.

Functions: To clear heart fire and prevent invasion of summer heat, strengthen spleen, promote digestion.

Indications: Summer diseases with such symptoms as fullness in chest, profuse sweating, irritability, thirst, tiredness and poor appetite.

Source:《卫生科普》4:1987

18.27 乌梅清暑饮 Wumei Qingshu Yin

Ingredients:

乌梅 Wumei, Smoked Plum (Fructus Mume) 15g

石斛 Shihu, Dendrobium (Herba Dendrobii) 10g

莲子心 Lianzi Xin, Lotus Plumule (Plumula Nelumbinis) 6g

竹叶卷心 Zhuyejuanxin, young Bamboo Leaf (Folium Phyllostachys Nigra), 30 pieces

西瓜翠衣 Xigua Cuiyi, Exocarp of Watermelon (Exocarpium Citrulli) 30g

Directions: Decoct dendrobium first, add the others later and continue boiling. Filter. Melt crystal sugar into the decoction before taking it.
Functions: To clear heat, quench thirst.
Indications: Summer diseases such as irritability and thirst.
Source:《百病饮食自疗》

18.28 清络饮 Qingluo Yin

Ingredients:
鲜荷叶 Xian Heye, Fresh Lotus Leaf (Folium Nelumbinis) 6g
鲜金银花 Xian Jinyinhua, Xian Honeysuckle Flower (Flos Lonicerae) 6g
鲜竹叶心 Xian Zhuyexin, Xian Bamboo Leaf (Folium Phyllostachys Nigra) 6g
鲜扁豆花 Xian Biandou Hua, Xian Hyacinth Bean Flower (Flos Dolichoris), a branch of
西瓜翠衣 Xigua Cuiyi, Exocarp of Watermelon (Exocarpium Citrulli) 6g
丝瓜皮 Sigua Pi, Towel Gourd Peel (Pericarpium Luffae) 6g

Directions: Decoct over high heat and then low heat for 5-10 minutes. Filter and drink.
Functions: Clear lung heat, treat summer diseases.
Indications: Headache and distention in head due to common cold in summer.
Source:《中国药膳大全》

18.29 清暑茶 I Qingshu Cha I

Ingredients:
六一散 Liuyisan [滑石 Huashi, Talc (Talcum)：甘草 Gancao, Liquorice Root (Radix Glycyrrhizae) = 6:1] 10g
薄荷 Bohe, Peppermint (Herba Menthae) 3g

Directions: Make as tea with boiling water. Take one dose every day.

Functions: To clear heat, dissolve damp.
Indications: Summer diseases due to damp-heat.
Source:《简易中医疗法》

18.30 清暑茶 II   Qingshu Cha II
Ingredients:
青蒿 Qinghao, Sweet Wormwood Herb (Herba Artemisiae Chinghao) 300g
薄荷 Bohe, Peppermint (Herba Menthae) 300g
荷叶 Heye, Lotus Leaf (Folium Nelumbinis) 300g
香薷 Xiangru, Mosla Herb (Herba Moslae) 300g
甘草 Gancao, Liquorice Root (Radix Glycyrrhizae) 90g

Directions: Stir-bake the first four on a low heat. Grind all materials into coarse powder. Sieve and wrap in bags with 13g in each. Use one bag each time, make as tea with boiling water.
Functions: To clear heat, treat summer diseases.
Indications: Sunstroke.
Source:《中草药制剂方法》

18.31 清暑茶 III   Qingshu Cha III
Ingredients:
金银花 Jinyinhua, Honeysuckle Flower (Flos Lonicerae) 9g
六一散 Liuyisan [滑石 Huashi, Talc (Talcum) : 甘草 Gancao, Liquorice Root (Radix Glycyrrhizae) = 6:1] 9g
绿豆衣 Ludou Yi, seed-coat of Mung Bean (Testa Phaseoli Radiati) 9g
薄荷 Bohe, Peppermint (Herba Menthae) 6g

Directions: Decoct and drink.
Functions: To clear heat, treat summer diseases.
Indications: Sunstroke.
Source:《浙江中医药》8:289, 1979

18.32 清暑明目茶 Qingshu Mingmu Cha

Ingredients:
白菊花 Baijuhua, White Chrysanthemum Flower (Flos Chrysanthemi) 10g
决明子 Jueming Zi, Cassia Seed (Semen Cassiae) 10g
槐花 Huai Hua, Pagodatree Flower (Flos Sophorae) 10g

Directions: Decoct and drink.

Functions: To clear heat, treat summer diseases, promote vision and refresh the mind.

Indications: Dizziness and blurred vision in summer, hypertension.

Source: 《瀚海颐生十二茶》

18.33 清暑解毒茶 Qingshu Jiedu Cha

Ingredients:
银花 Yinhua, Honeysuckle Flower (Flos Lonicerae) 10g
连翘 Lianqiao, Weeping Forsythia Capsule (Fructus Forsythiae) 10g
鲜荷叶 Xian Heye, Fresh Lotus Leaf (Folium Nelumbinis) 10g
鲜竹叶 Xian Zhuye, Fresh Bamboo Leaf (Folium Phyllostachys Nigra) 10g

Directions: Decoct and drink. Or make as tea with boiling water.

Functions: To clear heat, remove toxins.

Indications: Heat rash, summer boils.

Source: 《卫生科普》 4:1987

18.34 清暑益气饮 Qingshu Yiqi Yin

Ingredients:
麦冬 Maidong, Dwarf Lilyturf Tuber (Radix Ophiopogonis) 10g
鲜竹叶 Xian Zhuye, Fresh Bamboo Leaf (Folium Phyllostachys Nigra), 30 leaves
鲜荷梗 Xian Hegeng, Fresh Lotus Petiole (Petiolus Nelumbinis) 30g
西瓜翠衣 Xigua Cuiyi, Exocarp of Watermelon (Exocarpium Citrulli) 30g
粳米 Jingmi, Polished Round-Grained Nonglutinous Rice (Cultivarietas

Oryzae Sativae)
西洋参 Xiyangshen, American Ginseng (Radix Panacis Quinquefolii) 10g

Directions: Decoct the first five materials, filter and save the decoction. Decoct the sixth separately. Filter and save the decoction. Mix the two decoctions and take the mixture two or three times a day. Use for three successive days.

Functions: To clear heat, produce body fluid and reinforce *qi*.

Indications: Summer diseases with the manifestations of fever, coarse breathing, irritability, dark yellow urine, thirst, sweating, fatigue, listlessness, and weak pulse.

Source: 《百病饮食自疗》

18.35 淡盐糖水 Danyan Tangshui

Ingredients:
盐 Yan, Salt, a little
白糖 Baitang, White Sugar, desired amount

Directions: Make as tea with boiling water.

Functions: Same as glucose saline.

Indications: Profuse sweating and thirst of sunstroke.

Source: 《中国药膳学》

18.36 野秫根茶 Yeshugen Cha

Ingredients:
野秫根 Yeshugen, Rhizome of Wild Foxtail Millet (Rhizoma Setariae) 100g

Directions: Decoct and drink. Take one dose every day.

Functions: To clear heat, produce body fluid, quench thirst and treat irritability. To prevent sunstroke.

Source: 《民间验方》

18.37 雪梨饮 Xueli Yin

Ingredients:

雪梨 Xueli, Pear (Fructus Pyri) 200g (peeled, pitted, sliced)

冰糖 Bingtang, Crystal Sugar, desired amount

Directions: Put into iced boiled water. Let sit for four hours, then drink it.

Functions: To clear heat, quench thirst.

Indications: Common cold with fever and thirst. Lung *yin* deficiency causing dry throat, unproductive cough, hemoptysis, loss of voice, afternoon fever, night sweating, red tongue, thready rapid pulse.

Source: 《温病条辨》

18.38 焦大麦茶 Jiaodamai Cha

Ingredients:

焦大麦 Jiao Damai, Parched Barley (Fructus Hordei Vulgare) 10g

Directions: Make as tea with boiling water or decoct and drink.

Functions: To clear heat, strengthen stomach.

Indications: Sunstroke, fullness in chest, poor appetite.

Source: 《上海常用中草药》

18.39 绿豆酸梅茶 Ludou Suanmei Cha

Ingredients:

绿豆 Ludou, Mung Bean (Semen Phaseoli Radiati) 200g

酸梅 Suanmei, Smoked Plum (Fructus Mume) 100g

Directions: Decoct until cooked. Filter, mix white sugar into the fluid, cool, and drink.

Functions: To clear heat. It is used as a daily drink in summer.

Source: 《百病饮食自疗》

18.40 绿豆蜂蜜饮 Ludou Fengmi Yin

Ingredients:
绿豆 Ludou, Mung Bean (Semen Phaseoli Radiati) 200g
蜂蜜 Fengmi, Honey 100g

Directions: Decoct the bean. When cooked, filter and mix honey into the fluid. Take the mixture. Use daily.
Functions: To clear heat, remove toxins.
Indications: Various diseases caused by summer heat.
Source:《陕西中医交流验方汇编》

18.41 酸梅茶 Suanmei Cha

Ingredients:
酸梅 Suanmei, Smoked Plum (Fructus Mume), 20 pieces
冰糖 Bingtang, Crystal Sugar, desired amount

Directions: Make as tea with boiling water. Cool. Drink.
Functions: To produce body fluid, quench thirst. It is used as a daily drink in summer.
Source:《患者保健食谱》

18.42 蔗菊茶 Zhe Ju Cha

Ingredients:
甘蔗 Ganzhe, Sugarcane Stem (Caulis Saccharum Sinensis) 500g
菊花 Juhua, Chrysanthemum Flower (Flos Chrysanthemi) 50g

Directions: Cut the sugarcane stem into slices. Decoct both and drink.
Functions: To clear heat, produce body fluid and quench thirst.
Indications: Thirst due to damage of *yin* caused by summer heat.
Source:《中国药膳学》

18.43 积雪草茶 Jixuecao Cha

Ingredients:

积雪草 Jixuecao, Asiatic Pennywort Herb (Herba Centellae) 30g

Directions: Pestle into coarse powder, decoct and drink.

Functions: To clear heat, dissolve damp, remove toxins. To prevent and treat sunstroke.

Source:《简易中医疗法》

18.44 柠檬速溶饮 Ningmeng Surongyin

Ingredients:

鲜柠檬肉 Xian Ningmengrou, Fresh Lemon (Fructus Citri Limoniae), desired amount

Directions: Wrap with gauze. Twist into juice. Add ice and white sugar to taste before drinking. Take two times a day.

Functions: To clear heat, produce body fluid and quench thirst.

Indications: Thirst due to body fluid damage in febrile disease, vomiting in sunstroke, threatened abortion with abdominal pain and bleeding.

Source:《食物考》

18.45 鸡骨草茶 Jigucao Cha

Ingredients:

鸡骨草 Jigucao, Canton Love-Pea Vine (Herba Abri) 30g

Directions: Decoct and drink.

Functions: To clear heat, dissolve damp, promote detoxification and relieve pain. To prevent sunstroke.

Source:《全国中草药汇编》

18.46 鸡蛋花茶 Jidanhua Cha

Ingredients:

鸡蛋花 Jidanhua, Frangipani Flower (Flos Plumeriae Acutifoliae) 3-9g

Directions: Make as tea with boiling water.
Functions: To clear heat, dissolve damp. To prevent sunstroke.
Source:《中医大辞典·中药分册》

18.47 双皮茶 Shuangpi Cha

Ingredients:
冬瓜皮 Dongguapi, Chinese Waxgourd Peel (Exocarpium Benincasae)
西瓜皮 Xigua Pi, Exocarp of Watermelon (Exocarpium Citrulli)
In equal amounts.
Directions: Slice, decoct and drink.
Functions: To clear heat, induce diuresis and promote detoxification.
Indications: Thirst, scant dark-yellow urine and pediatric summer fever.
Source:《浙江中医》8:356, 1982

18.48 药王茶 Yaowangcha

Ingredients:
药王茶叶 Yaowangchaye, Bush Cinquefoil Leaf (Folium Potentillae Fructicosae) 12g
Directions: Make tea with boiling water.
Functions: To clear heat, replenish brain.
Indications: Palpitation, headache, and dizziness in summer.
Source:《全国中草药汇编》

18.49 藿香夏枯草茶 Huoxiang Xiakucao Cha

Ingredients:
藿香 Huoxiang, Cablia Patchouli Herb (Herba Pogostemonis) 10g
夏枯草 Xiakucao, Common Selfheal Fruit-Spike (Spica Prunellae) 10g
Directions: Pestle into coarse powder. Make as tea with boiling water.
Functions: To clear heat, dissolve damp.
Indications: Summer diseases.

Source:《常见病中医临床手册》

18.50 苏叶薄荷茶 Suye Bohe Cha

Ingredients:
紫苏叶 Zisu Ye, Perilla Leaf (Folium Perillae) 1,000g
薄荷 Bohe, Peppermint (Herba Menthae) 1,000g
佩兰叶 Peilan Ye, Fortune Eupatorium Leaf (Folium Eupatorii) 1,000g
藿香 Huoxiang, Cablia Patchouli Herb (Herba Pogostemonis) 1,000g
淀粉 Dianfen, Starch 200g
白糖 Baitang, White Sugar, desired amount

Directions: Grind the first four and screen. Melt sugar with 100ml warm boiled water. Mix starch into it. Use 200ml cooled boiled water to make starch into a paste. Pour 2,000ml boiling water into the paste and stir well. Mix the screened powder into the stirred paste. Make the paste into pieces of 10g each, dry, and store in a bottle. Use one or two pieces each time, two or three times a day, make as tea with boiling water.

Functions: To dispel wind cold, eliminate summer damp.

Indications: Common cold. Also to prevent sunstroke.

Source:《中草药制剂选编》

19 暑疖 For the Furuncle Due to Summer Heat

19.01 忍冬藤茶 Rendongteng Cha

Ingredients:
忍冬藤 Rendongteng, Honey-Suckle Stem (Caulis Lonicerae) 10g

Directions: Make as tea with boiling water. Use daily for seven days before the Dragon Boat Festival.

Functions: To clear heat, remove toxins. To prevent summer boils.

Source:《常用中草药》

19.02 银花露茶 Yinhualu Cha

Ingredients:
金银花 Jinyinhua, Honeysuckle Flower (Flos Lonicerae) 500g

Directions: Soak in water for two hours. Distill. Collect 1,600ml distilled water the first time, distil again and collect 800ml water the second time. Mix the distilled water, filter, and drink 50ml distillate, twice a day.

Functions: Clear heat, remove toxins, prevent and treat summer boils.

Source:《本草纲目拾遗》

19.03 银花绿豆茶 Yinhua Ludou Cha

Ingredients:
银花 Yinhua, Honeysuckle Flower (Flos Lonicerae) 30g
甘草 Gancao, Liquorice Root (Radix Glycyrrhizae) 3g
绿豆 Ludou, Mung Bean (Semen Phaseoli Radiati) 15g

Directions: Decoct and drink.

Functions: To clear heat, promote detoxification. To prevent and treat summer boils.

Source:《常见病验方选编》

20 咽喉炎、扁桃腺炎 For Pharyngotonsillitis

20.01 大海茶 Dahai Cha

Ingredients:
胖大海 Pangdahai, Boat-Fruited Sterculia Seed (Semen Sterculiae Lychnophorae), 5 pieces
甘草 Gancao, Liquorice Root (Radix Glycyrrhizae) 3g

Directions: Decoct. Add crystal sugar to taste before drinking.

Functions: To clear lung heat, relieve sore throat, dispel phlegm, control cough.

Indications: Common cold with cough, loss of voice, sore throat and

swollen and painful gums.
Source:《中国药膳学》

20.02 大海瓜子茶 Dahai Guazi Cha

Ingredients:
胖大海 Pangdahai, Boat-Fruited Sterculia Seed (Semen Sterculiae Lychnophorae), 3 pieces
冬瓜子 Dongguazi, Chinese Waxgourd Seed (Semen Benincasae) 10g
Directions: Decoct and drink the decoction.
Functions: To treat sore throat, moisten throat, dissolve damp, relieve swelling.
Indications: Loss of voice caused by laryngopharyngitis.
Source:《常见病验方研究参考资料》

20.03 土牛膝茶 Tuniuxi Cha

Ingredients:
土牛膝 Tuniuxi, Achyranthes Aspera Root (Radix Achyranthis Asperae) 30g
Directions: Pestle into coarse powder and decoct. Add crystal sugar to taste before drinking.
Functions: To clear heat-toxin, dissolve phlegm, relieve sore throat.
Indications: Diphtheria, pharyngitis.
Source:《常见病验方研究参考资料》

20.04 甘桔速溶饮 Gan Jie Surongyin

Ingredients:
生甘草 Sheng Gancao, Liquorice Root (Radix Glycyrrhizae) 60g
桔梗 Jiegeng, Platycodon Root (Radix Platycodi) 30g
白糖 Baitang, White Sugar 200g
Directions: Soak, decoct, pour out the decoction every 20 minutes and add water to decoct again. Repeat three times, remove the herbs and mix

the decoctions. Cook the mixed decoction over low heat until it becomes very thick. Remove from heat, cool, add white sugar. Dry, crush, and store in a bottle. Use 10g each time. Make as tea with boiling water.
Functions: To clear heat, treat throat diseases.
Indications: Pharyngolaryngitis.
Source:《伤寒论》

20.05 玄参青果茶 Xuanshen Qingguo Cha
Ingredients:
玄参 Xuanshen, Figwort Root (Radix Scrophulariae) 10g (sliced)
青果 Qingguo, Chinese White Olive (Fructus Canarii), 4 pieces (pestled)
Directions: Decoct and drink.
Functions: To relieve sore throat.
Indications: Pharyngolaryngitis, tonsillitis.
Source:《常见病验方研究参考资料》

20.06 玄麦甘桔汤 Xuanmai Gan Jie Tang
Ingredients:
玄参 Xuanshen, Figwort Root (Radix Scrophulariae) 15g
麦冬 Maidong, Dwarf Lilyturf Tuber (Radix Ophiopogonis) 15g
生甘草 Sheng Gancao, Liquorice Root (Radix Glycyrrhizae) 5g
桔梗 Jiegeng, Platycodon Root (Radix Platycodi) 10g
苦丁茶 Kudingcha, Holly Leaf (Folium Ilicis Cornutae) 10g
桑白皮 Sang Baipi, White Mulberry Root-Bark (Cortex Mori) 10g
Directions: Soak in a thermos bottle with boiled water for 30 minutes, add crystal sugar to taste before drinking as tea.
Functions: To moisten the lung, relieve sore throat.
Indications: Hoarse voice, cough, and dry throat after measles.
Source:《中药成药制剂手册》

20.07 加减清燥润肺饮 Jiajian Qingzao Runfei Yin

Ingredients:
石膏　Shigao, Gypsum (Gypsum Fibrosum) 10g
杏仁　Xing Ren, Apricot Seed (Semen Armeniacae Amarum) 5g
木蝴蝶　Muhudie, Oroxylum Seed (Semen Oroxyli) 3g

Directions: Decoct and filter. Add pear juice or sugarcane juice of a desired amount to the decoction before taking. Drink once or twice a day.

Functions: To clear heat, moisten the lung, produce body fluid and stop coughing.

Indications: Hoarse voice, dry throat, unproductive cough, red tongue, thready and rapid pulse due to dryness in the lung with damaged body fluid.

Source:《百病饮食自疗》

20.08 百两金茶 Bailiangjin Cha

Ingredients:
百两金　Bailiangjin, Crisped Ardisia Root (Radix Ardisiae Crispae) 10g

Directions: Make as tea with boiling water, or decoct and drink.

Functions: To clear heat, expel phlegm and dissolve damp.

Indications: Tonsillitis.

Source:《常用中成药》

20.09 冰糖木蝴蝶饮 Bingtang Muhudie Yin

Ingredients:
木蝴蝶　Muhudie, Oroxylum Seed (Semen Oroxyli) 3g
冰糖　Bingtang, Crystal Sugar, desired amount

Directions: Make as tea with boiling water.

Functions: To clear lung heat.

Indications: Chronic pharyngolaryngitis.

Source:《民间验方》

20.10 利咽茶 Liyan Cha

Ingredients:
金银花 Jinyinhua, Honeysuckle Flower (Flos Lonicerae) 15g
菊花 Juhua, Chrysanthemum Flower (Flos Chrysanthemi) 12g
桔梗 Jiegeng, Platycodon Root (Radix Platycodi) 10g
麦冬 Maidong, Dwarf Lilyturf Tuber (Radix Ophiopogonis) 10g
玄参 Xuanshen, Figwort Root (Radix Scrophulariae) 10g
木蝴蝶 Muhudie, Oroxylum Seed (Semen Oroxyli) 3g
甘草 Gancao, Liquorice Root (Radix Glycyrrhizae) 6g
胖大海 Pangdahai, Boat-Fruited Sterculia Seed (Semen Sterculiae Lychnophorae), 3 pieces

Directions: Soak for 10 minutes. Decoct over low heat for 20 minutes. Filter and collect the liquid. Add water to decoct again for 15 minutes and collect the liquid again. Mix the liquids and drink the mixture in two occasions in one day while warm after meal. Or make as tea with boiling water, cover and let stand for 15 minutes before drinking. One course of treatment consists of 20 days. Continue for two or three courses.

Functions: To clear heat, remove toxins and treat sore throat.
Indications: Tonsillitis, pharyngolaryngitis, pharyngoneurosis.
Source: 《陕西中医》 4:158, 1988

20.11 防疫清咽茶 Fangyi Qingyan Cha

Ingredients:
金银花 Jinyinhua, Honeysuckle Flower (Flos Lonicerae) 15g
杭菊花 Hangjuhua, Yellow Chrysanthemum (Flos Chrysanthemi) 10g
板蓝根 Banlangen, Isatis Root (Radix Isatidis) 20g
麦冬 Maidong, Dwarf Lilyturf Tuber (Radix Ophiopogonis) 10g
桔梗 Jiegeng, Platycodon Root (Radix Platycodi) 15g
甘草 Gancao, Liquorice Root (Radix Glycyrrhizae) 3g
茶叶 Chaye, Tea Leaf (Folium Camelliae Sinensis) 6g

Directions: Grind ingredients and wrap in three gauze-bags. Use one bag each time, add crystal sugar to taste and make as tea with boiling water.
Functions: To clear heat, remove toxins, treat sore throat, reduce swelling.
Indications: Pharyngitis.
Source:《北京中医》2:1985

20.12 金锁茶 Jinsuo Cha

Ingredients:
金锁 Jinsuo, Lambsquarters (Herba Chenopodii) 30g
马兰根 Malangen, Indian Kalimeris Root (Radix Kalimeridis) 30g
Directions: Pestle into coarse powder. Decoct and drink.
Functions: To clear heat, remove toxins, treat throat diseases, relieve swelling.
Indications: Tonsillitis.
Source:《上海中草药手册》

20.13 威灵仙茶 Weilingxian Cha

Ingredients:
威灵仙 Weilingxian, Clematis Root (Radix Clematidis) 30g
Directions: Decoct and drink.
Functions: To dissolve phlegm, remove stagnation.
Indications: Tonsillitis.
Source:《常见病中医临床手册》

20.14 咽喉茶 Yanhou Cha

Ingredients:
薄荷 Bohe, Peppermint (Herba Menthae) 2-3g
桔梗 Jiegeng, Platycodon Root (Radix Platycodi) 3-5g
生甘草 Sheng Gancao, Liquorice Root (Radix Glycyrrhizae) 3-5g

玄参 Xuanshen, Figwort Root (Radix Scrophulariae) 6-9g

胖大海 Pangdahai, Boat-Fruited Sterculia Seed (Semen Sterculiae Lychnophorae), 2-3 pieces

Directions: Make as tea with boiling water.

Functions: To replenish *yin*, reduce *xu*-fire.

Indications: Dry and sore throat, loss of voice. Take one or two doses a day. Stop if not effective after five doses.

Source:《祝您健康》3:47, 1988

20.15 消炎茶 Xiaoyan Cha

Ingredients:

蒲公英 Pugongying, Dandelion (Herba Taraxaci) 400g

银花 Yinhua, Honeysuckle Flower (Flos Lonicerae) 400g

薄荷 Bohe, Peppermint (Herba Menthae) 200g

甘草 Gancao, Liquorice Root (Radix Glycyrrhizae) 100g

胖大海 Pangdahai, Boat-Fruited Sterculia Seed (Semen Sterculiae Lychnophorae) 50g

淀粉 Dianfen, Starch 30g

Directions: Grind 200g of dandelion and honeysuckle flower together with peppermint, liquorice root and boat-fruited sterculia seed into fine powder. Decoct other 200g of dandelion and honeysuckle flower, filter. Add water to decoct a second time. Mix the decoctions. Boil to concentrate. Put starch into the concentrate and heat again to make a thick paste. Mix the powder with the thick paste. Screen the mixture to make granules. Dry the granules and store in a bottle. Use 10g each time and make as tea with boiling water.

Functions: To clear heat, promote detoxification, treat sore throat, and relieve swelling.

Indications: Pharyngolaryngitis, tonsillitis

Source:《吉林省中草药栽培和制剂》

20.16 清咽饮 II Qingyan Yin II

Ingredients:
乌梅肉 Wumeirou, Smoked Plum (Fructus Mume)
生甘草 Sheng Gancao, Liquorice Root (Radix Glycyrrhizae)
沙参 Shashen, Ladybell Root (Radix Adenophorae)
麦冬 Maidong, Dwarf Lilyturf Tuber (Radix Ophiopogonis)
桔梗 Jiegeng, Platycodon Root (Radix Platycodi)
玄参 Xuanshen, Figwort Root (Radix Scrophulariae), in equal amounts

Directions: Pestle into coarse powder. Use 15g each time and make as tea with boiling water. Take three times a day.
Functions: To clear heat, treat a sore throat.
Indications: Pharyngolaryngitis.
Source:《经验方》

20.17 清咽四味茶 Qingyan Siwei Cha

Ingredients:
石斛 Shihu, Dendrobium (Herba Dendrobii) 9g
玄参 Xuanshen, Figwort Root (Radix Scrophulariae) 9g
生甘草 Sheng Gancao, Liquorice Root (Radix Glycyrrhizae) 3g
银花 Yinhua, Honeysuckle Flower (Flos Lonicerae) 9g

Directions: Decoct and drink.
Functions: To replenish *yin*, clear heat, treat sore throat.
Indications: Chronic pharyngitis, dry and sore throat.
Source:《百病中医自我疗养丛书·咽喉炎·扁桃体炎》

20.18 丝瓜速溶饮 Sigua Surongyin

Ingredients:
经霜丝瓜 Jingshuang Sigua, Frosted Towel Gourd (Luffae Cylindricae), 1 piece
白糖 Baitang, White Sugar 500g

Directions: Remove the seeds, cut into small pieces. Decoct for one hour and filter. Boil again with low heat to concentrate. When the fluid becomes very thick, remove from heat and cool. Mix in white sugar. Dry, crush, and store in a bottle. Use 10g each time and make as tea with boiling water.
Functions: To clear heat, treat inflammation.
Indications: Acute and chronic pharyngitis and laryngitis, tonsillitis.
Source:《民间验方》

20.19 诃玉茶 He Yu Cha
Ingredients:
诃子 Hezi, Medicine Terminalia Fruit (Fructus Chebulae) 10g
玉竹 Yuzhu, Fragrant Solomonseal Rhizome (Rhizoma Polygonati Odorati) 10g
桔梗 Jiegeng, Platycodon Root (Radix Platycodi) 10g
木蝴蝶 Muhudie, Oroxylum Seed (Semen Oroxyli) 6g
Directions: Pestle and make as tea with boiling water.
Functions: A stringe lung, replenish *yin*, treat throat diseases.
Indications: Chronic laryngitis, hoarseness and dry throat.
Source:《常见病验方研究参考资料》

20.20 蜂蜜茶 I Fengmi Cha I
Ingredients:
茶叶 Chaye, Tea Leaf (Folium Camelliae Sinensis) 6g
蜂蜜 Fengmi, Honey, desired amount
Directions: Wrap tea in a gauze-bag, make tea with boiling water. Add honey before drinking. Gargle with and swallow every 30 minutes.
Functions: To replenish *yin*, treat sore throat.
Indications: Pharyngolaryngitis. Pharyngolaryngitis can be cured within two days. Continue use for three more days to consolidate relief.

Source:《健康文摘》4:29, 1985

20.21 绿茶梅花饮 Lucha Meihua Yin
Ingredients:
绿茶 Lucha, Green Tea 3g
玉蝴蝶 Yuhudie, Oroxylum Seed (Semen Oroxyli) 3g
绿梅花 Lu Meihua, White Mume Flower (Flos Mume Albus) 3g
冰糖 Bingtang, Crystal Sugar, desired amount
Directions: Make as tea with boiling water.
Functions: To clear heat, moisten throat.
Indications: Acute and chronic pharyngolaryngitis and loss of voice due to liver fire damaging lung.
Source:《新中医》3:42, 1985

20.22 绿合海糖茶 Lu He Hai Tang Cha
Ingredients:
绿茶 Lucha, Green Tea 3g
合欢花 Hehuan Hua, Albizzia Flower (Flos Albizziae) 3g
胖大海 Pangdahai, Boat-Fruited Sterculia Seed (Semen Sterculiae Lychnophorae), 2 seeds
冰糖 Bingtang, Crystal Sugar, desired amount
Directions: Make as tea with boiling water.
Functions: To clear lung heat, moisten dryness and treat the throat.
Indications: Laryngitis, hoarseness.
Source:《新中医》3:1985

20.23 酸浆草茶 Suanjiangcao Cha
Ingredients:
酸浆草 Suanjiang Cao, Downy Groundcherry Herb (Herba Physalis)
Directions: Pestle into coarse powder. Use 6g each day, add crystal sugar

to taste and make as tea with boiling water.
Functions: To clear heat, remove toxins and induce diuresis.
Indications: Acute and chronic tonsillitis and pharyngolaryngitis.
Source:《常见病验方研究参考资料》

20.24 凤衣冬蜜饮 Fengyi Dong Mi Yin

Ingredients:
凤凰衣 Fenghuangyi, Follicular Membrane of Hen's Egg (Membrana Follicularis Ovi) 6g
天冬 Tiandong, Cochinchinese Asparagus Root (Radix Asparagi) 12g
蜂蜜 Fengmi, Honey, 1 teaspoonful

Directions: Place all materials in a bowl, steam, and take the steamed mixture.
Functions: To replenish *yin*, treat throat disease.
Indications: Chronic laryngitis with hoarseness and sore throat.
Source:《中国食品》4:37, 1985

20.25 莲花茶叶茶 Lianhua Chaye Cha

Ingredients:
金莲花 Jinlianhua, Chinese Globeflower Flower (Flos Trollii) 6g
茶叶 Chaye, Tea Leaf (Folium Camelliae Sinensis) 6g

Directions: Make as tea with boiling water.
Functions: To clear heat, remove toxin and produce body fluid.
Indications: Chronic pharyngolaryngitis, tonsillitis.
Source:《百病中医自我疗养丛书·咽喉炎·扁桃体炎》

20.26 蝶菊茶蜜饮 Die Ju Cha Mi Yin

Ingredients:
绿茶 Lucha, Green Tea 6g
菊花 Juhua, Chrysanthemum Flower (Flos Chrysanthemi) 6g

玉蝴蝶 Yuhudie, Oroxylum Seed (Semen Oroxyli) 6g
蜂蜜 Fengmi, Honey, 1 teaspoonful

Directions: Decoct the seed for a short time. Make green tea and chrysanthemum flower as tea with boiling decoction. Cover and let stand. Add honey before drinking.

Functions: To replenish *yin*, clear heat, treat the throat.

Indications: Chronic laryngitis with hoarseness and sore throat.

Source:《中国食品》 4:37, 1985

20.27 橄榄冰糖饮 Ganlan Bingtang Yin

Ingredients:

生橄榄 Sheng Ganlan, Olive (Fructus Canarii), 20 pieces
冰糖 Bingtang, Crystal Sugar 30g

Directions: Pestle olives. Decoct and drink three times a day.

Functions: To replenish *yin*, treat the throat.

Indications: Chronic laryngitis, manifested as hoarseness and sore throat.

Source:《中国食品》 4:37, 1985

20.28 橄榄白萝卜茶 Ganlan Bailuobo Cha

Ingredients:

橄榄 Ganlan, Olive (Fructus Canarii), 10 pieces
白萝卜 Bailuobo, Radish Root (Radix Raphani)

Directions: Pestle. Make as tea with boiling water.

Functions: To replenish *yin*, treat the throat.

Indications: Sore throat.

Source:《王氏医案释注》

20.29 萝卜糖姜饮 Luobo Tang Jiang Yin

Ingredients:

鲜萝卜 Xian Luobo, Fresh Radish Root (Radix Raphani)

生姜 Sheng Jiang, Fresh Ginger (Rhizoma Zingiberis Recens)
In the ratio of 8 to 1.
Directions: Peel radish root and pestle to juice. Add white sugar to taste, decoct and drink.
Functions: To replenish *yin*, dissolve phlegm, dispel wind cold.
Indications: Loss of voice or even hoarseness, cough with phlegm, headache, nasal obstruction, sensitivity to cold, fever, white thin tongue coating, superficial pulse.
Source:《百病饮食自疗》

21 咳嗽、哮喘 For Coughs and Asthma

21.01 人参双花茶 Renshen Shuanghua Cha
Ingredients:
人参 Renshen, Ginseng (Radix Ginseng) 10g
金银花 Jinyinhua, Honeysuckle Flower (Flos Lonicerae) 10g
五味子 Wuweizi, Chinese Magnoliavine Fruit (Fructus Schisandrae) 10g
Directions: Decoct and drink as tea.
Functions: To replenish *qi*, nourish *yin*, clear lung heat.
Indications: Cough.
Source:《中医护理》

21.02 三子饮 Sanzi Yin
Ingredients:
瓜蒌子 Gualou Zi, Snakegourd Seed (Semen Trichosanthis) 10g
莱菔子 Laifuzi, Radish Seed (Semen Raphani) 10g
冬瓜子 Dongguazi, Chinese Waxgourd Seed (Semen Benincasae) 30g
Directions: Decoct and drink as tea two or three times a day.
Functions: To dispel phlegm, promote the lung in dispersing, relieve asthmatic breathing.

Indications: Asthmatic breathing with phlegm, fullness in chest, poor appetite, constipation, white and sticky tongue coating, rolling pulse.
Source:《百病饮食自疗》

21.03 三分茶 Sanfen Cha
Ingredients:
荞麦面 Qiaomai Mian, Buckwheat Flour (Pulvis Fagopyri Esculenti) 120g
茶叶 Chaye, Tea Leaf (Folium Camelliae Sinensis) 6g
蜂蜜 Fengmi, Honey 60g
Directions: Grind the tea leaves into a powder. Mix all ingredients to make paste. Use 20g each time and make as tea with boiling water.
Functions: To moisten the lung, stop cough, send *qi* downward, smooth intestines.
Indications: Cough and asthma.
Source:《儒门事亲》

21.04 三白茶 Sanbai Cha
Ingredients:
桑白皮 Sang Baipi, White Mulberry Root-Bark (Cortex Mori) 15g
百部 Baibu, Stemona Root (Radix Stemonae) 15g
白芍 Baishao, White Peony Root (Radix Paeoniae Alba) 15g
绿茶 Lucha, Green Tea 10g
Directions: Decoct. Add crystal sugar 15g to the decoction before drinking. Take one dose daily for five days is one course.
Functions: To clear heat, nourish the lung, send the lung *qi* downward and dissolve phlegm.
Indications: Whooping cough.
Source:《百病饮食自疗》

21.05 大蒜冰糖茶 Dasuan Bingtang Cha

Ingredients:
大蒜 Dasuan, Garlic Bulb (Bulbus Allii), 2 pieces

Directions: Pestle, add crystal sugar to taste, and make as tea with boiling water.

Functions: To promote the stomach, moisten the lung, clear toxic heat.

Indications: Whooping cough.

Source:《常见病验方研究参考资料》

21.06 小麦大枣饮 Xiaomai Dazao Yin

Ingredients:
浮小麦 Fuxiaomai, Light Wheat (Fructus Tritici Levis) 50g

大枣 Dazao, Chinese Date (Fructus Jujubae), 7 pieces

Directions: Decoct and drink the decoction.

Functions: To nourish the heart, stop sweating, reinforce *qi*, ease the mind.

Indications: Asthma with cold or heat phlegm, profuse sweating, and surging pulse.

Source:《洄溪医案》

21.07 川贝莱菔茶 Chuanbei Laifu Cha

Ingredients:
川贝母 Chuanbeimu, Tendrilleaf Fritillary Bulb (Bulbus Fritillariae Cirrhosae) 15g

莱菔子 Laifuzi, Radish Seed (Semen Raphani) 15g

Directions: Decoct and drink the decoction.

Functions: To moisten the lung, dissolve phlegm, send lung *qi* downward, control asthma.

Indications: Cough with phlegm due to bronchitis.

Source:《长寿之道》

21.08 川贝杏仁饮 Chuanbei Xingren Yin

Ingredients:
川贝母 Chuanbeimu, Tendrilleaf Fritillary Bulb (Bulbus Fritillariae Cirrhosae) 6g
杏仁 Xing Ren, Apricot Seed (Semen Armeniacae Amarum) 3g (peeled)

Directions: Decoct, add crystal sugar to taste, continue decocting with mild heat for 30 minutes and drink as tea.
Functions: To dissolve phlegm, stop coughing.
Indications: Infantile cough with phlegm.
Source:《成都国仁堂滋补餐厅》

21.09 止咳茶 Zhike Cha

Ingredients:
满山红花 Manshanhong Hua, Daurian Rhododendron Flower (Flos Rhododendri Daurici)
暴马子叶 Baomazi Ye, Manchurian Lilac Leaf (Folium Syringae)

In equal amounts.

Directions: Pestle, wrap in bags with 30g in each. Use one bag each time. Make as tea with boiling water.
Functions: To control coughing and asthma, dissolve phlegm.
Indications: Cough with phlegm due to chronic bronchitis.
Source:《防治慢性气管炎资料选编》

21.10 毛山茶(香风茶) Maoshancha (Xiangfengcha)

Ingredients:
毛山茶 Maoshancha, Shining Wintersweet Leaf (Folium Chimonanthi Nitentis) 9-18g

Directions: Make tea.
Functions: To clear heat, treat exterior syndromes, expel wind and remove toxins.

Indications: Cough due to invasion of wind-heat.
Source:《中医大辞典·中药分册》

21.11 玉米须桔皮茶 Yumixu Jupi Cha

Ingredients:
玉米须 Yumi Xu, Corn Stigma (Stigma Maydis) 30g
桔皮 Jupi, Tangerine Peel (Pericarpium Citri Reticulatae) 30g

Directions: Decoct. Drink.
Functions: To moisten the lung, stop coughing and dissolve phlegm.
Indications: Cough with phlegm.
Source:《常见病验方研究参考资料》

21.12 甘草醋茶 Gancao Cu Cha

Ingredients:
甘草 Gancao, Liquorice Root (Radix Glycyrrhizae) 6g
蜂蜜 Fengmi, Honey 30g
醋 Cu, Vinegar 10g

Directions: Make as tea with boiling water.
Functions: To moisten and astringe the lung, control cough.
Indications: Chronic bronchitis.
Source:《常见病验方研究参考资料》

21.13 甘草生姜汤 Gancao Shengjiang Tang

Ingredients:
甘草 Gancao, Liquorice Root (Radix Glycyrrhizae) 3g
生姜 Sheng Jiang, Fresh Ginger (Rhizoma Zingiberis Recens) 15-20g

Directions: Decoct and drink.
Functions: To eliminate wind-cold, dispel phlegm, control cough.
Indications: Cough due to invasion of exogenous pathogenic wind-cold.
Source:《百病饮食自疗》

21.14 冬瓜麦冬饮 Donggua Maidong Yin

Ingredients:
冬瓜子 Dongguazi, Chinese Waxgourd Seed (Semen Benincasae) 30g
麦冬 Maidong, Dwarf Lilyturf Tuber (Radix Ophiopogonis) 30g

Directions: Decoct, drink.
Functions: To reinforce *yin*, clear heat, dissolve phlegm.
Indications: Bronchitis.
Source:《湖北验方选集》

21.15 百药煎茶 Baiyaojian Cha

Ingredients:
五倍子 Wubeizi, Chinese Gall (Galla Chinensis) 500g
茶叶 Chaye, Tea Leaf (Folium Camelliae Sinensis) 30g
酵糟 Jiaozao, Distillers' Grains 120g

Directions: Pestle Chinese gall and grind into fine powder. Sift, add tea leaves and distillers' grains and pestle the mixture. Cut into pieces 3.5cm square. Keep in a jar till they are fermented with the surface changed to white. Dry and store in a dry cool place. Use one piece each time. Make as tea with boiling water, or dissolve in water and gargle.

Functions: To moisten the lung, dissolve phlegm, produce body fluid and quench thirst.

Indications: Prolonged cough with profuse and thick sputum, dry and sore throat.

Source:《本草蒙荃》

21.16 百部四味饮 Baibu Siwei Yin

Ingredients:
百部 Baibu, Stemona Root (Radix Stemonae) 15g
紫苏叶 Zisu Ye, Perilla Leaf (Folium Perillae) 10g
桑白皮 Sang Baipi, White Mulberry Root-bark (Cortex Mori) 10g

冰糖 Bingtang, Crystal Sugar 15g

Directions: Decoct the first three, filter and add the crystal sugar to the decoction before taking it. One dose a day. One week is one course of treatment.

Functions: To moisten the lung, stop coughing.

Indications: Early stage of whooping cough with symptoms such as fever, coughing, sneezing, and running nose.

Source:《百病饮食自疗》

21.17 杏梨饮 Xing Li Yin

Ingredients:

杏仁 Xing Ren, Apricot Seed (Semen Armeniacae Amarum) 10g (peeled, tip removed)

梨 Li, Pear (Fructus Pyri) (peeled, pitted, sliced), 1 piece

冰糖 Bingtang, Crystal Sugar, desired amount

Directions: Decoct by bringing to a boil and simmer for 30 minutes. Drink.

Functions: To clear heat, stop coughing.

Indications: Cough due to dryness in the lung.

Source:《成都同仁堂滋补餐厅》

21.18 杏仁冰糖饮 Xingren Bingtang Yin

Ingredients:

杏仁 Xing Ren, Apricot Seed (Semen Armeniacae Amarum) 30g

冰糖 Bingtang, Crystal Sugar 30g

Directions: Decoct and drink.

Functions: To relieve coughing and asthma.

Indications: Senile asthma.

Source:《中医验方汇编》第一辑

21.19 杏仁奶茶 Xingren Nai Cha

Ingredients:
杏仁 Xing Ren, Apricot Seed (Semen Armeniacae Amarum) 200g
白糖 Baitang, White Sugar 200g
牛奶 Niunai, Milk 250ml

Directions: Peel and grind apricot seeds, add water, filter, boil, add milk, boil again. Add sugar before taking the mixture.

Functions: To moisten the lung, stop coughing, relieve dryness, promote purgation.

Indications: Cough due to lung deficiency, constipation caused by body fluid deficiency and dryness in blood.

Precaution: Because the apricot seed contains hydrocyanic acid, exact dosage must be administered to avoid poisoning.

Source:《患者保健食谱》

21.20 皂荚芽茶 Zaojiaya Cha

Ingredients:
嫩皂荚芽 Nen Zaojia Ya, Young Chinese Honeylocust Spine (Spina Gleditsiae) 500g

Directions: Toast and grind into powder. Use 3g each time and, make as tea with boiling water.

Functions: To dissolve phlegm-damp.

Indications: Chronic bronchitis, cough with thick and sticky phlegm, asthmatic breathing and fullness in chest.

Source:《太平圣惠方》

21.21 沙参百合饮 Shashen Baihe Yin

Ingredients:
沙参 Shashen, Ladybell Root (Radix Adenophorae) 10g
百合 Baihe, Lily Bulb (Bulbus Lilii) 15g

Directions: Decoct and drink.

Functions: To moisten the lungs, stop coughing, nourish the stomach, produce body fluid.

Indications: Unproductive cough due to *yin* deficiency, or cough with little but sticky phlegm, dry mouth, red tongue with little coating, thready and rapid pulse.

Source: 《百病饮食自疗》

21.22 沙参梨皮饮 Shashen Lipi Yin

Ingredients:

沙参 Shashen, Ladybell Root (Radix Adenophorae) 10g

梨皮 Li Pi, Pear Pericarp (Pericarpium Pyri) 30g

Directions: Decoct and drink.

Functions: To expel wind-heat, moisten lung and stop coughing.

Indications: Cough with itching in throat, hemoptysis.

Source: 《百病饮食自疗》

21.23 沙参麦冬饮 Shashen Maidong Yin

Ingredients:

沙参 Shashen, Ladybell Root (Radix Adenophorae) 10g

麦冬 Maidong, Dwarf Lilyturf Tuber (Radix Ophiopogonis) 10g

生扁豆 Sheng Biandou, Hyacinth Bean (Semen Dolichoris) 10g

梨汁 Li Zhi, Pear Juice, desired amount

Directions: Decoct and add pear juice and crystal sugar to taste before drinking the decoction. Take two or three times a day.

Functions: To moisten the lungs, replenish *yin*, stop coughing, clear heart fire, relieve irritability, nourish stomach, produce body fluid.

Indications: Fever, unproductive cough and dry throat due to the damage of *yin* of the lung and stomach by wind-heat.

Source: 《百病饮食自疗》

21.24 车前根茶 Cheqiangen Cha

Ingredients:
鲜车前根 Xian Cheqian Gen, Fresh Plantain Root (Radix Plantaginis) 50g
冰糖 Bingtang, Crystal Sugar, desired amount

Directions: Decoct and drink. Or make as tea with boiling water.
Functions: To clear heat, moisten lung, dissolve phlegm, promote vision.
Indications: Whooping cough.
Source:《常见病验方研究参考资料》

21.25 芹菜根陈皮茶 Qincaigen Chenpi Cha

Ingredients:
芹菜根 Qincai Gen, Celery Root (Radix Apii), a handful
陈皮 Chenpi, Dried Tangerine Peel (Pericarpium Citri Reticulatae) 9g
饴糖 Yitang, Maltose 30g

Directions: Melt celery root, toast dried tangerine peel and maltose until they are slightly burnt. Decoct and drink. Fresh ginger can be added in case of cold.
Functions: To dissolve phlegm to stop cough.
Indications: Cough.
Source:《常见病验方研究参考资料》

21.26 定嗽定喘饮 Dingsou Dingchuan Yin

Ingredients:
山药 Shanyao, Common Yam Rhizome (Rhizoma Dioscoreae) 50g
石榴汁 Shiliu Zhi, Pomegranate-Seed Juice (Succus Granati Semen) 18g
甘蔗汁 Ganzhe Zhi, Sugarcane Stem Juice (Succus Saccharum Sinensis Caulis) 30g
蛋黄 Danhuang, Yolk, 4 pieces

Directions: Slice common yam, decoct over high heat and simmer for

20-30 minutes. Filter, mix pomegranate-seed and sugarcane stem juice with the decoction. Add yolk and decoct for a short time. Take the mixture.

Functions: To moisten the lungs, stop coughing.

Indications: Unproductive cough with dry throat.

Source:《医学衷中参西录》

21.27 柚子壳荷叶饮 Youzike Heye Yin

Ingredients:

柚皮　You Pi, Pummelo Peel (Exocarpium Citri Grandis) 30g (peeled)

荷叶　Heye, Lotus Leaf (Folium Nelumbinis) 3g

Directions: Decoct and add honey to taste before drinking.

Functions: To regulate lung *qi* and stop coughing.

Indications: Whooping cough.

Source:《常见病验方研究参考资料》

21.28 柿蒂茶 Shidi Cha

Ingredients:

柿蒂　Shi Di, Persimmon Calyx (Calyx Kaki), 3-5 pieces

冰糖　Bingtang, Crystal Sugar, desired amount

Directions: Make as tea with boiling water.

Functions: To send the lung *qi* downward, stop coughing.

Indications: Bronchitis, cough.

Source:《陕西中医》1:1985

21.29 胡萝卜大枣饮 Huluobo Dazao Yin

Ingredients:

胡萝卜　Huluobo, Carrot (Radix Dauci Sativae) 120g

红枣　Hongzao, Chinese Date (Fructus Jujubae), 12 pieces

Directions: Decoct and drink.

Functions: To moisten lung to stop cough.
Indications: Whooping cough.
Source:《岭南草药志》

21.30 宣肺饮 Xuanfei Yin

Ingredients:
生石膏 Sheng Shigao, Gypsum (Gypsum Fibrosum) 30g
冬瓜仁 Dongguaren, Chinese Waxgourd Seed (Semen Benincasae) 20g
杏仁泥 Xing Ren Ni, Mashed Apricot Seed (Semen Armeniacae Amarum) 10g
鲜竹叶 Xian Zhuye, Fresh Bamboo Leaf (Folium Phyllostachys Nigra), 10 pieces
竹沥 Zhuli, Bamboo Juice (Succus Bambosae) 20-30g

Directions: Decoct the first four and add bamboo joice before drinking. Drink it two or three times a day.
Functions: To promote lung in dispersing, clear heat, dissolve phlegm, redirect *qi* downward.
Indications: Asthma and cough with yellow thick phlegm, irritability and thirst due to heat in the lung.
Source:《百病饮食自疗》

21.31 姜枣饮 I Jiang Zao Yin I

Ingredients:
红糖 Hongtang, Brown Sugar 30g
红枣 Hongzao, Chinese Date (Fructus Jujubae) 30g
生姜 Sheng Jiang, Fresh Ginger (Rhizoma Zingiberis Recens) 15g

Directions: Decoct and drink. Should be accompanied by sweating for best effect.
Functions: To dispel wind-cold, relieve cough.
Indications: Cough due to invasion of wind-cold.
Source:《广东省中医验方交流汇编》

21.32 姜糖饮 II Jiang Tang Yin II

Ingredients:
生姜 Sheng Jiang, Fresh Ginger (Rhizoma Zingiberis Recens) 10g
饴糖 Yitang, Maltose 30g

Directions: Make fresh ginger as tea with boiling water, add maltose before drinking. Take while hot.

Functions: To dispel wind-cold, stop coughing.

Indications: Tracheitis manifested as cough with clear white phlegm, sensitivity to cold and nausea.

Source:《本草汇言》

21.33 扁柏叶茶 Bianbaiye Cha

Ingredients:
扁柏叶 Bianbaiye, Arborvitae Twig (Cacumen Biotae) 10g
红枣 Hongzao, Chinese Date (Fructus Jujubae), 7 pieces

Directions: Decoct and drink.

Functions: To dissolve phlegm, relieve coughing.

Indications: Chronic bronchitis.

Source:《常见病验方研究参考资料》

21.34 桑叶枇杷茶 Sangye Pipa Cha

Ingredients:
野菊花 Yejuhua, Wild Chrysanthemum Flower (Flos Chrysanthemi Indici) 10g
桑叶 Sangye, Mulberry Leaf (Folium Mori) 10g
枇杷叶 Pipa Ye, Loquat Leaf (Folium Eriobotryae) 10g

Directions: Pestle into coarse powder, decoct, and drink. Use daily for three or five days.

Functions: To clear heat, promote detoxification and relieve coughing.

Indications: Cough with yellow sputum in influenza.

Source:《中药临床手册》

21.35 桑杏饮 Sang Xing Yin

Ingredients:

桑叶 Sangye, Mulberry Leaf (Folium Mori) 10g

杏仁 Xing Ren, Apricot Seed (Semen Armeniacae Amarum) 10g (ground)

白茅根 Baimao Gen, Imperata Rhizome (Rhizoma Imperatae) 30g

雪梨汁 Xueli Zhi, Pear Juice (Succus Pyri Nivalis Fructus), desired amount

Directions: Decoct the first three, filter, add pear juice before drinking. Take two or three times a day.

Functions: To dispel wind, clear lung heat.

Indications: Hemoptysis, dry throat, fever, red tongue with thin yellow coating, superficial and rapid pulse caused by wind-heat.

Source: 《百病饮食自疗》

21.36 桑杏豆豉饮 Sang Xing Douchi Yin

Ingredients:

桑叶 Sangye, Mulberry Leaf (Folium Mori) 10g

杏仁 Xing Ren, Apricot Seed (Semen Armeniacae Amarum) 10g

淡豆豉 Dandouchi, Fermented Soybean (Semen Sojae Preparatum) 10g

Directions: Decoct and drink. Take two or three times a day.

Functions: To moisten the lungs, clear heat.

Indications: Unproductive cough or cough with little but thick sputum, dry throat, chest pain, fever, red tongue with yellow coating, thready and rapid pulse.

Source: 《百病饮食自疗》

21.37 桑菊杏仁饮 Sang Ju Xingren Cha

Ingredients:

桑叶 Sangye, Mulberry Leaf (Folium Mori) 10g

菊花 Juhua, Chrysanthemum Flower (Flos Chrysanthemi) 10g

杏仁 Xing Ren, Apricot Seed (Semen Armeniacae Amarum) 10g

Directions: Decoct and add white sugar to taste before drinking.
Functions: To dispel wind-heat, dissolve phlegm.
Indications: Hoarseness, cough with thick yellow phlegm, sore throat, yellow nasal discharge, thirst, headache, sensitivity to wind, fever, thin yellow tongue coating, superficial and rapid pulse due to wind-heat
Source:《百病饮食自疗》

21.38 化橘红茶 Huajuhong Cha
Ingredients:
化橘红 Huajuhong, Pummelo Peel (Exocarpium Citri Grandis), 1 slice
绿茶 Lucha, Green Tea 4.5g

Directions: Soak in boiled water, steam for 20 minutes, and make as tea with boiling water.
Functions: To relieve coughing, dissolve phlegm.
Indications: Cough with copious phlegm.
Source:《浙江中医药》8:289, 1979

21.39 桔梗甘草茶 Jiegeng Gancao Cha
Ingredients:
桔梗 Jiegeng, Platycodon Root (Radix Platycodi) 100g
甘草 Gancao, Liquorice Root (Radix Glycyrrhizae) 100g

Directions: Pestle into coarse powder, sift, wrap in bags with 10g in each. Use one bag each time, make as tea with boiling water.
Functions: To promote lung in dispersing, relieve coughing, dissolve phlegm.
Indications: Bronchitis.
Source:《常见病验方研究参考资料》

21.40 骨碎补茶 Gusuibu Cha
Ingredients:
骨碎补 Gusuibu, Fortune's Drynaria Rhizome (Rhizoma Drynariae) 30-

50g

Directions: Stir-bake with honey. Pestle into coarse powder, decoct and drink.

Functions: To reinforce kidney, moisten lung and relieve coughing.

Indications: Chronic bronchitis, cough with copious phlegm.

Source: 《常见病验方研究参考资料》

21.41 清心止嗽茶 Qingxin Zhisou Cha

Ingredients:
甘菊花 Ganjuhua, Chrysanthemum (Flos Chrysanthemi) 6g
霜桑叶 Shuangsangye, Mulberry Leaf (Folium Mori) 6g。
炙枇杷叶 Zhi Pipa Ye, Honey-Baked Loquat Leaf (Folium Eriobotryae) 6g
陈皮 Chenpi, Dried Tangerine Peel (Pericarpium Citri Reticulatae) 3g
酒黄芩 Jiu Huangqin, Scutellaria Root Prepared with Wine (Radix Scutellariae Praeparatum) 3g
生地黄 Sheng Dihuang, Dried Rehmannia Root (Radix Rehmanniae) 4.5g
焦枳壳 Jiao Zhiqiao, Parched Orange Fruit (Fructus Aurantii) 4.5g
鲜芦根 Xian Lugen, Fresh Reed Rhizome (Rhizoma Phragmitis) 10g

Directions: Wrap honey baked loquat leaves in a cloth bag. Pestle the remaining materials into coarse powder. Decoct all and drink.

Functions: To clear heat, relieve cough.

Indications: Cough with sticky phlegm, thirst, and sore throat of common cold due to wind-heat.

Source: 《慈禧光绪医方选议》

21.42 清燥润肺饮 I Qingzao Runfei Yin I

Ingredients:
石膏 Shigao, Gypsum (Gypsum Fibrosum) 15g
杏仁 Xing Ren, Apricot Seed (Semen Armeniacae Amarum) 6g
枇杷叶 Pipa Ye, Loquat Leaf (Folium Eriobotryae), 2 leaves (with fine

hair removed, baked with honey)
雪梨 Xueli, Pear (Fructus Pyri Nivalis), 1 pear (peeled and pestled)

Directions: Decoct the first three, add pear and filter. Store the decoction in a bottle and add honey to taste before drinking.

Functions: To clear heat, moisten the lungs and relieve coughing.

Indications: Non productive cough with fever, dry throat and nose, fullness and pain in chest and hypochondrium, irritability, thirst, red tongue with a thin and dry coating due to heat damaged lung.

Source: 《百病饮食自疗》

21.43 清燥润肺饮 II   Qingzao Runfei Yin II

Ingredients:
石膏 Shigao, Gypsum (Gypsum Fibrosum) 20g
麦冬 Maidong, Dwarf Lilyturf Tuber (Radix Ophiopogonis) 20g
沙参 Shashen, Ladybell Root (Radix Adenophorae) 30g
雪梨 Xueli, Pear (Fructus Pyri Nivalis), 2 or 3 pears

Directions: Decoct the first three, filter and save the decoction. Peel and pestle pear and add the pear juice before drinking. Take two or three times a day.

Functions: To clear lung heat, relieve *wei* syndrome.

Indications: *Wei* syndrome caused by body fluid damage due to lung heat, manifested as sudden onset of weakness of lower extremities, irritability, thirst, scant and dark yellow urine, constipation, red tongue with yellow coating, thready and rapid pulse in a febrile disease.

Source: 《百病饮食自疗》

21.44 雪羹汤 Xuegeng Tang

Ingredients:
海蛰 Haizhe, Jellyfish (Rhopilemae) 30g (soaked, washed, cut into small pieces)

鲜荸荠 Xian Biqi, Fresh Waternut Corm (Cormus Eleocharis Dulcis) 15g (peeled)

Directions: Decoct over low heat for one hour and drink.

Functions: To replenish *yin*, stop coughing, dissolve phlegm, promote digestion.

Indications: Chronic tracheitis due to *yin* deficiency manifested as cough with yellow sticky phlegm, thirst, and dry throat. Infantile indigestion with symptoms of poor appetite, emaciation, and diarrhea.

Source: 《古方选注》,《本草纲目拾遗》

21.45 陈皮饮 Chenpi Yin

Ingredients:
陈皮 Chenpi, Dried Tangerine Peel (Pericarpium Citri Reticulatae) 10g
白茯苓 Baifuling, Indian Bread (Poria) 15g
生姜 Sheng Jiang, Fresh Ginger (Rhizoma Zingiberis Recens), 3-5 slices

Directions: Decoct and drink.

Functions: To relieve coughing, dissolve phlegm.

Indications: Cough with sticky phlegm and difficulty in expectoration, fullness in chest, poor appetite, nausea, constipation, white sticky tongue coating, rolling pulse.

Source: 《百病饮食自疗》

21.46 鱼腥草饮 Yuxingcao Yin

Ingredients:
鲜鱼腥草 Xian Yuxingcao, Fresh Heartleaf Houttuynia Herb (Herba Houttuyniae) 30-60g

Directions: Decoct and drink.

Functions: To dissolve phlegm, relieve cough and pain.

Indications: Chest pain and fullness, cough with bloody or yellow thick phlegm, irritability, fever, red tongue with yellow and sticky coating,

rolling rapid pulse resulting from accumulation of phlegm-heat.
Source:《百病饮食自疗》

21.47 款冬花茶 Kuandonghua Cha

Ingredients:
款冬花 Kuandong Hua, Common Clotsfoot Flower (Flos Farfarae) 10g
冰糖 Bingtang, Crystal Sugar, desired amount

Directions: Make as tea with boiling water.
Functions: To clear heat, moisten the lungs, relieve cough, dissolve phlegm.
Indications: Cough and asthma in acute bronchitis.
Source:《常见病验方研究参考资料》

21.48 丝瓜花蜜饮 Siguahua Mi Yin

Ingredients:
丝瓜花 Sigua Hua, Towel Gourd Flower (Flos Luffae) 10g

Directions: Make as tea with boiling water. Add honey to taste before drinking. Take while hot. Three doses a day.
Functions: To clear lung heat, relieve cough.
Indications: Bronchitis due to lung heat manifested as cough with yellow phlegm, asthmatic breathing, chest pain and dry throat.
Source:《滇南本草》

21.49 黑芝麻茶 Heizhima Cha

Ingredients:
黑芝麻 Heizhima, Black Sesame (Semen Sesami Nigrum) 15g
冰糖 Bingtang, Crystal Sugar, desired amount

Directions: Toast and grind black sesame. Make as tea with boiling water.
Functions: To reinforce liver and kidney, moisten viscera.

Indications: Dry cough.
Source:《简易中医疗法》

21.50 无花果茶 Wuhuaguo Cha

Ingredients:

无花果 Wuhuaguo, Fig (Fructus Fici) 9g

Directions: Decoct and drink. Or crush to juice, make the juice as tea with boiling water.
Functions: To induce diuresis, relieve asthma.
Indications: Dysuria, asthma.
Source:《中医验方汇编》第一辑,《常见病验方研究参考资料》

21.51 滋胃和中茶 Ziwei Hezhong Cha

Ingredients:

朱拌竹茹 Zhu Ban Zhuru, Bamboo Shavings with Cinnabar (Caulis Bambusae in Taeniam cum Cinnabaris) 3g
鲜青果 Xian Qingguo, Fresh Chinese White Olive (Fructus Canarii) 10g
厚朴花 Houpu Hua, Officinal Magnolia Flower (Flos Magnoliae Officinalis) 1.5g
羚羊角 Lingyang Jiao, Pronghorn (Cornu Saigae Tataricae) 1.5g

Directions: Pestle, decoct and drink.
Functions: To dissolve phlegm, promote digestion.
Indications: Cough with copious yellow sticky phlegm, thirst, and poor appetite in elderly with *qi* deficiency and heat in lung.
Source:《慈禧光绪医方选议》

21.52 榆皮车前茶 Yupi Cheqian Cha

Ingredients:

榆树皮 Yushu Pi, Bark of Siberian Elm (Cortex Ulmi Pumilae) 10g
车前子 Cheqian Zi, Plantain Seed (Semen Plantaginis) 10g

Directions: Pestle, decoct and drink.

Functions: To clear heat, dispel phlegm and induce diuresis.
Indications: Cough due to heat in lung.
Source: 《常见病验方研究参考资料》

21.53 葫芦茶冰糖饮 Hulucha Bingtang Yin
Ingredients:
葫芦茶 Hulucha, Triquetrous Tadehagi Tickclover (Herba Desmodii Triquetri) 40g
冰糖 Bingtang, Crystal Sugar, desired amount
Directions: Decoct the first and add crystal sugar before drinking.
Functions: To dispel wind-heat, relieve cough.
Indications: Hoarse cough with sticky phlegm difficulty in expectorating, and sore throat caused by invasion of exogenous pathogenic wind-heat.
Source: 《饮食疗法》

21.54 酸石榴饮 Suanshiliu Yin
Ingredients:
鲜石榴汁 Xian Shiliu Zhi, Fresh Pomegranate-Seed Juice (Succus Granati Semen) 18g
山药 Shanyao, Common Yam Rhizome (Rhizoma Dioscoreae) 45g
甘蔗汁 Ganzhe Zhi, Sugarcane Stem Juice (Succus Saccharum Sinensis Caulis) 30g
生鸡子黄 Sheng Jizihuang, Yolk, 4 pieces
Directions: Decoct common yam, filter, cool the fluid. Mix the other three into the fluid. Take the mixture.
Functions: To relieve coughs and asthma.
Indications: Cough, asthma.
Precaution: After decocting yam, the fluid should be cool. Thus the yolk mixed into it will remain raw. If the yolk is cooked, it will not be effective in relieving cough and asthma.

Source:《医学衷中参西录》

21.55 银花芦根饮 Yinhua Lugen Cha

Ingredients:
芦根 Lugen, Reed Rhizome (Rhizoma Phragmitis) 30g
银花 Yinhua, Honeysuckle Flower (Flos Lonicerae) 10g

Directions: Decoct and drink.
Functions: To clear heat, relieve cough and dissolve phlegm.
Indications: Chest pain, asthma, cough with yellow sticky phlegm or blood, irritability, fullness in chest, fever, red tongue with yellow coating, rolling and rapid pulse caused by phlegm-heat.
Source:《百病饮食自疗》

21.56 润肺止咳茶 Runfei Zhike Cha

Ingredients:
玄参 Xuanshen, Figwort Root (Radix Scrophulariae) 60g
麦冬 Maidong, Dwarf Lilyturf Tuber (Radix Ophiopogonis) 60g
乌梅 Wumei, Smoked Plum (Fructus Mume) 24g
桔梗 Jiegeng, Platycodon Root (Radix Platycodi) 30g
甘草 Gancao, Liquorice Root (Radix Glycyrrhizae) 15g

Directions: Pestle into coarse powder, wrap in bags of 18g. Use one bag each time and make as tea with boiling water.
Functions: To moisten lung, relieve cough.
Indications: Cough with sticky phlegm due to *yin* deficiency causing interior heat and dryness in the lung.
Source:《中草药制剂方法》

21.57 橘皮饮 Jupi Yin

Ingredients:
橘皮 Jupi, Dried Tangerine Peel (Pericarpium Citri Reticulatae) 10g

杏仁 Xing Ren, Apricot Seed (Semen Armeniacae Amarum) 10g (peeled and tip removed)
老丝瓜 Lao Sigua, Dried Towel Gourd (Luffae Cylindricae) 10g

Directions: Decoct over high heat and then simmer for 20-30 minutes. Cool, filter and add white sugar to taste before drinking.
Functions: To regulate *qi*, remove phlegm.
Indications: Cough due to phlegm-damp.
Source:《民间验方》

21.58 橘皮茶 I   Jupi Cha I

Ingredients:
橘皮 Jupi, Dried Tangerine Peel (Pericarpium Citri Reticulatae) 10g

Directions: Cut into thread-like pieces. Make as tea with boiling water.
Functions: To regulate spleen, harmonize stomach, circulate *qi* and dissolve phlegm.
Indications: Chronic bronchitis manifested as cough with profuse white sticky phlegm, fullness and distention in the chest.
Source:《患者保健食谱》

21.59 橘红茶   Juhong Cha

Ingredients:
橘红 Juhong, Red Tangerine Peel (Exocarpium Citri Rubrum), 1 slice
绿茶 Lucha, Green Tea 4.5g

Directions: Make as tea with boiling water and then steam for 20 minutes. Drink the steamed tea.
Functions: To moisten lung, dissolve phlegm, regulate *qi*.
Indications: Cough with profuse sticky phlegm.
Source:《瀚海颐生十二茶》

21.60 双花杏蜜饮 Shuanghua Xing Mi Yin

Ingredients:
金银花 Jinyinhua, Honeysuckle Flower (Flos Lonicerae) 10g
菊花 Juhua, Chrysanthemum Flower (Flos Chrysanthemi) 10g
杏仁 Xing Ren, Apricot Seed (Semen Armeniacae Amarum) 10g (ground)
蜂蜜 Fengmi, Honey 30g

Directions: Decoct and add honey before drinking each time.

Functions: To clear heat, remove toxins, promote pus drainage and relieve pain.

Indications: Early stage of pulmonary abscess manifested as cough, chest pain, red tongue with yellow coating, superficial rolling and rapid pulse.

Source: 《百病饮食自疗》

21.61 罗布麻平喘茶 Luobuma Pingchuancha

Ingredients:
罗布麻叶 Luobuma Ye, Dogbane Leaf (Folium Apocyni Veneti) 10g
向日葵盘 Xiangrikui Pan, Sunflower Receptacle (Reseptaculum Helianthi) 5g

Directions: Make as tea with boiling water.

Functions: To relieve cough and asthma.

Indications: Bronchitis, asthma, allergic bronchial asthma.

Source: 《开卷有益》 4:35, 1988

21.62 罗汉果柿饼饮 Luohanguo Shibing Yin

Ingredients:
罗汉果 Luohanguo, Chinese Momordica Fruit (Fructus Momordicae), half a fruit
柿饼 Shi Bing, Prepared Persimmon (Fructus Kaki Praeparate), 2-3 pieces

Directions: Decoct and add crystal sugar before drinking. Drink 3 times a day.
Functions: To relieve cough and asthma, dissolve phlegm.
Indications: Cough with sticky phlegm, asthmatic breathing, irritability, flushed face and thirst.
Source:《饮食疗法》

21.63 萝卜茶 I Luobo Cha I
Ingredients:
经霜萝卜 Jingshuang Luobo, Frostbitten Radish Root (Radix Raphani) 100g
Directions: Slice, decoct and drink.
Functions: To promote digestion, circulate *qi* and expel phlegm.
Indications: Cough with phlegm, loss of voice, bleeding in pulmonary tuberculosis.
Source:《常见病验方研究参考资料》

21.64 萝卜饴糖饮 Luobo Yitang Yin
Ingredients:
萝卜 Luobo, Radish Root (Radix Raphani)
饴糖 Yitang, Maltose, 2-3 spoonful
Directions: Cut radish into small pieces and put into a bowl. Spread maltose on the pieces. Let stand over night. Take the resulting fluid.
Functions: To replenish *yin*, relieve cough.
Indications: Cough of acute and chronic bronchitis.
Source:《中国药膳学》

22 肺脓疡 For Pulmonary Suppuration

22.01 冬瓜藤饮 Dongguateng Yin

Ingredients:
冬瓜藤 Donggua Teng, Chinese Waxgourd Stem (Caulis Benincasae) 50-100g

Directions: Decoct, drink.

Functions: To clear heat, dissolve phlegm.

Indications: Diseases caused by heat in the lung and phlegm-heat.

Source:《浙江中医》8:356, 1982

22.02 冬瓜子芦根饮 Dongguazi Lugen Yin

Ingredients:
鲜芦根 Xian Lugen, Fresh Reed Rhizome (Rhizoma Phragmitis) 90g
冬瓜子 Dongguazi, Chinese Waxgourd Seed (Semen Benincasae) 90g

Directions: Decoct, drink.

Functions: To clear heat, dissolve phlegm-damp, drain pus, produce body fluid.

Indications: Pulmonary abscess.

Source:《湖北验方选集》

22.03 瓜蒌茶 Gualou Cha

Ingredients:
全瓜蒌 Quangualou, Snakegourd Fruit (Fructus Trichosanthis)

Directions: Steam, dry, cut into thread-like pieces. Use 30g each time, make as tea with boiling water.

Functions: To clear the lung heat, dissolve phlegm.

Indications: Pneumonia, bronchitis and cough with yellow sputum.

Source:《常见病验方研究参考资料》

23 高血压 For Hypertension

23.01 三子茶 Sanzi Cha

Ingredients:
荠菜子 Jicai Zi, Shepherds Purse Seed (Semen Capsellae) 6g
青葙子 Qingxiang Zi, Feather Cockscomb Seed (Semen Celosiae) 6g
决明子 Jueming Zi, Cassia Seed (Semen Cassiae) 6g

Directions: Grind all ingredients and wrap in a gauze bag. Make as tea with boiling water. Take one dose a day.
Functions: To soothe the liver, lower the blood pressure.
Indications: Hypertension, headache and dizziness.
Source:《实用中药学》

23.02 三宝茶 Sanbao Cha

Ingredients:
普洱茶 Puer Cha, Pu' er Tea (Camellia Cochinchinensis)
菊花 Juhua, Chrysanthemum Flower (Flos Chrysanthemi)
罗汉果 Luohanguo, Chinese Momordica Fruit (Fructus Momordicae)

In equal amounts.
Directions: Grind into coarse powder. Wrap in gauze bags with 20g in each. Use one bag each time. Make as tea with boiling water.
Functions: To lower blood pressure, reduce body weight.
Indications: Hypertension, hyperlipemia.
Source:《家用中成药》

23.03 三七花茶 Sanqihua Cha

Ingredients:
三七花 Sanqi Hua, Sanchi Flower (Flos Notoginseng) 5g

Directions: Make as tea with boiling water.
Functions: To clear heat, soothe the liver and lower blood pressure.

Indications: Hypertension.
Source:《云南中草药选》

23.04 山楂叶(花)茶 Shanzhaye(hua) Cha
Ingredients:
山楂叶 Shanzha Ye, Hawthorn Leaf (Folium Crataegi)   **or**
山楂花 Shanzha Hua, Hawthorn Flower (Flos Crataegi)

Directions: Cut and dry. Use 5g each time. Take 3-4 times a day. Make as tea with boiling water.
Functions: To promote digestion, remove food retention, activate blood circulation and remove blood stasis.
Indications: Hypertension, hyperlipemia.
Source:《中药大辞典》

23.05 山楂决明茶 Shanzha Jueming Cha
Ingredients:
山楂 Shanzha, Hawthorn Fruit (Fructus Crataegi) 10g
决明子 Jueming Zi, Cassia Seed (Semen Cassiae) 10g

Directions: Pestle into rough powder. Make as tea with boiling water.
Functions: To promote digestion, remove food retention, soothe the liver, lower blood pressure.
Indications: Hypertension.
Source:《实用中药学》

23.06 天麻菊花饮 Tianma Juhua Yin
Ingredients:
天麻 Tianma, Tall Gastrodia Tuber (Rhizoma Gastrodiae) 10g
菊花 Juhua, Chrysanthemum Flower (Flos Chrysanthemi) 10g

Directions: Decoct tall gastrodia tuber, add chrysanthemum flower, and continue to boil for five minutes. Drink the decoction twice a day.

Functions: To eliminate wind, relieve convulsions, clear toxic heat, soothe the liver, promote vision.

Indications: Windstroke due to liver and kidney *yin* deficiency and liver fire flaring up with symptoms of dizziness, tinnitus, deviation of mouth and eyes, stiffness of tongue, hemiplegia, red tongue with yellow coating, wiry and rolling pulse.

Source:《百病饮食自疗》

23.07 西瓜决明茶 Xigua Jueming Cha

Ingredients:
干西瓜翠衣 Gan Xigua Cuiyi, Dried Exocarp of Watermelon (Exocarpium Citrulli) 9g **or**
鲜西瓜翠衣 Xian Xigua Cuiyi, Fresh Exocarp of Watermelon (Exocarpium Citrulli) 30g
草决明 CaoJueming, Cassia Seed (Semen Cassiae) 9g

Directions: Make as tea with boiling water.

Functions: To clear heat, soothe the liver and lower blood pressure.

Indications: Hypertension.

Source:《中国药膳学》

23.08 西瓜翠衣茶 Xiguacuiyi Cha

Ingredients:
干西瓜翠衣 Gan Xigua Cuiyi, Dried Exocarp of Watermelon (Exocarpium Citrulli) 15-20g

Directions: Decoct and drink.

Functions: To clear heat, reduce fire.

Indications: Hypertension, red eyes, edema of nephritis, hot pain in urination, hepatitis.

Source:《黑龙江中医药》 5:57, 1984

23.09 向日葵叶饮 Xiangrikuiye Yin

Ingredients:
鲜向日葵叶 Xian Xiangrikui Ye, Fresh Sunflower Leaf (Folium Helianthi) 120g

Directions: Decoct and drink three times a day.

Functions: To soothe liver, promote vision, reduce liver *yang* and stop liver wind.

Indications: High blood pressure with dizziness.

Source:《江西中医药》12:1960

23.10 决明菊花茶 Jueming Juhua Cha

Ingredients:
草决明 CaoJueming, Cassia Seed (Semen Cassiae) 30g (ground)
野菊花 Yejuhua, Wild Chrysanthemum Flower (Flos Chrysanthemi Indici) 12g

Directions: Make as tea with boiling water.

Functions: To soothe liver by reducing its *yang*, lower blood pressure.

Indications: Headache of hypertension.

Source:《实用中药学》

23.11 旱芹车前茶 Hanqin Cheqian Cha

Ingredients:
鲜旱芹菜 Xian Hanqincai, Fresh Celery (Herba Apii) 100g
鲜车前草 Xian Cheqian Cao, Fresh Plantain Herb (Herba Plantaginis) 100g

Directions: Decoct and drink.

Functions: To soothe liver, clear heat, induce diuresis and lower blood pressure.

Indications: Dizziness and blurred vision in hypertension, edema.

Source:《上海常用中草药》

23.12 杜仲茶 Duzhong Cha

Ingredients:
杜仲 Duzhong, Eucommia Bark (Cortex Eucommiae) 15g
棕榈叶 Zongluye, Fortune Windmill Palm Leaf (Folium Trachycarpi) 30g
夏枯草 Xiakucao, Common Selfheal Fruit-spike (Spica Prunellae) 5g

Directions: Soak eucommia bark in salt water, toast and dry. Grind all materials together and make as tea with boiling water.

Functions: To reinforce kidney, soothe liver by reducing its *yang*.

Indications: Hypertension, headache and dizziness due to the deficiency of liver and kidney. It is effective in preventing windstroke.

Source:《常见病验方研究参考资料》

23.13 芹菜根茶 Qincaigen Cha

Ingredients:
芹菜根 Qincai Gen, Celery Root (Radix Apii) 60g

Directions: Decoct and drink.

Functions: Clear heat, dissolve damp, lower blood pressure and stop dizziness.

Indications: Insomnia, dizziness and hypertension.

Source:《常见病验方研究参考资料》

23.14 花生全草茶 Huashengquancao Cha

Ingredients:
干花生全草 Gan Huasheng Quancao, dried Peanut Herb (Herba Arachidis) 30-45g

Directions: Decoct and drink.

Functions: To lower blood pressure.

Indications: Hypertension.

Source:《中医教学》 4:45, 1977

23.15 胡桐叶茶 Hutongye Cha

Ingredients:
胡桐叶 Hutongye, Diversifolious Poplar Leaf (Folium Populi Diversifoliae) 10g

Directions: Make as tea with boiling water.
Functions: To lower blood pressure.
Indications: Hypertension.
Source:《全国中草药汇编》

23.16 苦丁茶 Kuding Cha

Ingredients:
苦丁茶 Kudingcha, Holly Leaf (Folium Ilicis Cornutae) 6g
菊花 Juhua, Chrysanthemum Flower (Flos Chrysanthemi) 6g
桑叶 Sangye, Mulberry Leaf (Folium Mori) 6g
白茅根 Baimao Gen, Imperata Rhizome (Rhizoma Imperatae) 6g
钩藤 Gouteng, Gambir Plant (Ramulus Uncariae cum Uncis) 6g

Directions: Decoct and drink.
Functions: To lower blood pressure.
Indications: Headache and dizziness of hypertension.
Source:《浙江中医药》 8:289, 1979

23.17 降压茶 I Jiangya Cha I

Ingredients:
野菊花 Yejuhua, Wild Chrysanthemum Flower (Flos Chrysanthemi Indici) 1,000g
夏枯草 Xiakucao, Common Selfheal Fruit-spike (Spica Prunellae) 1,500g
荠菜花 Jicai Hua, Shepherds Purse Flower (Flos Capsellae) 1,500g
决明子 Jueming Zi, Cassia Seed (Semen Cassiae) 2,000g
麦粉 Mai Fen, Wheat Flour (Pulvis Tritici Aestivi) 1,000g

白糖 Baitang, White Sugar, desired amount

Directions: Grind half of common selfheal fruit-spike, shepherds purse flower and cassia seed into a powder together with wild chrysanthemum flower. Decoct other half of the three ingredients twice. Mix the decoctions and concentrate to 2,500g. Add boiling water to wheat flour and sugar to make a thick paste. Mix the thick paste with the decoction and divide the mixture into 20g partions. Dry, and store in a bottle. Use one piece each time to make as tea with boiling water.
Functions: To clear heat, dispel wind, lower blood pressure.
Indications: Hypertension.
Source:《中草药制剂选编》

23.18 降压茶 II   Jiangya Cha II
Ingredients:
罗布麻叶 Luobuma Ye, Dogbane Leaf (Folium Apocyni Veneti) 6g
川芎 Chuanxiong, Sichuan Lovage Rhizome (Rhizoma Chuanxiong) 6g
钩藤 Gouteng, Gambir Plant (Ramulus Uncariae cum Uncis) 3g
Directions: Decoct and drink.
Functions: To lower blood pressure.
Indications: Hypertension.
Source:《健康文摘》 3:20, 1985

23.19 香蕉根茶 Xiangjiaogen Cha
Ingredients:
香蕉根 Xiangjiao Gen, Dwarf Banana Root (Radix Musae Nanae) 30-60g
Directions: Slice, decoct and drink.
Functions: To clear heat, remove toxins, induce diuresis and relieve swelling.
Indications: Hypertension.

Source: 《常见病验方研究参考资料》

23.20 桑树根茶 Sangshugen Cha

Ingredients:
桑根 Sang Gen, Mulberry Root (Radix Mori Albae) 9g

Directions: Pestle into coarse powder. Decoct and drink as tea.

Functions: To eliminate wind, clear obstructed meridians, lower blood pressure, improve vision.

Indications: Hypertension.

Source: 《野外工作人员卫生防病手册》

23.21 桑根白皮茶 Sanggenbaipi Cha

Ingredients:
桑白皮 Sang Baipi, White Mulberry Root-Bark (Cortex Mori) 30g

Directions: Decoct and drink as tea.

Functions: To lower blood pressure, induce diuresis.

Indications: Obesity, dizziness and vertigo due to hypertension with phlegm-damp, oliguria and edema.

Source: 《肘后备急方》

23.22 桑菊枸杞饮 Sang Ju Gouqi Yin

Ingredients:
桑叶 Sangye, Mulberry Leaf (Folium Mori) 9g
菊花 Juhua, Chrysanthemum Flower (Flos Chrysanthemi) 9g
枸杞子 Gouqi Zi, Barbary Wolfberry Fruit (Fructus Lycii) 9g
决明子 Jueming Zi, Cassia Seed (Semen Cassiae) 6g

Directions: Decoct and drink.

Functions: To control dizziness, improve vision.

Indications: Dizziness and blurred vision.

Source: 《中国药膳学》

23.23 夏枯草茶 Xiakucao Cha

Ingredients:
夏枯草 Xiakucao, Common Selfheal Fruit-Spike (Spica Prunellae) 30g

Directions: Pestle into coarse powder. Make as tea with boiling water.
Functions: To control liver fire, relieve *qi* stagnation.
Indications: Early stage of hypertension with headache and dizziness.
Source:《常见病验方研究参考资料》

23.24 夏枯草荷叶茶 Xiakucao Heye Cha

Ingredients:
夏枯草 Xiakucao, Common Selfheal Fruit-Spike (Spica Prunellae) 10g
荷叶 Heye, Lotus Leaf (Folium Nelumbinis) 12g

Directions: Decoct and drink.
Functions: To replenish yin of liver and kidney, pacify liver *yang*.
Indications: Windstroke with deviation of mouth, stiffness of tongue, hemiplegia and red tongue with yellow coating, wiry and rolling pulse.
Source:《百病饮食自疗》

23.25 侧柏叶茶 Cebaiye Cha

Ingredients:
侧柏叶 Cebaiye, Chinese Arborvitae Twig and Leaf (Cacumen Platycladi) 6g
白糖 Baitang, White Sugar, desired amount

Directions: Make as tea with boiling water.
Functions: To lower blood pressure.
Indications: Hypertension.
Source:《常见病验方研究参考资料》

23.26 梧桐茶 Wutong Cha

Ingredients:
鲜梧桐叶 Xian Wutong Ye, fresh Phoenix Tree Leaf (Folium Firmianae)

30g (collected before it blossoms)

Directions: Cut into thread-like pieces, rinse with boiling water once, then make as tea.

Functions: To dispel wind, dissolve damp, lower blood pressure.

Indications: Hypertension, arteriosclerosis.

Source:《常见病验方研究参考资料》

23.27 清热理气茶 Qingre Liqi Cha

Ingredients:

甘菊花 Ganjuhua, Chrysanthemum (Flos Chrysanthemi) 9g

霜桑叶 Shuangsangye, Mulberry Leaf (Folium Mori) 9g

炒谷芽 Chao Guya, Parched Rice Sprout (Fructus Oryzae Germinatus) 9g

橘红 Juhong, Red Tangerine Peel (Exocarpium Citri Rubrum) 4.5g

炒枳壳 Chao Zhiqiao, Parched Orange Fruit (Fructus Aurantii) 4.5g

鲜芦根 Xian Lugen, Fresh Reed Rhizome (Rhizoma Phragmitis) 10g

炒建曲 Chao Jianqu, Parched Medicated Leaven (Massa Fermentata Medicinalis) 6g

羚羊角 Lingyang Jiao, Pronghorn (Cornu Saigae Tataricae) 1.5g

Directions: Pestle, decoct and drink. Take one dose a day.

Functions: To clear heat, promote vision, regulate *qi* and harmonize middle *jiao*.

Indications: Early stage of hypertension with dizziness, blurred vision, red complexion, nausea, and vomiting.

Source:《慈禧光绪医方选议》

23.28 望江南茶 Wangjiangnan Cha

Ingredients:

望江南 Wangjiangnan, Coffee Senna Seed (Semen Cassiae Occidentalis)

Directions: Toast to brown and grind into powder. Use 3g each time and

add sugar to taste. Make as tea with boiling water. Take three doses a day.
Functions: To clear liver fire, promote vision, strengthen stomach and loosen bowels.
Indications: Hypertension with headache.
Source:《全国中草药汇编》

23.29 菊花钩藤饮 I Juhua Gouteng Yin I
Ingredients:
白菊花 Baijuhua, White Chrysanthemum Flower (Flos Chrysanthemi) 10g
钩藤 Gouteng, Gambir Plant (Ramulus Uncariae cum Uncis) 10g
Directions: Decoct and drink.
Functions: To replenish *qi* and blood, remove obstruction of meridians.
Indications: Sequela of windstroke manifested as deviation of mouth, salivation, slurred voice, hemiplegia, numbness of extremities, listlessness, pale tongue with blood spots, white or sticky tongue coating, thready hesitant or weak pulse caused by *qi* and blood deficiency and obstruction of meridians.
Source:《百病饮食自疗》

23.30 菊花钩藤饮 II Juhua Gouteng Yin II
Ingredients:
白菊花 Baijuhua, White Chrysanthemum Flower (Flos Chrysanthemi) 10g
霜桑叶 Shuangsangye, Mulberry Leaf (Folium Mori) 10g
钩藤 Gouteng, Gambir Plant (Ramulus Uncariae cum Uncis) 10g
Directions: Decoct and drink. Take two times a day.
Functions: To restore consciousness.
Indications: The tense syndrome of windstroke manifested as sudden loss of consciousness, trismus, clenched fists, stiffness of limbs, retention of urine and feces, coarse breathing, flushed face, red tongue with yellow coating, string-taut rolling and rapid pulse.

Source:《百病饮食自疗》

23.31 菊槐绿茶饮 Ju Huai Lucha Yin
Ingredients:
菊花 Juhua, Chrysanthemum Flower (Flos Chrysanthemi) 10g
槐花 Huai Hua, Pagodatree Flower (Flos Sophorae) 3g
绿茶 Lucha, Green Tea 3g
Directions: Make as tea with boiling water.
Functions: To clear heat, soothe liver.
Indications: Hypertension.
Source:《民间验方》

23.32 菊藤茶 Ju Teng Cha
Ingredients:
菊花 Juhua, Chrysanthemum Flower (Flos Chrysanthemi) 10g
夏枯草 Xiakucao, Common Selfheal Fruit-spike (Spica Prunellae) 10g
钩藤 Gouteng, Gambir Plant (Ramulus Uncariae cum Uncis) 10g
Directions: Pestle, make as tea with boiling water. Take one dose a day.
Functions: To clear heat, soothe the liver, lower blood pressure.
Indications: Dizziness of hypertension.
Source:《民间饮食疗法》

23.33 黄瓜藤茶 Huangguateng Cha
Ingredients:
黄瓜藤 Huanggua Teng, Cucumber Stem (Caulis Cucumeris sativi) 100g
Directions: Cut into small pieces, decoct and drink.
Functions: To clear heat, induce diuresis, soothe the liver, normalize the secretion and excretion of bile.
Indications: Hypertension.
Source:《宁夏科技普及》

23.34 钩藤茶 Gouteng Cha

Ingredients:
钩藤 Gouteng, Gambir Plant (Ramulus Uncariae cum Uncis)

Directions: Pestle. Use 30g as tea with boiling water twice a day.
Functions: To clear heat, soothe liver and stop liver wind.
Indications: Hypertension.
Source: 《常用中草药手册》

23.35 葛根槐花茶 Gegen Huaihua Cha

Ingredients:
葛根 Ge Gen, Kudzuvine Root (Radix Puerariae) 30g
槐花 Huai Hua, Pagodatree Flower (Flos Sophorae) 15g
茺蔚子 Chongweizi, Motherwort Fruit (Fructus Leonuri) 15g

Directions: Pestle, make as tea with boiling water.
Functions: To clear heat, cool blood, lower blood pressure.
Indications: Hypertension.
Source: 《湖北中医杂志》 1:1985

23.36 槐花茶 Huaihua Cha

Ingredients:
槐花 Huai Hua, Pagodatree Flower (Flos Sophorae) 6g

Directions: Make as tea with boiling water.
Functions: To clear liver fire, cool blood, stop bleeding.
Indications: Hypertension, encephalorrhagia.
Source: 《常见病验方研究参考资料》

23.37 银菊茶 Yin Ju Cha

Ingredients:
银花 Yinhua, Honeysuckle Flower (Flos Lonicerae) 20-30g
菊花 Juhua, Chrysanthemum Flower (Flos Chrysanthemi) 20-30g

桑叶 Sangye, Mulberry Leaf (Folium Mori) 15g
山楂 Shanzha, Hawthorn Fruit (Fructus Crataegi) 10-20g

Directions: Use the first three to make as tea with boiling water for headache. Use the first two and hawthorn fruit to make as tea with boiling water for arteriosclerosis and hyperlipemia.

Functions: To clear heat, pacify liver, lower blood pressure.

Indications: Headache and dizziness of hypertension, arteriosclerosis, hyperlipemia.

Source:《新中医杂志》2:1972

23.38 豨莶草茶 Xixiancao Cha

Ingredients:
豨莶草 Xixian Cao, Siegesbeckia Herb (Herba Siegesbeckiae) 15g
糖 Tang, Sugar, desired amount

Directions: Decoct and drink.

Functions: To dispel wind, dissolve damp, remove obstruction of meridians and, lower blood pressure.

Indications: Hypertension, dizziness and insomnia with dream-disturbed sleep.

Source:《常见病验方研究参考资料》

23.39 橘红茯苓饮 Juhong Fuling Yin

Ingredients:
橘红 Juhong, Red Tangerine Peel (Exocarpium Citri Rubrum) 15g
茯苓 Fuling, Indian Bread (Poria) 20g

Directions: Decoct and drink.

Functions: To dissolve phlegm, promote resuscitation.

Indications: Tense syndrome of windstroke due to accumulation of phlegm.

Source:《百病饮食自疗》

23.40 橘杏丝瓜饮 Ju Xing Sigua Yin

Ingredients:
干橘皮 Gan Jupi, Dried Tangerine Peel (Pericarpium Citri Reticulatae) 10g
杏仁 Xing Ren, Apricot Seed (Semen Armeniacae Amarum), 10 pieces (peeled and tip removed)
老丝瓜 Lao Sigua, Dried Towel Gourd (Luffae Cylindricae), 1 piece

Directions: Decoct over high heat and then simmer for 20 minutes. Cool, filter, and take the fluid.

Functions: To clear lung heat, dispel wind cold.

Indications: Common cold of wind-cold type.

Source:《民间验方》

23.41 猪毛菜茶 Zhumaocai Cha

Ingredients:
猪毛菜 Zhumaocai, Common Russianthistle Herb (Herba Salsolae Collinae) 15g

Directions: Decoct and drink.

Functions: To soothe liver, lower blood pressure.

Indications: Hypertension, headache due to the hyperactivity of liver *yang*.

Source:《实用中药学》

23.42 萝芙木根茶 Luofumugen Cha

Ingredients:
萝芙木根 Luofumu Gen, Devilpepper Root (Radix Rauwolfiae Verticillatae)

Directions: Cut into small pieces, dry in the sun. Use 50g each day, add white sugar to taste, decoct and drink.

Functions: To clear heat, activate blood, lower blood pressure.

Indications: Early stage hypertension, palpitations and headache.
Source:《常见病验方研究参考资料》

23.43 荠菜茶 Jicai Cha

Ingredients:
荠菜 Jicai, Shepherds Purse (Herba Capsellae)

Directions: Collect at the end of spring, wash, dry, cut into small pieces. Use 10-15g each time (15-30g a day) and make as tea with boiling water.
Functions: To clear heat, induce diuresis and lower blood pressure.
Indications: Dizziness and headache due to hyperactivity of liver *yang* in hypertension.
Source:《常见病验方研究参考资料》

23.44 罗布麻降压茶 Luobuma Jiangyacha

Ingredients:
鲜罗布麻叶 Xian Luobuma Ye, Fresh Dogbane Leaf (Folium Apocyni Veneti) 5g
白菊花 Baijuhua, White Chrysanthemum Flower (Flos Chrysanthemi) 5g
Directions: Make as tea with boiling water.
Functions: To clear heat, subdue liver fire and promote vision.
Indications: Hypertension, sunstroke, and dizziness in summer.
Source:《开卷有益》 4:35, 1988

23.45 罗布麻速溶饮 Luobuma Surongyin

Ingredients:
罗布麻叶 Luobuma Ye, Dogbane Leaf (Folium Apocyni Veneti) 500g
Directions: Decoct, collecting the decocted fluid every 20 minutes. Add water to decoct again. Decoct three times. Mix all decocted fluid and boil until very thick. Remove from heat, cool, add 500g of white sugar. Stir, dry, crush and store in a bottle. Use 10g each time and make as tea with

boiling water.
Functions: To calm mind, lower blood pressure.
Indications: Chronic bronchitis, hypertension, coronary heart disease, neurasthenia and insomnia.
Source:《新疆中草药手册》

23.46 罗布麻叶茶 Luobumaye Cha
Ingredients:
罗布麻叶 Luobuma Ye, Dogbane Leaf (Folium Apocyni Veneti)
Directions: Make as tea with boiling water. Take three or four times a day. Use for three or six days each time.
Functions: To lower blood pressure, induce diuresis, pacify liver, calm mind.
Indications: Dizziness and headache of hypertension.
Source:《中药大辞典》

23.47 蚕豆花茶 Candouhua Cha
Ingredients:
蚕豆花 Candou Hua, Broadbean Flower (Flos Viciae Fabae) 30g
Directions: Soak in boiled water. Drink as tea.
Functions: To astringe floating yang.
Indications: Hypertensive dizziness, morbid leukorrhagia. Only long-term use gives good result.
Source: 中医研究院《中医验方汇编》第一辑

24 头痛 For a Headache

24.01 巴豆茶 Badou Cha
Ingredients:
春茶 Chuncha, Tea Leaf (Folium Camelliae Sinensis)

167

巴豆 Badou, Croton Fruit (Fructus Crotonis), 40 pieces

Directions: Toast croton fruit until brown, grind into powder, decoct 3g of the powder each time together with tea leaves, and drink after a meal.

Functions: To remove cold phlegm, relieve water retention.

Indications: Headache.

Source:《医方大成》

24.02 杏菊饮 I   Xing Ju Yin I

Ingredients:
杏仁 Xing Ren, Apricot Seed (Semen Armeniacae Amarum) 6g (peeled, tip removed, ground)
菊花 Juhua, Chrysanthemum Flower (Flos Chrysanthemi) 6g

Directions: Decoct by bringing to the boil and simmer for three to five minutes. Drink.

Functions: To expel wind, clear heat.

Indications: Headache due to wind-heat, headache and dizziness caused by the liver fire.

Source:《民间验方》

24.03 杏菊饮 II   Xing Ju Yin II

Ingredients:
杏仁 Xing Ren, Apricot Seed (Semen Armeniacae Amarum) 6g (peeled, tip removed, ground)
菊花 Juhua, Chrysanthemum Flower (Flos Chrysanthemi) 6g

Directions: Decoct apricot seeds and use the boiling decoction to make chrysanthemum flower as tea.

Functions: To relieve cough and asthma, expel wind, clear heat, soothe the liver and improve vision.

Indications: Headache, dizziness, epigastric fullness, nausea, vomiting, white and sticky tongue coating, rolling or wiry rolling pulse caused by

phlegm.
Source:《百病饮食自疗》

24.04 辛夷花茶 Xinyihua Cha

Ingredients:
辛夷 Xinyi, Biond Magnolia Flower (Flos Magnoliae) 2g
苏叶 Suye, Perilla Leaf (Folium Perillae) 6g

Directions: Pestle and wrap in a gauze-bag. Make as tea with boiling water.

Functions: To dispel wind-cold, remove nasal obstruction.

Indications: Nasal diseases and related headache.

Source:《全国中草药汇编》

24.05 青葙子速溶饮 Qingxiangzi Surongyin

Ingredients:
青葙子 Qingxiang Zi, Feather Cockscomb Seed (Semen Celosiae) 300g

Directions: Soak in cool water. Decoct, filter, keep the decoction for use. Add water to decoct again. Repeat three times. Mix the decoctions and continue to boil with low heat until it becomes very thick. Remove from heat, add 400g white sugar to make a thick paste. Dry, crush, and store in a bottle. Use 10g each time and make as tea with boiling water. Take three doses a day.

Functions: To pacify liver *yang*.

Indications: Unilateral headache, hypertension, red swollen and painful eyes.

Source:《福建中草药》

24.06 香附川芎茶 Xiangfu Chuanxiong Cha

Ingredients:
香附子 Xiangfuzi, Nutgrass Galingale Rhizome (Rhizoma Cyperi) 3g

川芎 Chuanxiong, Szechwan Lovage Rhizome (Rhizoma Chuanxiong) 3g
茶叶 Chaye, Tea Leaf (Folium Camelliae Sinensis) 3g

Directions: Pestle into coarse powder. Make as tea with boiling water.

Functions: To soothe liver, regulate *qi*, relieve pain.

Indications: Headache due to liver *qi* stagnation.

Source:《中国药膳学》

24.07 菊花茶 Juhua Cha

Ingredients:
菊花 Juhua, Chrysanthemum Flower (Flos Chrysanthemi) 15g
白糖 Baitang, White sugar   **or**   蜂蜜 Fengmi, Honey, desired amount

Directions: Make as tea with boiling water.

Functions: To clear heat, remove toxins, lower blood pressure, ease mind, promote vision, soothe liver to expel its wind.

Indications: Headache, redness of eyes, and dry throat from invasion of exogenous pathogenic wind-heat. Headache and dizziness from liver wind.

Source:《祝您健康》 6:1988

24.08 菊花龙井茶 Juhua Longjing Cha

Ingredients:
菊花 Juhua, Chrysanthemum Flower (Flos Chrysanthemi) 10g
龙井茶 Longjingcha, Dragon Well tea 3g

Directions: Infuse tea with boiling water.

Functions: To dispel wind-heat, remove fire from liver, promote vision.

Indications: Early stage of hypertension, headache caused by liver fire flaring up.

Source:《辽宁中医》 2:1985

24.09 棕榈槐花茶 Zonglu Huaihua Cha

Ingredients:
鲜棕榈叶 Xian Zongluye, Fresh Fortune Windmill Palm Leaf (Folium Trachycarpi) 30g
槐花 Huai Hua, Pagodatree Flower (Flos Sophorae) 10g

Directions: Pestle, make as tea with boiling water.
Functions: To remove heat from liver, cool blood.
Indications: Headache of hypertension.
Source:《实用中药学》

24.10 葛根茶 Gegen Cha

Ingredients:
葛根 Ge Gen, Kudzuvine Root (Radix Puerariae) 30g

Directions: Slice, decoct and drink.
Functions: To expel pathogenic factors to induce mild perspiration, relieve irritability.
Indications: Headache of hypertension.
Source:《长寿之道》

24.11 橘皮茶 II Jupi Cha II

Ingredients:
陈皮 Chenpi, Dried Tangerine Peel (Pericarpium Citri Reticulatae) 6g
茶叶 Chaye, Tea Leaf (Folium Camelliae Sinensis), a little

Directions: Decoct the peel. Use the boiling fluid, infuse the tea, and then drink.
Functions: To dissolve phlegm.
Indications: Headache due to phlegm, with dizziness, fullness in the chest and epigastrium, nausea, vomiting, white sticky tongue coating, rolling or wiry rolling pulse.
Source:《百病饮食自疗》

25 冠心病 For Coronary Atherosclerotic Heart Disease

25.01 丹参茶 Danshen Cha

Ingredients:

丹参 Danshen, Danshen Root (Radix Salviae Miltiorrhizae) 6g

Directions: Decoct and drink the decoction once or twice a day.

Functions: To activate blood circulation, remove stasis, ease the mind and relieve irritability.

Indications: Irritability, insomnia and coronary heart disease.

Source:《中国药膳学》

25.02 玉竹速溶饮 Yuzhu Surongyin

Ingredients:

玉竹 Yuzhu, Fragrant Solomonseal Rhizome (Rhizoma Polygonati Odorati) 250g

白糖 Baitang, White Sugar 500g

Directions: Soak. Decoct for one hour. Pour out the decoction every 20 minutes, add water to decoct again. Remove the herb and concentrate the decoction over low heat. When it becomes very thick, remove from heat and cool. Add white sugar. Dry, crush, and store in a bottle. Use 10g each time infusing with warm boiled water. Take three times a day.

Functions: To replenish *yin*, moisten dryness, relieve irritability, tonify the heart.

Indications: Rheumatic heart disease, cor pulmonale, coronary heart disease and cardiac failure.

Source:《中国药物志》

25.03 柿叶降脂茶 Shiye Jiangzhi Cha

Ingredients:

嫩柿叶 Nen Shi Ye, Young Leaves of Male Persimmon (Folium Kaki), collected before the Summer Solstice.

Directions: Soak the leaves in boiling water for two minutes, remove, cut into thread-like pieces, dry in the sun. Make as tea with boiling water at 90 ℃.

Functions: Promote body resistance, resist cancers, prevent and treat hypertension and hyperlipemia, quench thirst, moisten throat, refresh the mind, and prolong life because of its rich Vitamin C. Long-term use is suggested for prolonging life.

Source:《开卷有益》4:34, 1988

25.04 降脂茶 Jiangzhi Cha

Ingredients:
荷叶 Heye, Lotus Leaf (Folium Nelumbinis) 10g
山楂 Shanzha, Hawthorn Fruit (Fructus Crataegi) 15g
五味子 Wuweizi, Chinese Magnoliavine Fruit (Fructus Schisandrae) 5g
冰糖 Bingtang, Crystal Sugar, desired amount

Directions: Make as tea with boiling water.
Functions: To lower blood lipid.
Indications: Coronary heart disease.
Source:《健康文摘》3:20, 1985

25.05 菊楂决明饮 Ju Zha Jueming Yin

Ingredients:
菊花 Juhua, Chrysanthemum Flower (Flos Chrysanthemi) 3g
山楂 Shanzha, Hawthorn Fruit (Fructus Crataegi) 15g
草决明 Cao Jueming, Cassia Seed (Semen Cassiae) 15g

Directions: Make as tea with boiling water.
Functions: To lower blood pressure.
Indications: Hypertension with coronary heart disease.
Source:《民间验方》

25.06 银杏叶茶 Yinxingye Cha

Ingredients:

银杏叶 Yingxing Ye, Ginkgo Leaf (Folium Ginkgo) 5g

Directions: Make as tea with boiling water.

Functions: To reinforce heart, astringe lung, dissolve damp, stop diarrhea.

Indications: Arteriosclerosis, angina pectoris, hyperlipemia, dysentery, enteritis.

Source: 《健康与食物》

26 糖尿病 For Diabetes Mellitus

26.01 山药茶 Shanyao Cha

Ingredients:

生山药 Sheng Shanyao, Common Yam Rhizome (Rhizoma Dioscoreae) 120g

Directions: Peel, slice, decoct, and drink the decoction.

Functions: To strengthen the spleen, reinforce *yang*, quench thirst.

Indications: Diabetes.

Source: 《山西省中医验方秘方汇集》第一辑

26.02 止消渴速溶饮 Zhixiaoke Surongyin

Ingredients:

鲜冬瓜皮 Xian Dongguapi, Fresh Chinese Waxgourd Peel (Exocarpium Benincasae) 1,000g (peeled)

西瓜皮 Xigua Pi, Exocarp of Watermelon (Exocarpium Citrulli) 1,00g (peeled)

天花粉 Tianhuafen, Snakegourd Root (Radix Trichosanthis) 250g (pestled and soaked)

Directions: Decoct for one hour. Remove the herbs and continue

decocting until the fluid becomes very thick. Remove from heat, cool, add 500g white sugar. Dry, crush, and store in a bottle. Use 10g each time. Make as tea with boiling water.
Functions: To induce diuresis, relieve edema.
Indications: Diabetes.
Source:《民间验方》

26.03 田螺茶 Tianluo Cha

Ingredients:
田螺 Tianluo, River-snail (Cipangopaludinae)
Directions: Decoct, drink.
Functions: To clear heat, quench thirst.
Indications: Diabetes. Also eaten as soup in regular diet.
Source:《中医大辞典·中药分册》

26.04 冬瓜瓤汤 Dongguarang Tang

Ingredients:
冬瓜瓤 Donggua Rang, Chinese Waxgourd Pulp (Pulpa Benincasae) (seeds removed)
Directions: Dry the pulp. Use 30g of the dry pulp each time, decoct, drink.
Functions: To induce diuresis, relieve edema.
Indications: Thirst with fever, irritability and edema with oliguria.
Source:《太平圣惠方》

26.05 生地石膏茶 Shengdi Shigao Cha

Ingredients:
生地黄 Sheng Dihuang, Dried Rehmannia Root (Radix Rehmanniae) 30g.
石膏 Shigao, Gypsum (Gypsum Fibrosum) 60g

Directions: Decoct, drink.
Functions: To clear heat, reinforce *yin* and quench thirst.
Indications: Diabetes.
Source:《千家妙方》

26.06 加减三花饮 Jiajian, Sanhua Yin

Ingredients:
丝瓜花 Sigua Hua, Towel Gourd Flower (Flos Luffae), 20 pieces
扁豆花 Biandou Hua, Hyacinth Bean Flower (Flos Dolichoris), 20 pieces
南瓜花 Nangua Hua, Pumpkin Flower (Flos Cucurbitae), 5 pieces
莲子心 Lianzi Xin, Lotus Plumule (Plumula Nelumbinis) 10g
乌梅 Wumei, Smoked Plum (Fructus Mume) 10g
鲜竹叶卷心 Xian Zhuyejuanxin, Fresh Bamboo Leaf (Folium Phyllostachys Nigra), 30 pieces
鲜荷梗 Xian Hegeng, Fresh Lotus Petiole (Petiolus Nelumbinis) 20g

Directions: Decoct for 20 minutes, filter, and add white sugar to taste before drinking.
Functions: To clear the heart fire, replenish the kidney water.
Indications: Irritability and thirst with a dark red tongue and a yellow dry coating caused by the summer heat damaging the heart and kidney.
Source:《百病饮食自疗》

26.07 消渴茶 Xiaoke Cha

Ingredients:
玉竹 Yuzhu, Fragrant Solomonseal Rhizome (Rhizoma Polygonati Odorati) 15g
麦冬 Maidong, Dwarf Lilyturf Tuber (Radix Ophiopogonis) 15g
黄芪 Huangqi, Milkvetch Root (Radix Astragali) 100g
通草 Tongcao, Ricepaper Plant Pith (Medulla Tetrapanacis) 100g

茯苓　Fuling, Indian Bread (Poria) 50g
干姜　Gan Jiang, Dried Ginger (Rhizoma Zingiberis) 50g
葛根　Ge Gen, Kudzuvine Root (Radix Puerariae) 50g
桑白皮　Sang Baipi, White Mulberry Root-Bark (Cortex Mori) 50g
牛蒡根　Niubang Gen, Great Burdock Root (Radix Arctii) 150g
地黄　Dihuang, Rehmannia Root (Radix Rehmanniae) 30g
枸杞根　Gouqi Gen, Barbary Wolfberry Root (Radix Lycii) 30g
银花藤　Yinhuateng, Honeysuckle Stem (Caulis Lonicerae) 30g
薏苡仁　Yiyi Ren, Coix Seed (Semen Coicis) 30g
菝葜　Baqia, Chinaroot Greenbrier (Rhizoma Smilacis Chinensis) 24g
樗椿根白皮　Chuchun Genbaipi, Ailanthus Bark (Cortex Ailanthi)

Directions: Pestle the first 14 materials into a coarse powder. Cut the last one into thread-like pieces and decoct. Mix the powder into the decoction and divide into portions each about 13g. Dry and store in a bottle. Use one or two pieces everyday. Add a little salt, and make as tea with boiling water.

Functions: To clear heat, prevent dehydration, reinforce *qi*, replenish *yin*.

Indications: Diabetes manifested as eating, drinking and urinating a lot, weight loss, pale complexion, shortness of breath, tiredness, dizziness, tinnitus, weakness and pain in the lumbus and knees.

Source:《外台秘要》

26.08 皋芦叶茶　Gaoluye Cha

Ingredients:
皋芦叶　Gaolu Ye, Leaf of Bigleaf Tea (Folium Camelliae Macrophyllae), a handful

Directions: Decoct and drink.
Functions: To clear heat, quench thirst.
Indications: Diabetes, headache and irritability.
Source:《普济方》

26.09 益胃茶 II Yiwei Cha II

Ingredients:
北沙参 Beishashen, Coastal Glehnia Root (Radix Glehniae) 15g
麦冬 Maidong, Dwarf Lilyturf Tuber (Radix Ophiopogonis) 15g
生地黄 Sheng Dihuang, Dried Rehmannia Root (Radix Rehmanniae) 15g
玉竹 Yuzhu, Fragrant Solomonseal Rhizome (Rhizoma Polygonati Odorati) 5g
冰糖 Bingtang, Crystal Sugar, desired amount

Directions: Pestle into coarse powder, decoct and drink.
Functions: To reinforce the stomach, produce body fluid.
Indications: Irritability and thirst of a febrile disease, diabetes with polydipsia.
Source:《中国药膳学》

26.10 淮山药茶 Huaishanyao Cha

Ingredients:
淮山药 Huaishanyao, Common Yam Rhizome (Rhizoma Dioscoreae) 30-50g

Directions: Decoct and drink.
Functions: To reinforce spleen and stomach, strengthen lung and kidney.
Indications: Diabetes, frequency and polyuria in elderly.
Source:《长寿之道》

26.11 麦冬乌梅饮 Maidong Wumei Yin

Ingredients:
麦冬 Maidong, Dwarf Lilyturf Tuber (Radix Ophiopogonis) 20g
炒乌梅 Chao Wumei, Parched Smoked Plum (Fructus Mume) 6g

Directions: Decoct and add crystal sugar to taste before drinking the decoction. Take it two or three times a day.
Functions: To produce body fluid, quench thirst.

Indications: Diabetes insipidus.
Source:《中国药膳学》

26.12 菝葜叶茶 Baqiaye Cha

Ingredients:
菝葜叶 Baqia Ye, Chinaroot Greenbrier Leaf (Folium Smilacis Chinensis) 30g

Directions: Cut into thread-like pieces. Decoct and drink.
Functions: To dispel wind, dissolve damp.
Indications: Diabetes.
Source:《中医大辞典·中药分册》

26.13 蚕茧茶 Canjian Cha

Ingredients:
蚕茧 Can Jian, Silkworm Cocoon (Coccum Bombycis) 50g (pupae removed)

Directions: Decoct and drink.
Functions: To cool blood, quench thirst.
Indications: Polyuria and polydipsia diabetes.
Source:《中医护理》

26.14 糯米草茶 Nuomicao Cha

Ingredients:
糯米草 Nuomicao, Hirsute Gonostegia Herb (Herba Gonostegiae Hirtae)

Directions: Cut off both ends. Bake until outer part becomes charred and inner part remains unchanged. Use 2.4g each day and make as tea with boiling water.
Functions: To clear heat, dissolve damp.
Indications: Thirst caused by stomach heat.
Source:《中医验方汇编》第一辑

26.15 糯稻杆茶 Nuodaogan Cha

Ingredients:
糯稻秆 Nuodao Gan, Glutinous Rice Culm (Caulis Oryzae Glutinosae) 10g

Directions: Cut into small pieces, toast to brown, wrap with cloth and make as tea with boiling water.

Functions: To astringe *yin*, quench thirst.

Indications: Thirst of diabetes.

Source:《中医验方汇编》第一辑

27 肝炎、黄疸 For Hepatitis

27.01 石花茶 Shihua Cha

Ingredients:
石花 Shihua, Parmelia Saxatilis (Parmelia Saxatilis) 30g

Directions: Make as tea with boiling water.

Functions: To clear heat, dissolve damp.

Indications: Jaundice.

Source:《中医大辞典·中药分册》

27.02 金鸡饮 Jin Ji Yin

Ingredients:
金钱草 Jinqiancao, Christina Loosestrife (Herba Lysimachiae) 30g

鸡内金 Jineijin, Chicken's Gizzard-skin (Endothelium Corneum Gigeriae Galli) 10g

红花 Honghua, Safflower (Flos Carthami) 3g

Directions: Decoct and drink two or three times a day.

Functions: To clear heat, induce diuresis, dispel wind and relieve edema.

Indications: Chronic jaundice with ashen yellow skin and sclera, accompanied by poor appetite, abdominal distention, purple tongue with blood spots, thready and hesitant pulse.

Source:《百病饮食自疗》

27.03 消黄茶 Xiaohuang Cha

Ingredients:

车前草 Cheqian Cao, Plantain Herb (Herba Plantaginis) 15g

半边莲 Banbianlian, Chinese Lobelia Herb (Herba Lobeliae Chinensis) 15g

茵陈 Yinchen, Virgate Wormwood Herb (Herba Artemisiae Scopariae) 15g

Directions: Decoct and add white sugar to taste before drinking.

Functions: To clear heat, induce diuresis and relieve jaundice.

Indications: Icteric hepatitis.

Source: 《常见病验方研究参考资料》

27.04 柴甘茅根茶 Chai Gan Maogen Cha

Ingredients:

柴胡 Chaihu, Chinese Thorowax Root (Radix Bupleuri) 50g

甘草 Gancao, Liquorice Root (Radix Glycyrrhizae) 10g

白茅根 Baimao Gen, Imperata Rhizome (Rhizoma Imperatae) 50g

Directions: Pestle into coarse powder, decoct and drink.

Functions: To soothe liver, clear heat, induce diuresis.

Indications: Jaundice accompanied by an exterior syndrome.

Source: 《本草纲目》

27.05 茵陈茶 Yinchen Cha

Ingredients:

茵陈 Yinchen, Virgate Wormwood Herb (Herba Artemisiae Scopariae) 60g

Directions: Decoct and drink.

Functions: To clear heat, dissolve damp, relieve jaundice and lower blood pressure.

Indications: Jaundice, hypertension, hyperlipemia.

Source: 《中医杂志》 1:1980

27.06 茵陈香芦茶 Yinchen Xiang Lu Cha

Ingredients:
茵陈 Yinchen, Virgate Wormwood Herb (Herba Artemisiae Scopariae) 30g
香薷 Xiangru, Mosla Herb (Herba Moslae) 30g
芦根 Lugen, Reed Rhizome (Rhizoma Phragmitis) 45g

Directions: Pestle into coarse powder, decoct and drink.
Functions: To clear heat, relieve jaundice.
Indications: Icteric hepatitis.
Source: 《常见病验方研究参考资料》

27.07 茵陈陈皮茶 Yinchen Chenpi Cha

Ingredients:
茵陈 Yinchen, Virgate Wormwood Herb (Herba Artemisiae Scopariae) 10g
陈皮 Chenpi, Dried Tangerine Peel (Pericarpium Citri Reticulatae) 10g

Directions: Decoct and drink.
Functions: To clear heat, dissolve damp, relieve jaundice.
Indications: Jaundice caused by damp-heat with bright yellow skin, fever, thirst, scant and dark yellow urine, pain in the right hypochondrium, nausea, vomiting, epigastric pain and distention, constipation, red tongue with a yellow and sticky coating, wiry and rapid pulse.
Source: 《百病饮食自疗》

27.08 茵陈红糖饮 Yinchen Hongtang Yin

Ingredients:
茵陈 Yinchen, Virgate Wormwood Herb (Herba Artemisiae Scopariae) 15g
红糖 Hongtang, Brown Sugar 30g

Directions: Decoct the first, add the second before drinking.
Functions and **Indications:** Same as No. 27.07.
Source: 《百病饮食自疗》

27.09 茵陈银花饮 Yinchen Yinhua Yin

Ingredients:
茵陈 Yinchen, Virgate Wormwood Herb (Herba Artemisiae Scopariae) 15g
银花 Yinhua, Honeysuckle Flower (Flos Lonicerae) 10g

Directions: Decoct and drink.
Functions and **Indications:** Same as No. 27.07.
Source:《百病饮食自疗》

27.10 退黄饮 Tuihuang Yin

Ingredients:
早稻草 Zaodaocao, Rice Straw (Herba Oryzae Sativae) 60g
薏苡根 Yiyi Gen, Coix Root (Radix Coicis) 30g

Directions: Decoct and drink.
Functions: To clear heat, dissolve damp.
Indications: Jaundice.
Source:《常见病验方研究参考资料》

27.11 马鞭草茶 Mabiancao Cha

Ingredients:
马鞭草 Mabiancao, European Verbena Herb (Herba Verbenae) 30g

Directions: Pestle into coarse powder, wrap in a cloth-bag, make as tea with boiling water. Add white sugar to taste before drinking.
Functions: To clear heat, remove toxins, activate blood circulation, remove blood stasis, induce diuresis and relieve swelling.
Indications: Icteric hepatitis.
Source:《常见病验方研究参考资料》

27.12 清肝利黄茶 Qinggan Lihuang Cha

Ingredients:
排钱树根 Paiqianshugen, Beatiful Phyllodium Root (Radix Phyllodii

Pulchelli) 30g
茵陈 Yinchen, Virgate Wormwood Herb (Herba Artemisiae Scopariae) 10g
积雪草 Jixuecao, Asiatic Pennywort Herb (Herba Centellae) 10g
车前草 Cheqian Cao, Plantain Herb (Herba Plantaginis) 10g
甘草 Gancao, Liquorice Root (Radix Glycyrrhizae) 10g

Directions: Pestle, decoct and drink.
Functions: To clear heat, dissolve damp, relieve jaundice.
Indications: Icteric hepatitis.
Source:《全国中草药汇编》

27.13 荸荠茶 Biqi Cha

Ingredients:
鲜荸荠 Xian Biqi, Fresh Waternut Corm (Cormus Eleocharis Dulcis) 250g
Directions: Pestle, decoct and drink.
Functions: To clear heat, dissolve damp, remove retention.
Indications: Jaundice due to damp-heat.
Source:《中国药膳学》

27.14 硝黄茶 Xiao Huang Cha

Ingredients:
大黄 Dahuang, Rhubarb (Radix et Rhizoma Rhei) 10g
元明粉 Yuanmingfen, Exsiccated Sodium Sulfate (Natrii Sulfas Exsiccatus) 6g
白糖 Baitang, White Sugar, desired amount

Directions: Pestle the first ingredient into coarse powder. Make as tea with boiling water, filter, and drink the tea.
Functions: To clear heat, dissolve damp, regulate *qi* of *fu*-organs.
Indications: Jaundice.
Source:《江苏中医杂志》4:1981

27.15 雄花茶 Xionghua Cha

Ingredients:
雄花 Xionghua, Largeflowered Lychnis (Herba Lychnis) 60g
Directions: Decoct and drink.
Functions: Normalize the secretion and excretion of bile to relieve jaundice.
Indications: Icteric hepatitis, cholecystitis.
Source: 河北《中医验方汇选》内科第二集

27.16 无花果叶茶 Wuhuaguoye Cha

Ingredients:
无花果叶 Wuhuaguo Ye, Fig Leaf (Folium Fici) 10g
白糖 Baitang, White Sugar, desired amount
Directions: Make as tea with boiling water.
Functions: To clear heat, treat inflammation.
Indications: Jaundice.
Source:《常见病验方研究参考资料》

27.17 菟丝草茶 Tusicao Cha

Ingredients:
菟丝草 Tusicao, Dodder Herb (Herba Cuscutae) 20-30g
白糖 Baitang, White Sugar, desired amount
Directions: Make as tea with boiling water.
Functions: To clear heat, cool blood, induce diuresis, remove toxins.
Indications: Icteric hepatitis.
Source:《民间验方》

27.18 滑石红糖茶 Huashi Hongtang Cha

Ingredients:
滑石 Huashi, Talc (Talcum) 12g

Directions: Wrap in a cloth-bag, decoct, filter. Add brown sugar to taste and boil again for a little while. Drink.

Functions: To clear heat, normalize the secretion and excretion of bile.

Indications: Jaundice with bright yellow skin and eyes accompanied by fever, thirst, dark yellow and scant urine, right hypochondrium pain, nausea, vomiting, distention in epigastrium, constipation, red tongue with yellow sticky coating, string-taut and rapid pulse.

Source:《百病饮食自疗》

27.19 榕树叶茶 Rongshuye Cha

Ingredients:

榕树叶 Rongshu Ye, Leaf of Smallfruit Fig (Folium Aerio Fici Microcarpae) 10g

白糖 Baitang, White Sugar, desired amount

Directions: Decoct and drink.

Functions: To clear heat, promote detoxification, activate blood and remove stasis.

Indications: Jaundice.

Source:《常见病验方研究参考资料》

27.20 螃蟹饮 Pangxie Yin

Ingredients:

鲜螃蟹 Xian Pangxie, living Crab (Eriocheiris Sinensis), 2 crabs

Directions: Put into boiling water, reduce heat and simmer for 40-50 minutes. Take the fluid.

Functions: To clear heat, promote detoxification.

Indications: Pain in chest and stomach, irritability, poor appetite, dermatitis rhus, jaundice.

Source:《民间验方》

28 胃炎 For Gastritis

28.01 石斛茶 Shihu Cha

Ingredients:
鲜石斛 Xian Shihu, Fresh Dendrobium (Herba Dendrobii)

Directions: Make as tea with boiling water.
Functions: To clear heat, produce body fluid and nourish the stomach *yin*.
Indications: Burning epigastric pain, dry throat.
Source:《常见病验方研究参考资料》

28.02 加减人参乌梅汤 Jiajian Renshen Wumei Tang

Ingredients:
乌梅 Wumei, Smoked Plum (Fructus Mume) 15g
白糖参 Baitang Shen, Scaled, Thick-Sugar-Juice Soaked, and Dried Ginseng (Radix Ginseng) 10g
淮山药 Huaishanyao, Common Yam Rhizome (Rhizoma Dioscoreae) 30g
冰糖 Bingtang, Crystal Sugar, desired amount

Directions: Decoct and drink.
Functions: To nourish *yin*, reinforce the stomach.
Indications: Epigastric pain of deficiency type, namely, a dull pain in the stomach with a dry throat, constipation, red tongue with little coating, thready and wiry pulse.
Source:《百病饮食自疗》

28.03 竹茹芦根茶 Zhuru Lugen Cha

Ingredients:
竹茹 Zhuru, Bamboo Shavings (Caulis Bambusae in Taeniam) 30g
芦根 Lugen, Reed Rhizome (Rhizoma Phragmitis) 30g
生姜 Sheng Jiang, Fresh Ginger (Rhizoma Zingiberis Recens) 10g

Directions: Decoct and drink.

Functions: To clear heat, redirect *qi* downward.
Indications: Hiccups, vomiting.
Source:《备急千金要方》

28.04 羊乳饮 Yangru Yin

Ingredients:
羊奶 Yangnai, Sheep Milk, one cup
竹沥 Zhuli, Bamboo Juice (Succus Bambosae), two spoonfuls
蜂蜜 Fengmi, Honey, two spoonfuls
韭菜汁 Jiucai Zhi, Tuber Onion Juice (Succus Allii Tuberosi), one spoonful
Directions: Boil the first one, add the rest and drink when it is warm.
Functions: To harmonize the stomach by reinforcing its *yin*.
Indications: Vomiting, poor appetite, red tongue, thready and rapid pulse due to stomach *yin* deficiency.
Source:《百病饮食自疗》

28.05 枇杷饮 Pipa Yin

Ingredients:
枇杷叶 Pipa Ye, Loquat Leaf (Folium Eriobotryae) 10g
芦根 Lugen, Reed Rhizome (Rhizoma Phragmitis) 10g
Directions: Decoct over low heat for 20-30 minutes.
Functions: To clear heat, stop vomiting.
Indications: Vomiting caused by heat in the stomach and the perversion of the stomach *qi*.
Source:《民间验方》

28.06 柚子鸡蛋饮 Youzi Jidan Yin

Ingredients:
柚子 Youzi, Pummelo (Fructus Citri Grandis), one piece (cut into 2)
白糖 Baitang, White Sugar 15g

鸡蛋 Jidan, Egg, one piece

Directions: Decoct pummelo, make the egg as tea with the decoction. Add white sugar before drinking.
Functions: To regulate stomach *qi*.
Indications: Stomach *qi* stagnation.
Source:《中医杂志》2:1966

28.07 香橼茶 Xiangyuan Cha

Ingredients:
陈香橼 Chen Xiangyuan, Dried Citron Fruit (Fructus Citri), one fruit
Directions: Decoct and drink.
Functions: To regulate *qi*, relieve pain.
Indications: Gastric pain due to *qi* stagnation.
Source:《常见病验方研究参考资料》

28.08 扁豆益胃饮 Biandou Yiwei Yin

Ingredients:
炒扁豆 Chao Biandou, Parched Hyacinth Bean (Semen Dolichoris)
党参 Dangshen, Pilose Asiabell Root (Radix Codonopsis Pilosulae)
玉竹 Yuzhu, Fragrant Solomonseal Rhizome (Rhizoma Polygonati Odorati)
山楂 Shanzha, Hawthorn Fruit (Fructus Crataegi)
乌梅 Wumei, Smoked Plum (Fructus Mume)
All in equal amounts.
Directions: Decoct and add white sugar to taste before drinking.
Functions: To strengthen spleen and stomach, produce body fluid.
Indications: Hypochlorhydria.
Source:《中国药膳学》

28.09 高粱叶茶 Gaoliangye Cha

Ingredients:
高粱叶 Gaoliang Ye, Sorghum Leaf (Folium Sorghi Vulgaris) 1,500g-2,500g

Directions: Decoct and drink.
Functions: To harmonize stomach, relieve vomiting and pain.
Indications: Gastric pain, vomiting.
Source: 《常见病验方研究参考资料》

28.10 健胃茶 III   Jianwei Cha III

Ingredients:
徐长卿 Xuchangqing, Paniculate Swallowwort Root (Radix Cynanchi Paniculati) 4g
麦冬 Maidong, Dwarf Lilyturf Tuber (Radix Ophiopogonis) 3g
橘叶 Juye, Tangerine Leaf (Folium Citri Reticulatae) 3g
白芍 Baishao, White Peony Root (Radix Paeoniae Alba) 3g
生甘草 Sheng Gancao, Liquorice Root (Radix Glycyrrhizae) 2g
玫瑰花 Meigui Hua, Rose (Flos Roasae Rugosae) 1.5g
绿茶 Lucha, Green Tea 1.5g

Directions: Pestle into coarse powder. Make as tea with boiling water. Take one dose every day for three months.
Functions: To replenish *yin*, nourish stomach, soothe liver and activate blood circulation.
Indications: Superficial gastritis of *xu*-heat type with burning pain in the epigastric region.
Source: 《新中医》 9:1981

28.11 健胃茶 IV   Jianwei Cha IV

Ingredients:
徐长卿 Xuchangqing, Paniculate Swallowwort Root (Radix Cynanchi Paniculati) 3g
麦冬 Maidong, Dwarf Lilyturf Tuber (Radix Ophiopogonis) 3g
丹参 Danshen, Danshen Root (Radix Salviae Miltiorrhizae) 3g
黄芪 Huangqi, Milkvetch Root (Radix Astragali) 4.5g

乌梅 Wumei, Smoked Plum (Fructus Mume) 1.5g
生甘草 Sheng Gancao, Liquorice Root (Radix Glycyrrhizae) 1.5g
绿茶 Lucha, Green Tea 1.5g

Directions: Pestle into coarse powder, make as tea with boiling water. Take one dose every day for three months.

Functions: To reinforce *qi*, strengthen spleen, replenish *yin* and nourish stomach.

Indications: Atrophic gastritis of *xu*-heat type.

Source:《新中医》9:1981

28.12 黄连食醋白糖山楂饮 Huanglian Shicu Baitang Shanzha Yin

Ingredients:

黄连 Huanglian, Coptis Root (Rhizoma Coptidis) 500g
食醋 Shicu, Vinegar 500 ml
白糖 Baitang, White Sugar 500g
山楂 Shanzha, Hawthorn Fruit (Fructus Crataegi) 1,000g

Directions: Soak in 4,000 ml boiled water for seven days (Don't use plastic utensil!). Take three times a day, 50ml each time, after meals.

Functions: To strengthen spleen and stomach.

Indications: Atrophic gastritis.

Source:《中医杂志》6:28, 1986

28.13 醋浸生姜饮 Cuqin Shengjiang Yin

Ingredients:

生姜 Sheng Jiang, Fresh Ginger (Rhizoma Zingiberis Recens)

Directions: Slice, soak in vinegar for 24 hours. Use three slices each time, add brown sugar, and make as tea with boiling water.

Functions: To promote appetite, stop vomiting, relieve pain.

Indications: Poor appetite, vomiting, gastric pain.

Source:《食医心镜》

28.14 绿豆饮 Ludou Yin

Ingredients:
绿豆 Ludou, Mung Bean (Semen Phaseoli Radiati) 30-60g

Directions: Decoct and drink.

Functions: To clear stomach heat.

Indications: Vomiting, fever, irritability, thirst, red tongue with yellow coating, forceful and rapid pulse due to accumulation of heat in stomach.

Source:《普济方》

29 消化道溃疡 For Digestive Tract Peptic

29.01 白糖茶 Baitang Cha

Ingredients:
茶叶 Chaye, Tea Leaf (Folium Camelliae Sinensis) 120-300g
白糖 Baitang, White sugar 120-300g

Directions: Decoct, settle, remove the sediment. Store the decoction in a bottle. After 6-12 days, it is ready to take if the color has changed to that of old red wine. Use one spoonful each time, heat, take while warm, twice a day.

Functions: To promote ulcer healing.

Indications: Peptic ulcer.

Source: 江苏《中医秘方汇编》第一集

29.02 胃溃疡茶 Weikuiyang Cha

Ingredients:
枸杞子 Gouqi Zi, Barbary Wolfberry Fruit (Fructus Lycii) 312g
海螵蛸 Haipiaoxiao, Cuttlefish Bone (Os Sepiellae seu Sepiae) 156g
延胡索 Yanhusuo, Yanhusuo (Rhizoma Corydalis) 62g
紫珠草 Zizhucao, Taiwan Beautyberry Herb (Herba Callicarpae Pedunculatae) 62g
甘草 Gancao, Liquorice Root (Radix Glycyrrhizae) 62g

乌药 Wuyao, Combined Spicebush Root (Radix Linderae) 92g
陈皮 Chenpi, Dried Tangerine Peel (Pericarpium Citri Reticulatae) 77g
白芍 Baishao, White Peony Root (Radix Paeoniae Alba) 30g

Directions: Grind dried tangerine peel into powder. Decoct the first two for one hour, add the rest and continue to decoct for 1.5 hours. Filter and add water to decoct again for another 1.5 hours. Mix the decoctions to concentrate to thick paste. Put the powder into the paste to make granules, dry, sift, and store in 20 plastic bags. Use one bag each time, pour into a cup and make as tea with boiling water.

Functions: To reduce gastric acidity, stop bleeding, treat inflammation, stop pain.

Indications: Gastric ulcer, duodenal ulcer.

Source:《浙江中草药制剂技术》

29.03 糖蜜红茶饮 Tang Mi Hongcha Yin

Ingredients:

红茶 Hongcha, Black Tea 5g
蜂蜜 Fengmi, Honey, desired amount
红糖 Hongtang, Brown Sugar, desired amount

Directions: Make tea with boiling water, cover and let sit for 10 minutes. Add honey and brown sugar. Drink the tea hot. Take three doses a day before meals.

Functions: To dispel cold, relieve pain.

Indications: Gastric ulcer, duodenal ulcer.

Source:《民间验方》

30 泄泻、肠炎、痢疾 For Diarrhea, Enteritis and Dysentery

30.01 一味薯预饮 Yiwei Shuyu Yin

Ingredients:

生山药 Sheng Shanyao, Common Yam Rhizome (Rhizoma Dioscoreae)

120g

Directions: Peel and cut into slices. Decoct by bringing to a boil and then simmer for 40-50 minutes. Filter and add white sugar to taste. Drink the decoction.

Functions: To reinforce the spleen and kidney.

Indications: Poor appetite, diarrhea, seminal emission, frequent urination.

Source: 《医学衷中参西录》

30.02 山楂红白糖茶 Shanzha Hongbaitang Cha

Ingredients:

山楂 Shanzha, Hawthorn Fruit (Fructus Crataegi) 90g

红糖 Hongtang, Brown Sugar 30g

白糖 Baitang, White Sugar 30g

Directions: Decoct and take four times a day.

Functions: To remove retention and stasis, inhibit Bacillus dysenteriae.

Indications: Dysentery.

Source: 《中医验方汇选》内科第一集

30.03 止泻茶 I Zhixie Cha I

Ingredients:

茶叶 Chaye, Tea Leaf (Folium Camelliae Sinensis) 15g

炮姜 Pao Jiang, Baked Ginger (Rhizoma Zingiberis) 3g

食盐 Shiyan, Salt 3g

粳米 Jingmi, Polished Round-Grained Nonglutinous Rice (Cultivarietas Oryzae Sativae) 30g

Directions: Decoct and drink the decoction.

Functions: To warm middle *jiao*, expel cold and strengthen spleen and stomach.

Indications: Loose stools, diarrhea.

Source: 《新中医》 2:5, 1980

30.04 止泻茶 II Zhixie Cha II

Ingredients:
绿茶 Lucha, Green Tea 9g
玫瑰花 Meigui Hua, Rose (Flos Roasae Rugosae) 6g
茉莉花 Moli Hua, Arabian Jasmine Flower (Flos Jasmini Sambac) 3g
金银花 Jinyinhua, Honeysuckle Flower (Flos Lonicerae) 9g
陈皮 Chenpi, Dried Tangerine Peel (Pericarpium Citri Reticulatae) 6g
甘草 Gancao, Liquorice Root (Radix Glycyrrhizae) 3g

Directions: Make as tea with boiling water.
Functions: Anti-inflammatory, analgesia, to treat incontinence of stool, and prolapse of rectum, regulate *qi*, promote digestion, activate blood circulation, stop bleeding, induce diuresis, clear heat, remove toxin.
Indications: Gastroenteritis, dysentery, diarrhea and indigestion. External use: Cleanse skin infections.
Source:《新中医》2:5, 1980

30.05 木槿花速溶饮 Mujinhua Surongyin

Ingredients:
木槿花 Mujin Hua, Shrubalthea Flower (Flos Hibisci) 500g
白糖 Baitang, White Sugar 500g

Directions: Decoct for one hour, remove the herb, continue to decoct with low heat till the decoction becomes very thick. Remove from heat. Cool the decoction and add white sugar, dry, crush, and store in a bottle. Use 10g each time, twice a day. Make as tea with boiling water.
Functions: To clear heat, cool blood, remove toxins, reduce swelling.
Indications: Dysentery, hematochezia.
Source:《福建民间草药》

30.06 六和茶 Liuhe Cha

Ingredients:
藿香 Huoxiang, Cablia Patchouli Herb (Herba Pogostemonis) 45g
杏仁 Xing Ren, Apricot Seed (Semen Armeniacae Amarum) 45g
木瓜 Mugua, Common Floweringqince Fruit (Fructus Chaenomelis) 45g
苍术 Cangzhu, Swordlike Atractylodes Rhizome (Rhizoma Atractylodis) 45g
川朴 Chuanpu, Officinal Magnolia Bark (Cortex Magnoliae Officinalis) 30g
党参 Dangshen, Pilose Asiabell Root (Radix Codonopsis Pilosulae) 30g
半夏 Banxia, Pinellia Tuber (Rhizoma Pinelliae) 60g
赤茯苓 Chifuling, Indian Bread (Poria) 60g
扁豆 Biandou, Hyacinth Bean (Semen Dolichoris) 60g
砂仁 Sharen, Villous Amomum Fruit (Fructus Amomi) 15g
甘草 Gancao, Liquorice Root (Radix Glycyrrhizae) 15g
茶叶 Chaye, Tea Leaf (Folium Camelliae Sinensis) 120g

Directions: Powder all ingredients. Use 9g each time. Put together with 3g ginger and jujube, five pieces, and make as tea with boiling water.

Functions: To strengthen the spleen and stomach, regulate *qi*, dissolve damp.

Indications: Weakness of the spleen and stomach with symptoms of retention of food and phlegm, abdominal distention, and loose stools.

Source:《全国中成药处方集》

30.07 石榴叶茶 Shiliuye Cha

Ingredients:
石榴叶 Shiliu Ye, Pomegranate Leaf (Folium Granati) 60g
生姜 Sheng Jiang, Fresh Ginger (Rhizoma Zingiberis Recens) 15g
食盐 Shiyan, Salt 3g

Directions: Toast ingredients until black, decoct and drink.

Functions: To warm the middle *jiao*, stop diarrhea.

Indications: Enterogastritis.

Source:《常见病验方选编》

30.08 石榴皮茶 Shiliupi Cha

Ingredients:

石榴皮 Shiliupi, Pomegranate Rind (Pericarpium Granati)

Directions: Decoct and drink. Or make as tea with boiling water. Use 15g each day until the dysentery ceases.

Functions: To relieve dysentery and diarrhea, stop bleeding, expel intestinal parasites.

Indications: Bacillary dysentery, amebic dysentery and chronic colitis.

Source:《民间验方》

30.09 冬瓜叶饮 Dongguaye Yin

Ingredients:

冬瓜叶 Donggua Ye, Chinese Waxgourd Leaf (Folium Benincasae) 30-50g

Directions: Decoct, drink.

Functions: To remove damp, stop diarrhea

Indications: dysentery, diarrhea.

Source:《浙江中医》8:356, 1982

30.10 地锦草茶 Dijincao Cha

Ingredients:

地锦草 Dijin Cao, Creeping Euphorbia (Herba Euphorbiae Humifusae)

Directions: Dry. Use 75g every day. Decoct. Add sugar to taste before drinking.

Functions: To clear heat, cool blood, dissolve damp, stop dysentery.

Indications: Bacillary dysentery.

Source:《百病中医自我疗养丛书·痢疾》

30.11 芝麻茶 Zhima Cha

Ingredients:
白芝麻 Baizhima, White Sesame (Semen Sesami) 30g
冰糖 Bingtang, Crystal Sugar, desired amount

Directions: Make as tea with boiling water.
Functions: To clear heat, dissolve damp.
Indications: Dysentery.
Source: 福建《中医验方》第二集

30.12 车前蜂蜜饮 Cheqian Fengmi Yin

Ingredients:
车前草 Cheqian Cao, Plantain Herb (Herba Plantaginis) 30g
蜂蜜 Fengmi, Honey, desired amount

Directions: Decoct the herb, filter, add honey to the decoction. Drink while warm.
Functions: To clear heat, induce diuresis, dissolve damp, remove toxins.
Indications: Dysentery due to damp-heat, scanty and dark yellow urine.

Ginger juice can be added to the decoction to prevent indigestion caused by the sweet and greasy property of the honey. This decoction should not be used if the patient suffers from spleen deficiency and fullness in the epigastric region.

Source:《新中医》5:41, 1983

30.13 柚皮茶 I Youpi Cha I

Ingredients:
柚皮 You Pi, Pummelo Peel (Exocarpium Citri Grandis) 9g
细茶叶 Xichaye, Tea Leaf (Folium Camelliae Sinensis) 6g
生姜 Sheng Jiang, Fresh Ginger (Rhizoma Zingiberis Recens), 2 slices

Directions: Decoct and drink.
Functions: To warm middle *jiao*, dispel cold and relieve pain.

Indications: Acute gastroenteritis.
Source:《常见病验方研究参考资料》

30.14 苦瓜根茶 Kuguagen Cha

Ingredients:
鲜苦瓜根 Xian Kugua Gen, Fresh Momordica Charantia Root (Radix Momordicae Charantiae) 30g
Directions: Cut into small pieces, decoct and drink.
Functions: To clear heat, remove toxins.
Indications: Diarrhea in summer.
Source:《常见病验方选编》

30.15 马齿苋绿豆汤 Machixian Ludou Tang

Ingredients:
马齿苋 Machixian, Purslane Herb (Herba Portulacae) 30g **or**
鲜马齿苋 Xian Machixian, Fresh Purslane Herb (Herba Portulacae) 120g
绿豆 Ludou, Mung Bean (Semen Phaseoli Radiati) 30-60g
Directions: Decoct and drink. Take one dose a day. Use daily for three or four days.
Functions: To clear heat, dissolve damp, regulate the *ying* system and stop bleeding.
Indications: Hematochezia due to damp-heat.
Source:《饮食疗法》

30.16 马齿苋槟榔茶 Machixian Binglang Cha

Ingredients:
马齿苋 Machixian, Purslane Herb (Herba Portulacae) 10g
槟榔 Binglang, Areca Seed (Semen Arecae) 10g
Directions: Decoct and drink.
Functions: To clear heat, dissolve damp.

Indications: Dysentery with abdominal pain, tenesmus and burning anal pain.
Source:《百病饮食自疗》

30.17 苋菜茶 Xiancai Cha

Ingredients:
铁苋菜 Tiexiancai, Herb of Copperleaf (Herba Acalyphae) 30g
Directions: Decoct and drink.
Functions: To clear heat, dissolve damp.
Indications: Dysentery post measles with fever, abdominal pain with blood and mucus in the stools.
Source:《百病饮食自疗》

30.18 陈醋茶 Chencu Cha

Ingredients:
茶叶 Chaye, Tea Leaf (Folium Camelliae Sinensis) 3g
陈醋 Chencu, Mature Vinegar, 1ml
Directions: Make tea and filter. Save the fluid, add mature vinegar before drinking. Take three doses a day.
Functions: To harmonize stomach, stop dysentery and remove stasis.
Indications: Toothache, dysentery and abdominal pain of pediatric ascariasis.
Source:《烟酒茶俗》

30.19 健脾饮 Jianpi Yin

Ingredients:
橘皮 Jupi, Dried Tangerine Peel (Pericarpium Citri Reticulatae) 10g
荷叶 Heye, Lotus Leaf (Folium Nelumbinis), a half leaf
炒山楂 Chao Shanzha, Parched Hawthorn Fruit (Fructus Crataegi) 3g
生麦芽 Sheng Mai Ya, Germinated Barley (Fructus Hordei Germinatus) 15g

Directions: Decoct over high heat and then low heat for 30 minutes. Filter and add white sugar to taste before taking decoction.
Functions: To strengthen spleen, remove food retention.
Indications: Poor appetite and abdominal distention due to weakness of spleen in transportation and transformation causing indigestion.
Source:《民间验方》

30.20 无花果糖饮 Wuhuaguo Tang Yin

Ingredients:
鲜无花果 Xian Wuhuaguo, fresh Fig (Fructus Fici), 2-3 fruit
Directions: Pestle, decoct and add white and brown sugar to taste before drinking.
Functions: To treat inflammation, relieve pain, strengthen stomach and cure dysentery.
Indications: Dysentery, hemorrhoids.
Source:《河北卫生》 7:1959

30.21 棕榈花茶 Zongluhua Cha

Ingredients:
棕榈花 Zongluhua, Fortune Windmill Palm Flower (Flos Trachycarpi) 30g
Directions: Make as tea with boiling water. Use daily for three days.
Functions: Hemostasis.
Indications: Bacillary dysentery manifested as more blood than white mucus in stools, enterorrhagia, functional uterine bleeding.
Source:《常见病验方研究参考资料》

30.22 绿茶蜜饮 Lucha Mi Yin

Ingredients:
绿茶 Lucha, Green Tea 5g
蜂蜜 Fengmi, Honey, desired amount

Directions: Make tea with boiling water, add honey before drinking. Take two or three doses a day.
Functions: To clear heat, stop dysentery.
Indications: Bacillary dysentery.
Source:《民间验方》

30.23 姜枣饮 II   Jiang Zao Yin II

Ingredients:
干姜 Gan Jiang, Dried Ginger (Rhizoma Zingiberis) 5-10g
红枣 Hongzao, Chinese Date (Fructus Jujubae), 10 pieces
饴糖 Yitang, Maltose, desired amount

Directions: Decoct the dried ginger and date and add maltose before drinking the decoction. Take twice a day.
Functions: To strengthen spleen, harmonize stomach.
Indications: Dull pain in abdomen, loose stools, listlessness, shortness of breath, sensitivity to cold, poor appetite, pale tongue with a white coating, deep and thready pulse.
Source:《百病饮食自疗》

30.24 姜糖茶 II   Jiang Tang Cha II

Ingredients:
细茶 Xicha, Tea Leaf (Folium Camelliae Sinensis) 15g
生姜 Sheng Jiang, Fresh Ginger (Rhizoma Zingiberis Recens) 6g
红糖 Hongtang, Brown Sugar 30g

Directions: Make as tea with boiling water. Take two doses a day.
Functions: To clear heat, dissolve damp.
Indications: Dysentery.
Source:《锦方实验录》

30.25 姜茶饮 Jiang Cha Yin

Ingredients:
绿茶 Lucha, Green Tea 3g
干姜 Gan Jiang, Dried Ginger (Rhizoma Zingiberis) 3g (cut into thread-like pieces)

Directions: Make as tea with boiling water.
Functions: To warm middle *jiao*, relieve pain.
Indications: Acute gastroenteritis manifested as vomiting, diarrhea and irritability.
Source:《圣济总录》

30.26 姜茶速溶饮 Jiang Cha Surongyin

Ingredients:
红茶 Hongcha, Black Tea 200g
鲜生姜汁 Xian Sheng Jiang Zhi, Fresh Ginger Juice (Succus Zingiberis Rhizoma Recens) 200g
白糖 Baitang, White Sugar 500g

Directions: Decoct black tea for 20 minutes, filter and add water to decoct again. Repeat three times. Mix the decoctions and boil the mixture until it becomes very thick. Add fresh ginger juice to the thick paste, heat, remove from heat, cool and add white sugar. Dry, crush, and store in a closed container. Use 10g each time and make as tea with boiling water. Take three doses a day.
Functions: To dispel heat, stop pain.
Indications: Enteritis, bacillary dysentery and abdominal pain.
Source:《民间验方》

30.27 姜茶乌梅饮 Jiang Cha Wumei Yin

Ingredients:
生姜 Sheng Jiang, Fresh Ginger (Rhizoma Zingiberis Recens) 10g (cut into thread-like pieces)

乌梅肉 Wumeirou, Smoked Plum (Fructus Mume) 30g
绿茶 Lucha, Green Tea 5g
红糖 Hongtang, Brown Sugar, desired amount

Directions: Make as tea with boiling water.

Functions: To dispel damp-heat.

Indications: Bacillary dysentery, Amebic dysentery.

Source:《世医得效方》

30.28 萝卜茶 II   Luobo Cha II

Ingredients:
茶叶 Chaye, Tea Leaf (Folium Camelliae Sinensis) 5g
白萝卜 Bailuobo, Radish Root (Radix Raphani) 100g

Directions: Make tea. Slice radish root, decoct with salty water, add tea to the decoction before taking it. Take twice a day.

Functions: To clear heat, dispel wind, relieve pain and swelling.

Indications: Summer boils.

Source:《烟酒茶俗》

30.29 萝卜姜蜜茶 Luobo Jiang Mi Cha

Ingredients:
白萝卜汁 Bailuobo Zhi, Radish Juice (Succus Raphani), a winecup of
生姜汁 Sheng Jiang Zhi, Fresh Ginger Juice (Succus Zingiberis Rhizoma Recens), half a teaspoonful
蜂蜜 Fengmi, Honey 30g
陈茶 Chencha, Tea Leaf (Folium Camelliae Sinensis) 3g

Directions: Infuse with one cup of warm boiled water and drink. Use three times a day.

Functions: To clear heat, remove toxins.

Indications: Dysentery.

Source: 中医研究院《中医验方汇编》第一辑

31 眩晕头重 For Dizziness and Heaviness of Head

31.01 生姜蔻仁汤 Shengjiang Kouren Tang

Ingredients:
生姜 Sheng Jiang, Fresh Ginger (Rhizoma Zingiberis Recens) 15g
蔻仁 Kouren, Round Cardamon Fruit (Fructus Amomi Rotundus) 10g
Directions: Decoct for five minutes, drink twice a day.
Functions: To dry damp, dispel phlegm, strengthen spleen and harmonize stomach.
Indications: Dizziness, heaviness in the head, nausea, with a soft and rolling pulse due to retention of phlegm in the middle *jiao*.
Source:《百病饮食自疗》

31.02 清眩饮 Qingxuan Yin

Ingredients:
泽泻 Zexie, Oriental Waterplantain Rhizome (Rhizoma Alismatis) 9g
白术 Baizhu, Largehead Atractylodes Rhizome (Rhizoma Atractylodis Macrocephalae) 9g
荷叶蒂 Heye Di, Lotus Base (Pedicellus Nelumbinis), 5 bases
菊花 Juhua, Chrysanthemum Flower (Flos Chrysanthemi) 6g
佩兰叶 Peilan Ye, Fortune Eupatorium Leaf (Folium Eupatorii) 3g
Directions: Soak, decoct and drink.
Functions: To dissolve phlegm-damp.
Indications: Dizziness, heaviness in head and body due to phlegm-damp.
Source:《浙江中医药》8:289, 1979

31.03 藿香苡仁饮 Huoxiang Yiren Yin

Ingredients:
苡仁 Yiren, Coix Seed (Semen Coicis) 15g
扁豆 Biandou, Hyacinth Bean (Semen Dolichoris) 15g

藿香 Huoxiang, Cablia Patchouli Herb (Herba Pogostemonis) 6g
厚朴花 Houpu Hua, Officinal Magnolia Flower (Flos Magnoliae Officinalis) 6g
鲜荷叶 Xian Heye, Fresh Lotus Leaf (Folium Nelumbinis) or
西瓜汁 Xigua Zhi, Watermelon Juice (Succus Citrulli)

Directions: Decoct the first two, add cablia patchouli herb, filter, save fluid. Mix watermelon juice or fresh lotus leaves into the fluid before drinking. Take several times a day.

Functions: To clear and dissolve damp-heat of *qi* stage in febrile disease which is more damp than hot.

Indications: Febrile disease in *qi* stage with symptoms of sensitivity to cold, little sweating, fever, constricted heaviness in the head, tiredness, fullness in chest and epigastrium, loose stools, turbid urine, white sticky coating of tongue, soft and slow pulse.

Source: 《百病饮食自疗》

32 鼻衄 For Epistaxis

32.01 三鲜饮 Sanxian Yin

Ingredients:
鲜白茅根 Xian Baimao Gen, Fresh Lalang Grass Rhizome (Rhizoma Imperatae) 120g
鲜藕 Xian Ou, Fresh Lotus Rhizome (Nelumbinis Rhizomatis) 120g
鲜小蓟根 Xian Xiaoji Gen, Fresh Field Thistle Root (Radix Cephalanoploris) 60g

Directions: Decoct and drink the decoction.

Functions: Cool blood, stop bleeding, clear heat, dissolve phlegm.

Indications: Hematemesis, epistaxis, hemoptysis.

Source: 《医学衷中参西录》

32.02 玉米花茶 Yumihua Cha

Ingredients:
玉米花 Yumi Hua, Corn Flower (Flos Maydis) 10g

Directions: Make as tea with boiling water.

Functions: Hemostasis.

Indications: Epistaxis (nose-bleed).

Source:《常见病验方研究参考资料》

32.03 白茅花茶 Baimaohua Cha

Ingredients:
白茅花 Baimao Hua, Imperata Flower (Flos Imperatae) 10g

Directions: Decoct, drink.

Functions: Hemostasis.

Indications: Epistaxis, hematuria.

Source:《常见病验方研究参考资料》

32.04 白茅根茶 Baimaogen Cha

Ingredients:
白茅根 Baimao Gen, Imperata Rhizome (Rhizoma Imperatae) 100g

Directions: Pestle, decoct, drink.

Functions: To clear heat, cool blood, stop bleeding, induce diuresis.

Indications: Epistaxis, hemoptysis, hematemesis, gingiva bleeding, hematuria.

Source:《上海常用中药手册》

32.05 地骨皮茶 Digupi Cha

Ingredients:
地骨皮 Digupi, Chinese Wolfberry Root-Bark (Cortex Lycii) 20g

Directions: Make as tea with boiling water.

Functions: To clear heat, cool blood.

Indications: Epistaxis, gingiva bleeding.
Source:《常见病验方研究参考资料》

32.06 鸡蛋清白糖饮 Jidanqing Baitang Yin
Ingredients:
鸡蛋清 Jidan Qing, Egg White, 2 egg's
白糖 Baitang, White Sugar 30g
Directions: Stir egg white, add white sugar and stir again. Make as tea with boiling water. Drink.
Functions: To cool blood, stop bleeding.
Indications: Infantile epistaxis.
Source:《河南省中医秘方验方汇编》

32.07 萝卜叶茶 II Luoboye Cha II
Ingredients:
干萝卜叶 Gan Luobo Ye, Dried Radish Leaf (Folium Raphani) 15-20g
Directions: Decoct and drink.
Functions: To dispel wind heat, stop bleeding, treat dysentery.
Indications: Sore throat due to invasion of wind heat, epistaxis, dysentery.
Source: 福建《中医验方》

33 咳血、吐血 For Hemoptysis and Spitting Blood

33.01 小蓟根茶 Xiaojigen Cha
Ingredients:
小蓟根 Xiaoji Gen, Field Thistle Root (Radix Cirsii) 30-60g
Directions: Pestle, decoct and drink the decoction.
Functions: Hemostasis.
Indications: Hematemesis, hemoptysis, hematuria.

Source:《医学衷中参西录》

33.02 五君子饮 Wujunzi Yin
Ingredients:
茯苓 Fuling, Indian Bread (Poria) 12g
山药 Shanyao, Common Yam Rhizome (Rhizoma Dioscoreae) 12g
藕 Ou, Lotus Rhizome (Nelumbinis Rhizomatis) 120g
大枣 Dazao, Chinese Date (Fructus Jujubae) 10g
百合 Baihe, Lily Bulb (Bulbus Lilii) 10g

Directions: Decoct by bringing to a boil and then simmer for 30-40 minutes. Filter and add white sugar to the decoction before drinking it.
Functions: To reinforce the spleen and lung.
Indications: Cough with blood phlegm, poor appetite and loose stools.
Source:《民间验方》

33.03 止血茶 Zhixue Cha
Ingredients:
鲜梨 Xian Li, Fresh Pear (Fructus Pyri), 1 piece (pitted)
鲜藕 Xian Ou, Fresh Lotus Rhizome (Nelumbinis Rhizomatis) 500g (joint removed)
鲜荷叶 Xian Heye, Fresh Lotus Leaf (Folium Nelumbinis), 1 piece (base removed)
柿饼 Shi Bing, Prepared Persimmon (Fructus Kaki Praeparate), 1 piece (base removed)
大枣 Dazao, Chinese Date (Fructus Jujubae), 10 pieces (pitted)
鲜白茅根 Xian Baimao Gen, Fresh Lalang Grass Rhizome (Rhizoma Imperatae) 30g (heart removed)
Directions: Decoct and drink the decoction.
Functions: To cool blood, stop bleeding, astringe the lung, control cough.
Indications: Cough with bloody phlegm.

Source:《中医秘方验方》

33.04 玉米须冰糖茶 Yumixu Bingtang Cha

Ingredients:
玉米须 Yumi Xu, Corn Stigma (Stigma Maydis) 60g
冰糖 Bingtang, Crystal Sugar 60g

Directions: Decoct. Drink.

Functions: To soothe liver, clear heat, moisten lung, dissolve phlegm, stop cough and remove toxins.

Indications: Cough due to the dryness of lung, hemoptysis.

Source:《福建中医验方》

33.05 四花饮 Sihua Yin

Ingredients:
银花 Yinhua, Honeysuckle Flower (Flos Lonicerae) 10g
菊花 Juhua, Chrysanthemum Flower (Flos Chrysanthemi) 10g
栀子花 Zhizi Hua, Cape Jasmine Flower (Flos Gardeniae) 10g
白菜花 Baicai Hua, Peking Cabbage Flower (Flos Brassicae Pekinensis) 10g
雪梨 Xueli, Pear (Fructus Pyri Nivalis), 2 pears (made into juice)

Directions: Decoct the first four. Mix the decoction with the pear juice. Take the mixed fluid two or three times a day.

Functions: To eliminate wind-heat, moisten the lung, control coughing, soothe the liver, clear the accumulated heat in the stomach.

Indications: Cough, hemoptysis, hematemesis due to accumulated heat in the stomach and/or attack of the stomach by the liver fire.

Source:《百病饮食自疗》

33.06 加味三七饮 Jiawei Sanqi Yin

Ingredients:
三七 Sanqi, Sanchi (Radix Notoginseng) 10g

鲜橙汁 Xian Cheng Zhi, Fresh Orange Juice (Succus Citri Sinensis)
藕汁 Ou Zhi, Lotus Juice (Succus Nelumbinis Rhizomatis)

Directions: Make as tea with warm boiled water.

Functions: To stop bleeding, remove blood stasis, relieve pain.

Indications: Hematemesis due to liver fire affecting the stomach with symptoms of bitter taste in mouth, hypochondriac pain, irritability, hot temper, dream-disturbed sleep, restlessness, dark red tongue, wiry and rapid pulse.

Source:《百病饮食自疗》

33.07 仙鹤草茶 Xianhecao Cha

Ingredients:

仙鹤草 Xianhecao, Hairvein Agrimonia Herb (Herba Agrimoniae) 15-30g

红糖 Hongtang, Brown Sugar, desired amount

Directions: Decoct and drink.

Functions: To clear heat, cool blood, stop bleeding, reinforce the stomach, tonify the body.

Indications: Hemoptysis, hematemesis.

Source:《常见病验方研究参考资料》

33.08 荷叶饮 I Heye Yin I

Ingredients:

鲜荷叶 Xian Heye, Fresh Lotus Leaf (Folium Nelumbinis), a half leaf **or**
干荷叶 Gan Heye, Dried Lotus Leaf (Folium Nelumbinis) 15g

绿豆 Ludou, Mung Bean (Semen Phaseoli Radiati) 30g

竹茹 Zhuru, Bamboo Shavings (Caulis Bambusae in Taeniam) 10g

鲜茅根 Xian Maogen, Fresh Lalang Grass Rhizome (Rhizoma Imperatae) 30-60g **or**
干茅根 Gan Maogen, Dried Imperata Rhizome (Rhizoma Imperatae) 15g

Directions: Decoct the mung beans first. When cooked, add lotus leaves, bamboo shavings and rhizome. Boil again, filter, and drink. Take two or three times a day.

Functions: To clear heat, stop bleeding.

Indications: Fullness and distending pain in chest and abdomen, hematemesis, hematochezia, constipation, red tongue with yellow and sticky coating, rolling and rapid pulse due to accumulated heat in stomach.

Source:《百病饮食自疗》

33.09 麦冬茅根饮 Maidong Maogen Yin

Ingredients:
麦冬 Maidong, Dwarf Lilyturf Tuber (Radix Ophiopogonis) 15g
茅根 Maogen, Lalang Grass Rhizome (Rhizoma Imperatae) 12g
百合 Baihe, Lily Bulb (Bulbus Lilii) 15g

Directions: Decoct and add crystal sugar to taste before drinking.

Functions: To produce body fluid, relieve cough.

Indications: Non-productive cough, hemoptysis.

Source:《中国药膳学》

33.10 黄花菜饮 Huanghuacai Yin

Ingredients:
黄花菜 Huanghuacai, Foldleaf Daylily Root (Radix Hemerocallidis Plicatae) 60g
鲜藕 Xian Ou, Fresh Lotus Rhizome (Nelumbinis Rhizomatis) 60g (sliced)
茅根 Maogen, Lalang Grass Rhizome (Rhizoma Imperatae) 15g

Directions: Decoct and drink. Or, decoct daylily root and grass rhizome, crush fresh lotus rhizome into juice. And add the juice to the decoction before drinking. Take two or three times a day.

Functions: To clear heat, cool blood, stop bleeding.
Indications: Cough with bloody expectorant caused by heat in lung, hematemesis due to accumulated heat in stomach or liver fire influencing stomach.
Source:《食物与治病》

33.11 双荷汤 Shuanghe Tang
Ingredients:
鲜荷叶 Xian Heye, Fresh Lotus Leaf (Folium Nelumbinis) 100g
鲜藕节 Xian Ou Jie, fresh Lotus Node (Nodus Nelumbinis Rhizomatis) 200g
蜂蜜 Fengmi, Honey 50g
Directions: Pestle all materials. Decoct for one hour, and drink two or three times a day.
Functions: To cool blood, stop bleeding.
Indications: Hematemesis, hematochezia.
Source:《太平圣惠方》

33.12 藕节茶 Oujie Cha
Ingredients:
藕节 Ou Jie, Lotus Node (Nodus Nelumbinis Rhizomatis), 10 nodes
Directions: Decoct and drink.
Functions: To cool blood, stop bleeding.
Indications: Various bleeding diseases.
Source:《民间便方》

33.13 藕节茅根茶 Oujie Maogen Cha
Ingredients:
藕节 Ou Jie, Lotus Node (Nodus Nelumbinis Rhizomatis), 9 nodes
桑叶 Sangye, Mulberry Leaf (Folium Mori) 15g
白茅根 Baimao Gen, Imperata Rhizome (Rhizoma Imperatae) 15g

Directions: Pestle into coarse powder, decoct and drink.
Functions: To dispel wind, clear heat, cool blood, stop bleeding.
Indications: Hemoptysis, hematemesis.
Source:《常见病验方研究参考资料》

33.14 蚕豆花冰糖茶 Candouhua Bingtang Cha

Ingredients:
蚕豆花 Candou Hua, Broadbean Flower (Flos Viciae Fabae) 9g
Directions: Decoct, filter and melt a little crystal sugar into it. Drink two or three times a day.
Functions: To astringe lung, control bleeding.
Indications: Bloody Cough.
Source:《现代实用中药》

34 便血 For Hematochezia

34.01 木耳芝麻茶 Muer Zhima Cha

Ingredients:
黑木耳 Heimuer, Jew's Ear (Auricularia) 60g
黑芝麻 Heizhima, Black Sesame (Semen Sesami Nigrum) 15g
Directions: Divide each into two parts. One part is well-baked, and the other part is used raw. Mix the baked with the raw. Use 10-15g each time. Make as tea with boiling water.
Functions: Cool blood, stop bleeding, moisten intestines, relieve constipation.
Indications: Hematochezia due to hemorrhoids (pile bleeding).
Source:《医学指南》

34.02 加味槐花饮 Jiawei Huaihua Yin

Ingredients:
粳米 Jingmi, Polished Round-Grained Nonglutinous Rice (Cultivarietas

Oryzae Sativae) 30g
赤小豆 Chixiaodou, Rice Bean (Semen Phaseoli) 10g
槐花 Huai Hua, Pagodatree Flower (Flos Sophorae) 10g (ground)
红糖 Hongtang, Brown Sugar, desired amount

Directions: Decoct the first two, filter, add the rest to the decoction before taking it.

Functions: To clear heat, cool blood, stop bleeding.

Indications: Hematochezia accompanied by hesitant bowel movement, bitter taste in mouth, yellow and sticky tongue coating, soft and rapid pulse caused by accumulation of heat in the intestines.

Source:《百病饮食自疗》

34.03 旱莲草红枣汤 Hanliancao Hongzao Tang

Ingredients:
鲜旱莲草 Xian Hanliancao, Fresh Eclipta (Herba Ecliptae) 50g
红枣 Hongzao, Chinese Date (Fructus Jujubae), 8-10 pieces

Directions: Decoct and drink.

Functions: To cool blood, stop bleeding.

Indications: Hematochezia.

Source:《饮食疗法》

34.04 秋梨椿根皮茶 Qiuli Chungenpi Cha

Ingredients:
秋梨 Qiuli, Pear 360g
茶叶 Chaye, Tea Leaf (Folium Camelliae Sinensis) 30g
椿根皮 Chun Genpi, Chinese Toona Root-Bark (Cortex Toonae Sinensis Radicis) 360g
白糖 Baitang, White Sugar 250g

Directions: Decoct the first three and add white sugar before drinking.

Functions: To cool blood, stop bleeding.

Indications: Hematochezia.
Source: 《中医实用效方选》

34.05 黄花菜红糖饮 Huanghuacai Hongtang Yin

Ingredients:
黄花菜 Huanghuacai, Foldleaf Daylily Root (Radix Hemerocallidis Plicatae) 120g
红糖 Hongtang, Brown Sugar 120g

Directions: Decoct and add brown sugar before drinking the decoction.
Functions: To clear heat, remove stasis.
Indications: Hemorrhoids (cure in early stage, relieve pain in later stage).
Source: 《山西省中医验方秘方汇集》第一辑

34.06 蜂蜜木瓜饮 Fengmi Mugua Yin

Ingredients:
蜂蜜 Fengmi, Honey 6g
木瓜粉 Mugua Fen, Common Flowering Quince Fruit Powder (Pulvis Chaenomelis Fructus) 6g

Directions: Melt honey with boiling water, add the powder before drinking. Take one dose in the morning and evening respectively. Use daily for chronic cases.
Functions: To moisten bowels, stop bleeding.
Indications: Hematochezia of many years duration.
Source: 《中医验方汇选》内科第二集

34.07 槐花饮 Huaihua Yin

Ingredients:
陈槐花 Chen Huai Hua, Dried Pagodatree Flower (Flos Sophorae) 10g
粳米 Jingmi, Polished Round-Grained Nonglutinous Rice (Cultivarietas

Oryzae Sativae) 30g

红糖 Hongtang, Brown Sugar, desired amount

Directions: Bake the flower and grind into powder. Decoct together with the rice using high heat and then simmer for 40 minutes. Filter, save the fluid. Add brown sugar. Take the mixture.

Functions: To cool blood, stop bleeding.

Indications: Hematochezia due to invasion of wind heat.

Source:《民间验方》

34.08 槐叶茶 Huaiye Cha

Ingredients:

嫩槐叶 Nen Huai Ye, Young Pagodatree Leaf (Folium Sophorae)

Directions: Steam, dry. Use 15g each day, add sugar to taste and make as tea with boiling water.

Functions: To clear heat, stop bleeding.

Indications: Hematochezia due to hemorrhoids.

Source:《食医心镜》

34.09 槐角茶 Huaijiao Cha

Ingredients:

槐角 Huai Jiao, Pagodatree Fruit (Fructus Sophorae)

红糖 Hongtang, Brown Sugar, desired amount

Directions: Toast together in an iron pan with sand. Remove from sand and clean with a dry towel. Grind into coarse powder. Make as tea with boiling water.

Functions: To clear heat, moisten liver, cool blood and stop bleeding.

Indications: Hematochezia of hemorrhoids.

Precaution: Contra indicated in pregnancy.

Source:《中医杂志》 7:1983

34.10 槐芽茶 Huaiya Cha

Ingredients:
嫩槐芽 Nen Huai Ya, Pagodatree Flower-Bud (Flos Sopharae)
Directions: Steam. Bake. Use 5g each time and make as tea with boiling water.
Functions: To clear heat, cool blood, stop bleeding.
Indications: Enterorrhagia.
Source:《普济方》

34.11 绿豆芽白皮饮 Ludouya Baipi Yin

Ingredients:
绿豆芽 Ludou Ya, Mung Bean Sprout (Semen Phaseoli Radiati Germinatus) 120g
红糖 Hongtang, Brown Sugar 120g
椿根皮 Chun Genpi, Chinese Toona Root-Bark (Cortex Toonae Sinensis Radicis) 120g
Directions: Decoct. Drink morning and evening. One dose a day.
Functions: Clear heat, stop bleeding.
Indications: Hematochezia.
Source:《浙江中医杂志》4:1966

35 血尿、泌尿系感染 For Hematuria and Urinary System Infection

35.01 二鲜饮 Erxian Yin

Ingredients:
鲜藕 Xian Ou, Fresh Lotus Rhizome (Nelumbinis Rhizomatis) 120g
鲜白茅根 Xian Baimao Gen, Fresh Lalang Grass Rhizome (Rhizoma Imperatae) 120g
Directions: Cut into small pieces. Decoct and drink the decoction.

Functions: To cool blood, stop bleeding, clear heat, remove stasis.
Indications: Hematuria, burning with urination, abdominal pain, hemoptysis.
Source:《医学衷中参西录》

35.02 二花茶 Erhua Cha
Ingredients:
荠菜花 Jicai Hua, Shepherds Purse Flower (Flos Capsellae) 10-15g
蚕豆花 Candou Hua, Broadbean Flower (Flos Viciae Fabae) 10-15g
Directions: Make as tea with boiling water.
Functions: To cool blood, stop bleeding, lower blood pressure.
Indications: Hypertension.
Source:

35.03 人字草茶 Renzicao Cha
Ingredients:
人字草 Renzicao, Japan Clover Herb (Herba Kummerowiae Striatae) 60g
Directions: Pestle and make as tea with boiling water.
Functions: To clear heat, dissolve damp, cool blood, stop bleeding.
Indications: Hematuria.
Source:《简易中医疗法》

35.04 大小蓟速溶饮 Daxiaoji Surongyin
Ingredients:
鲜大蓟 Xian Daji, Japanese Thistle (Herba seu Radix Cirsii Japonici)   **or**
鲜小蓟 Xian Xiaoji, Fresh Field Thistle Herb (Herba Cirsii) 2,500g
白糖 Baitang, White Sugar 500g
Directions: Decoct by bringing to boil and then simmer for one hour. Remove the herbs and continue decocting till the fluid becomes very thick. Remove from heat. Mix white sugar into the decoction. Dry, grind,

and store in a bottle. Use 10g each time and take three times a day. Dissolve in boiling water.

Functions: To cool blood, stop bleeding, remove blood stasis.

Indications: Bleeding diseases.

Source:《太平圣惠方》

35.05 甘竹茶 Gan Zhu Cha

Ingredients:

甘草梢 Gancao Shao, Liquorice Stem-Tip (Apex Glycyrrhizae) 9g

竹叶 Zhuye, Bamboo Leaf (Folium Phyllostachys Nigra) 5g

Directions: Make as tea with boiling water.

Functions: To clear heat, dissolve damp.

Indications: Frequent, urgent, and painful urination due to accumulation of damp-heat in the urinary bladder.

Source:《中医护理》

35.06 白果冬瓜子饮 Baiguo Dongguazi Yin

Ingredients:

白果 Baiguo, Ginkgo Seed (Semen Ginkgo), 10 pieces (peeled)

冬瓜子 Dongguazi, Chinese Waxgourd Seed (Semen Benincasae) 30g

莲子肉 Lianzirou, Lotus Seed (Semen Nelumbinis) 15g

胡椒 Hujiao, Pepper Fruit (Fructus Piperis) 15g

白糖 Baitang, White Sugar, desired amount

Directions: Decoct the first three to boiling and then simmer for 30-40 minutes. Filter, remove the herbs, add the last two to the decoction and store the mixture in a jar. Take as tea.

Functions: Induce diuresis for treating stranguria.

Indications: Cloudy urine, frequent, urgent, urination in small amounts with continuous leakage.

Source:《食物与食治》

35.07 半边钱茶 Banbianqian Cha

Ingredients:
半边钱 Banbianqian, Obcordate Christia Herb (Herba Christiae Obcordatae) 60g

Directions: Decoct and drink.
Functions: To induce diuresis.
Indications: Urinary disturbances including pain, dysuria, and leakage.
Source:《常见中草药汇编》

35.08 加减小蓟饮 Jiajian Xiaoji Yin

Ingredients:
小蓟 Xiaoji, Field Thistle Herb (Herba Cirsii) 10g
竹叶 Zhuye, Bamboo Leaf (Folium Phyllostachys Nigra) 10g
藕节 Ou Jie, Lotus Node (Nodus Nelumbinis Rhizomatis) 10g

Directions: Decoct. Filter. Add the pear juice and watermelon juice to the decoction before taking it.
Functions: To clear the damp-heat of the lower *jiao*, nourish *yin*, relieve the hyperactivity of the heart fire, stop bleeding.
Indications: Dark yellow urine with a burning sensation in urination, hematuria, irritability, thirst, red tongue and rapid pulse.
Source:《百病饮食自疗》

35.09 竹茅饮 Zhu Mao Yin

Ingredients:
淡竹叶 Danzhuye, Lophatherum Herb (Herba Lophatheri) 10g
白茅根 Baimao Gen, Imperata Rhizome (Rhizoma Imperatae) 10g

Directions: Make as tea with boiling water.
Functions: To clear heat, produce body fluid, cool blood, induce diuresis.
Indications: Hematuria.
Source:《江西草药》

35.10 向日葵根茶 Xiangrikuigen Cha

Ingredients:

向日葵根 Xiangrikui Gen, Sunflower Root (Radix Helianthi) 7-15g

Directions: Decoct and drink.

Functions: To induce diuresis, stop pain.

Indications: Urinary infection with oliguria.

Source:《河北中医验方汇选》内科第二集

35.11 豆豉茶 Douchi Cha

Ingredients:

豆豉 Douchi, Prepared Soybean (Semen Sojae Fermentatum), a pinch of

Directions: Decoct and drink.

Functions: To clear heat.

Indications: Hematuria.

Source:《常见病验方研究参考资料》

35.12 旱莲草茶 Hanliancao Cha

Ingredients:

旱莲草 Hanliancao, Eclipta (Herba Ecliptae) 20g

车前草 Cheqian Cao, Plantain Herb (Herba Plantaginis) 20g

白糖 Baitang, White Sugar, desired amount

Directions: Decoct and drink.

Functions: To clear heat, induce diuresis, cool blood, stop bleeding.

Indications: Hematuria.

Source:《民间便方》

35.13 尿利清茶 Niaoliqing Cha

Ingredients:

艾 Ai, Argy Wormwood (Artemisiae Argyi) 45g (root and stem collected in May)

风尾草 Fengweicao, Phoenix-Tail Fern (Herba Pteridis Multifidae) 15g
白茅根 Baimao Gen, Imperata Rhizome (Rhizoma Imperatae) 15g
蜂蜜 Fengmi, Honey 10g

Directions: Decoct the first three, add the last one before drinking. Drink twice a day before meal.
Functions: To clear heat, dissolve damp, cool blood, remove toxins and induce diuresis.
Indications: Urinary tract infection, pyelonephritis and cystitis.
Source:《江西中医药》4:1980

35.14 车前海金饮 Cheqian Haijin Yin

Ingredients:
鲜车前草 Xian Cheqian Cao, fFresh Plantain Herb (Herba Plantaginis) 30-60g
海金沙 Haijinsha, Japanese Climbing Fern Spore (Spora Lygodii) 6-10g (wrapped in a cloth-bag)

Directions: Decoct and drink two or three times a day.
Functions: To clear heat, induce diuresis.
Indications: Stranguria marked by chyluria.
Source:《百病饮食自疗》

35.15 玫瑰花灯心茶 Meiguihua Dengxin Cha

Ingredients:
玫瑰花瓣 Meigui Huaban, Rose (Flos Roasae Rugosae) 6-10g
灯心草 Dengxincao, Common Rush (Medulla Junci) 2-3g

Directions: Decoct common rush and make rose as tea with the decoction.
Functions: To soothe liver, regulate *qi*.
Indications: Abdominal pain with red tongue and wiry pulse due to liver *qi* stagnation.
Source:《百病饮食自疗》

35.16 茅根车前饮 Maogen Cheqian Yin

Ingredients:
白茅根 Baimao Gen, Imperata Rhizome (Rhizoma Imperatae) 50g
车前子 Cheqian Zi, Plantain Seed (Semen Plantaginis) 50g
白糖 Baitang, White Sugar 25g
Directions: Decoct and drink.
Functions: To cool blood to stop bleeding, clear heat to induce diuresis.
Indications: Hematuria.
Source:《中国药膳学》

35.17 茅根竹蔗饮 Maogen Zhuzhe Yin

Ingredients:
白茅根 Baimao Gen, Imperata Rhizome (Rhizoma Imperatae) 50-120g
竹蔗 Zhuzhe, Sugarcane Stem (Caulis Saccharum Sinensis) 100-300g
Directions: Decoct and drink.
Functions: To replenish *yin*, reduce *xu*-fire, clear heat, induce diuresis.
Indications: Hematuria due to heat in lower *jiao* and heart fire hyperactivity.
Source:《百病饮食自疗》

35.18 马齿苋饮 Machixian Yin

Ingredients:
鲜马齿苋 Xian Machixian, fresh Purslane Herb (Herba Portulacae)
Directions: Crush and use juice to make as tea with boiling water.
Functions: To clear heart fire, dispel lower jiao heat.
Indications: Hematuria accompanied by irritability, thirst, red face, mouth ulcer, insomnia, red tongue and rapid pulse due to lower *jiao* heat or heart fire.
Source:《百病饮食自疗》

35.19 马齿苋红糖茶 Machixian Hongtang Cha

Ingredients:
马齿苋 Machixian, Purslane Herb (Herba Portulacae) 200-250g **or** 鲜马齿苋 Xian Machixian, Fresh Purslane Herb (Herba Portulacae) 400-500g
红糖 Hongtang, Brown Sugar 150g

Directions: Decoct and drink while hot. Take three times a day.
Functions: To clear heat, dissolve damp.
Indications: Acute urinary infection, pyelonephritis.
Source:《吉林中医药》3:29, 1985

35.20 茵地茶 Yin Di Cha

Ingredients:
茵陈 Yinchen, Virgate Wormwood Herb (Herba Artemisiae Scopariae) 30g
生地黄 Sheng Dihuang, Dried Rehmannia Root (Radix Rehmanniae) 30g

Directions: Decoct and drink.
Functions: To nourish kidney, clear heat, dissolve damp.
Indications: Cystitis.
Source:《常见病验方研究参考资料》

35.21 清淋茶 Qinglin Cha

Ingredients:
野葡萄藤 Yeputaoteng, Stem and Leaf of Hairy Grape (Caulis et Folium Vitis Quinquangularis) 10-15g
竹圆荽 Zhuyuansui, Japanese Climbing Fern Herb (Herba Lygodii) 10-15g
淡竹叶 Danzhuye, Lophatherum Herb (Herba Lophatheri) 10-15g
麦冬 Maidong, Dwarf Lilyturf Tuber (Radix Ophiopogonis) 10-15g
灯心草 Dengxincao, Common Rush (Medulla Junci) 10-15g

乌梅 Wumei, Smoked Plum (Fructus Mume) 10-15g
当归 Danggui, Chinese Angelica (Radix Angelicae Sinensis) 10-15g
红枣 Hongzao, Chinese Date (Fructus Jujubae), 10 dates

Directions: Pestle, decoct and drink. Take one dose every day.

Functions: To clear heat, cool blood, induce diuresis, treat urinary disturbances.

Indications: Hematuria accompanied by urinary disturbances, such as pain in the urethra and lower abdomen, and urgent urination.

Source: 《本草纲目》

35.22 清明柳叶速溶饮 Qingming Liuye Surongyin

Ingredients:

嫩柳叶 Nen Liu Ye, Young Leaves of Babylon Weeping Willow (Folium Salicis Babylonicae) 1,000g (collected during Pure Brightness, namely, 5th solar term)
白糖 Baitang, White Sugar 500g

Directions: Decoct for one hour, filter and boil the decoction again over low heat until it becomes very thick. Remove from heat, cool and mix white sugar into it. Dry, crush, and store in a bottle. Use 10g each time and make as tea with boiling water.

Functions: To clear heat, dissolve damp.

Indications: Urinary infection with urgency and frequency, and turbid urine.

Source: 《濒湖集简方》

35.23 淡竹叶灯心茶 Danzhuye Dengxin Cha

Ingredients:

淡竹叶 Danzhuye, Lophatherum Herb (Herba Lophatheri) 10g
灯心草 Dengxincao, Common Rush (Medulla Junci), a pinch of
通草 Tongcao, Ricepaper Plant Pith (Medulla Tetrapanacis) 3g

Directions: Pestle. Make as tea with boiling water.
Functions: To clear heart fire, induce diuresis, remove damp-heat of lower *jiao*.
Indications: Oliguria.
Source:《常见病中医临床手册》

35.24 扁蓄茶 Bianxu Cha

Ingredients:
扁蓄 Bianxu, Common Knotgrass Herb (Herba Polygoni Avicularis) 15-30g **or** 扁蓄叶 Bianxu Ye, Common Knotgrass Leaf (Folium Polygoni Avicularis) 15-30g
Directions: Steam, toast, and infuse as tea with boiling water.
Functions: To clear heat, dissolve damp, treat urinary disturbances.
Indications: Urinary disturbances due to accumulation of damp-heat in urinary tract and retention of urine.
Source:《实用中药学》

35.25 满天星茶 Mantianxing Cha

Ingredients:
满天星 Mantianxing, Sphagnum Teres Herb (Herba Sphagnum Teres) 30g
Directions: Pestle and make as tea with boiling water.
Functions: To clear heat, dissolve damp, induce diuresis and remove obstruction from urinary tract.
Indications: Retention of urine.
Source:《祖国医学采风录》

35.26 蒲公英茶 Pugongying Cha

Ingredients:
蒲公英 Pugongying, Dandelion (Herba Taraxaci) 60g
Directions: Pestle into coarse powder, decoct and drink.

Functions: To clear heat, promote detoxification and dissolve damp.
Indications: Cystitis due to damp-heat, urinary infection.
Source:《全国中草药汇编》

35.27 凤眼草茶 Fengyancao Cha
Ingredients:
凤眼草 Fengyancao, Ailanthus Samara (Fructus Ailanthi) 30g
Directions: Make as tea with boiling water.
Functions: To clear heat, cool blood, treat morbid leukorrhea.
Indications: Hematuria accompanied by urinary disturbances, such as urethral and lower abdominal pain, urgent urination, etc.
Source:《四川中医》12:1985

35.28 绿豆芽白糖饮 Ludouya Baitang Yin
Ingredients:
绿豆芽 Ludou Ya, Mung Bean Sprout (Semen Phaseoli Radiati Germinatus) 100g
白糖 Baitang, White Sugar 60g
Directions: Use the juice of bean sprout to melt white sugar, and take the mixture.
Functions: To relieve urinary disturbances (Linzheng).
Indications: The early stage of urinary disturbances.
Source:《山西省中医验方秘方汇集》第一辑

35.29 灯心柿饼汤 Dengxin Shibing Tang
Ingredients:
灯心草 Dengxincao, Common Rush (Medulla Junci) 6g
柿饼 Shi Bing, Prepared Persimmon (Fructus Kaki Praeparate), 2 pieces
Directions: Decoct and add white sugar to taste before drinking.
Functions: To clear heat, cool blood, stop bleeding.

Indications: Hematuria.
Source: 《饮食疗法》

35.30 糠壳老茶 Kangkelao Cha

Ingredients:
糠壳 Kangke, Rice Pericarp (Pericarpium Oryzae Germinatus) 30g
Directions: Decoct and drink.
Functions: To dissolve damp-heat, induce diuresis.
Indications: Urethritis, dysuria and edema.
Source:《实用中药学》

35.31 糯稻根须饮 Nuodaogenxu Yin

Ingredients:
糯稻根须 Nuodao Genxu, Glutinous Rice Root (Radix Oryzae Glutinosae) 250g
Directions: Decoct 30g each time and drink.
Functions: To reinforce *qi*, clear heat, treat urinary diseases.
Indications: Painful, frequent and urgent urination, hematuria.
Source:《常见病验方研究参考资料》

36 泌尿系结石 For Urinary System Calculi

36.01 三金茶 Sanjin Cha

Ingredients:
金钱草 Jinqiancao, Christina Loosestrife (Herba Lysimachiae) 10g
海金沙 Haijinsha, Japanese Climbing Fern Spore (Spora Lygodii) 10g (wrapped in a gauze bag)
鸡内金 Jineijin, Chicken's Gizzard-Skin (Endothelium Corneum Gigeriae Galli) 15g
Directions: Decoct and drink the decoction.

Functions: To clear heat, dissolve damp, help discharge urinary stone.
Indications: Urinary stone with painful and difficult urination.
Source:《百病饮食自疗》

36.02 玉米根叶茶 Yumigenye Cha

Ingredients:
玉米根 Yumi Gen, Corn Root (Radix Maydis) 30g
玉米叶 Yumi Ye, Corn Leaf (Folium Maydis) 30g
Directions: Decoct. Drink.
Functions: To clear heat, dissolve damp.
Indications: Frequent oliguria with constant leakage of urine, stranguria due to renal calculus.
Source:《本草纲目》

36.03 石苇车前茶 Shiwei Cheqian Cha

Ingredients:
石韦 Shiwei, Shearers Pyrrosia Leaf (Folium Pyrrosiae) 20-60g
车前草 Cheqian Cao, Plantain Herb (Herba Plantaginis) 30-60g
栀子 Zhizi, Cape Jasmine Fruit (Fructus Gardeniae) 30g
甘草 Gancao, Liquorice Root (Radix Glycyrrhizae) 9-15g
Directions: Pestle, decoct, drink.
Functions: To clear heat, induce diuresis and assist passage of renal calculus.
Indications: Urinary stone.
Source:《全国中草药汇编》

36.04 佛耳草茶 Foercao Cha

Ingredients:
佛耳草 Foercao, Cudweed Herb (Herba Gnaphalii Affinis) 30g
Directions: Decoct and drink.

Functions: To clear heat, induce diuresis.
Indications: Renal calculus.
Source: 河南医学院《验方集锦》

36.05 谷皮藤茶 Gupiteng Cha

Ingredients:
谷皮藤 Gupiteng, Kazinoki Papermulberry Stem (Caulis Broussonetiae) 250g
绿豆 Ludou, Mung Bean (Semen Phaseoli Radiati) 60g
Directions: Decoct and drink.
Functions: To clear heat, induce diuresis and stop cough.
Indications: Renal calculus, cough due to the heat in the lung.
Source: 《常见中草药汇编》

36.06 金钱草茶 Jinqiancao Cha

Ingredients:
金钱草 Jinqiancao, Christina Loosestrife (Herba Lysimachiae) 60g
Directions: Pestle into a coarse powder. Make as tea with boiling water.
Functions: To clear heat, remove stones and induce diuresis.
Indications: Urethral stone, cystolith, urinary tract infection.
Source: 《上海中医杂志》 10:1985

36.07 荸荠内金饮 Biqi Neijin Yin

Ingredients:
荸荠 Biqi, Waternut Corm (Cormus Eleocharis Dulcis) 120g
鸡内金 Jineijin, Chicken's Gizzard-Skin (Endothelium Corneum Gigeriae Galli) 15g
Directions: Decoct and drink.
Functions: To remove damp-heat, aid in passage of a stone.
Indications: Renal calculus with dark yellow and turbid urine and pain during urination.

Source:《百病饮食自疗》

36.08 葱白琥珀饮 Congbai Hupo Yin
Ingredients:
葱白 Cong Bai, Onion (Bulbus Allii Fistulosi) 100g
琥珀末 Hupo Mo, Amber Powder (Pulvis Succinum) 1-1.5g
Directions: Decoct onion, filter, swallow amber powder with the warm decoction. Take two times a day.
Functions: To help pass renal stones.
Indications: Renal calculus manifested as fine granules in urine, brown-yellow turbid urine, painful and urgent urination, interruption of urination in mid-stream, abdominal and lumbar pain, red tongue with thin yellow coating, slightly rapid pulse.
Source:《百病饮食自疗》

36.09 薏苡仁汤 Yiyiren Tang
Ingredients:
薏苡仁 Yiyi Ren, Coix Seed (Semen Coicis) 60g
Directions: Decoct and drink.
Functions: To induce diuresis.
Indications: Jaundice, renal calculus.
Source:《杨氏经验方》

37 肾炎、水肿 For Nephritis and Edema

37.01 二陈竹叶茶 Erchen Zhuye Cha
Ingredients:
陈皮 Chenpi, Dried Tangerine Peel (Pericarpium Citri Reticulatae) 10g
陈瓢 Chen Piao, Old Bottle Gourd Peel (Pericarpium Lagenariae) 10g
鲜竹叶 Xian Zhuye, Fresh Bamboo Leaf (Folium Phyllostachys Nigra),

20 pieces
Directions: Decoct and add white sugar to taste before drinking.
Functions: To alleviate edema by diuresis.
Indications: Edema.
Source:《西安市中医验方汇编》

37.02 大麦秸茶 Damaijie Cha
Ingredients:
大麦秸 Damaijie, Barley Straw (Caulis Hordei Vulgare) 30-60g
Directions: Decoct and drink the decoction.
Functions: To strengthen the spleen, dissolve damp, relieve edema.
Indications: Nephritis.
Source:《常见病验方研究参考资料》

37.03 山扁豆草茶 Shanbiandoucao Cha
Ingredients:
山扁豆草 Shanbiandou Cao, Senna (Herba Cassiae Mimosoidis) 10-15g
Directions: Decoct and drink the decoction.
Functions: To clear toxic heat, induce diuresis.
Indications: Edema due to nephritis.
Source:《全国中草药汇编》

37.04 五皮饮 Wupi Yin
Ingredients:
生姜皮 Sheng Jiang Pi, Fresh Ginger Peel (Rhizoma Zingiberis Recens Peel)
桑白皮 Sang Baipi, White Mulberry Root-Bark (Cortex Mori)
橘皮 Jupi, Dried Tangerine Peel (Pericarpium Citri Reticulatae)
大腹皮 Dafupi, Areca Peel (Pericarpium Arecae)
茯苓皮 Fulingpi, Indian Bread Peel (Cutis Poriae)
All in equal amounts.

Directions: Pestle, decoct 10g each time, drink the decoction.
Functions: To induce diuresis, dissolve damp.
Indications: Edema (especially facial) with heaviness and soreness of joints, and oliguria.
Source:《华氏中藏经》

37.05 玉米芯茶 Yumixin Cha

Ingredients:
玉米芯 Yumi Xin, Corncob (Pedunculus Maydis) 60g
Directions: Pestle. Decoct. Drink.
Functions: To strengthen the spleen, dissolve damp, induce diuresis.
Indications: Chyluria.
Source:《广东省中医验方交流汇编》

37.06 玉米须茶 Yumixu Cha

Ingredients:
玉米须 Yumi Xu, Corn Stigma (Stigma Maydis) 50g
Directions: Decoct for 20-30 minutes. Drink the decoction twice a day.
Functions: To soothe the liver, clear heat, lower blood pressure and induce diuresis.
Indications: Nephritis, edema, dizziness due to hypertension, diabetes, jaundice, dysuria, stranguria due to renal calculus.
Source:《实用经效单方》

37.07 玉米须速溶饮 Yumixu Surongyin

Ingredients:
鲜玉米须 Xian Yumi Xu, Fresh Corn Stigma (Stigma Maydis) 1,000g
Directions: Decoct for one hour, remove the herb, continue to decoct until the decoction is very thick. Remove from heat, cool, mix 500g of white sugar into the decoction. Dry, crush and store in a bottle. Use 10g

each time infusing with warm boiled water. Take three times a day.
Functions: To alleviate water retention, lower blood pressure.
Indications: Edema of nephritis, lumbago due to renal calculus, hematuria.
Source: 《民间验方》

37.08 向日葵花茶 Xiangrikuihua Cha

Ingredients:

向日葵花 Xiangrikui Hua, Sunflower Flower (Flos Helianthi) 30g

麦秸 Maijie, Wheat Straw (Caulis Tritici Aestivi) 30g

Directions: Make as tea with boiling water, or decoct and drink.
Functions: To induce diuresis, lower blood pressure.
Indications: Edema of nephritis.
Source: 《常见病验方研究参考资料》

37.09 车前草茶 Cheqiancao Cha

Ingredients:

车前草 Cheqian Cao, Plantain Herb (Herba Plantaginis) 20g

Directions: Decoct and drink.
Functions: To clear heat, dissolve damp, induce diuresis.
Indications: Chronic pyelonephritis, cystitis, retention of urine, chronic nephritis, hypertension.
Source: 《中医杂志》2:1985

37.10 尿感茶 Niaogan Cha

Ingredients:

海金沙 Haijinsha, Japanese Climbing Fern Spore (Spora Lygodii) 1,600g

律草 Lucao, Japanese Hop Herb (Herba Humuli Scandentis) 1,600g

连钱草 Lianqiancao, Longtube Ground Ivy Herb (Herba Glechomae)

1,600g
风尾草 Fengweicao, Phoenix-tail fern (Herba Pteridis Multifidae) 1,600g

Directions: Grind 40 percent of ground ivy herb into fine powder. Decoct all the other materials. Concentrate the decoction to thick paste. Add the powder to the paste. Dry granules and wrap into 100 bags. Use half a bag each time to make as tea with boiling water. Take three doses a day.

Functions: To clear heat, dissolve damp.

Indications: Pyelonephritis, pyelitis, nephritis and urinary stone.

Source:《浙江中草药制剂技术》

37.11 茅根菠萝速溶饮 Maogen Boluo Surongyin

Ingredients:

鲜茅根 Xian Maogen, Fresh Lalang Grass Rhizome (Rhizoma Imperatae) 250g

菠萝汁 Boluo Zhi, Pineapple Juice 500g

白糖 Baitang, White Sugar 500g

Directions: Decoct grass rhizome for 30 minutes, filter, boil the decoction again over low heat until very thick. Add pineapple juice, heat again, remove from heat, cool, mix white sugar into thick paste. Dry, crush, and store in a bottle. Use 10g each time and make as tea with boiling water. Take three doses a day.

Functions: To cool blood, induce diuresis.

Indications: Nephritis.

Source:《民间验方》

37.12 海金砂草茶 Haijinshacao Cha

Ingredients:

海金沙草 Haijinsha Cao, Japanese Fern Herb (Herba Lygodii) 60g

冰糖 Bingtang, Crystal Sugar 15g

Directions: Decoct Japanese fern herb, filter and add crystal sugar before drinking the decoction.

Functions: To clear heat, promote detoxification and induce diuresis to treat stranguria.

Indications: Acute cystitis, pyelonephritis
Source:《福建民间草药》

37.13 菩提树根茶 Putishugen Cha

Ingredients:
菩提树根 Putishu Gen, Miquel Linden Root (Radix Tilia Miquelianae) 250g

Directions: Pestle into coarse powder. Use 30g each time, decoct and add white sugar to taste before drinking.

Functions: To induce sweating, reinforce insufficiency of the body.
Indications: Edema of nephritis.
Source:《常见病验方研究参考资料》

37.14 萱草根茶 Xuancaogen Cha

Ingredients:
萱草根 Xuancao Gen, Daylily Root (Radix Hemerocallis) 20g

Directions: Pestle, decoct and drink.
Functions: To induce diuresis, cool blood.
Indications: Dysuria, edema.
Source:《本草纲目》

37.15 粳稻根饮 Jingdaogen Yin

Ingredients:
早稻根 Zaodaogen, Rice Root (Radix Oryzae Sativae) 180-240g

Directions: Decoct and drink.
Functions: To clear heat, induce diuresis.

Indications: Entire body edema.
Source: 江西《锦方实验录》

37.16 蓄兰茶 Xu Lan Cha

Ingredients:
扁蓄 Bianxu, Common Knotgrass Herb (Herba Polygoni Avicularis) 10-15g
马兰根 Malangen, Indian Kalimeris Root (Radix Kalimeridis) 10-15g
茜草 Qiancao, India Madder Root and Rhizome (Radix et Rhizoma Rubiae) 10-15g
甘草 Gancao, Liquorice Root (Radix Glycyrrhizae) 10-15g

Directions: Pestle into coarse powder, decoct and drink.
Functions: To clear heat, cool blood, induce diuresis.
Indications: Chronic pyelitis and pyelonephritis.
Source:《中医杂志》 2:1985

37.17 蚕豆饮 Candou Yin

Ingredients:
数年陈蚕豆 Shunian Chen Candou, Old Broad Bean (Semen Viciae Fabae) 120g
红糖 Hongtang, Brown Sugar 90g

Directions: Decoct and drink.
Functions: To strengthen spleen and stomach, promote purgation, relieve swelling.
Indications: Dysuria, swelling of nephritis.
Source: 中医研究院《中医验方汇编》第一辑

37.18 蚕豆壳茶 Candouke Cha

Ingredients:
蚕豆壳 Candou Ke, Broadbean Testa (Testa Viciae Fabae) 30g

Directions: Toast to brown. Make as tea with boiling water.

Functions: To induce diuresis, dissolve damp.
Indications: Swelling of nephritis.
Source:《西安市中医验方汇编》

38 自汗、盗汗 For Spontaneous Sweating and Night Sweat

38.01 止汗饮 Zhihan Yin

Ingredients:
浮小麦 Fuxiaomai, Light Wheat (Fructus Tritici Levis) 30g
糯稻根 Nuodao Gen, Glutinous Rice Root (Radix Oryzae Glutinosae) 30g
Directions: Decoct and drink the decoction.
Functions: To clear deficient heat, ease the mind.
Indications: Spontaneous sweating, night sweating.
Source:《常见病验方研究参考资料》

38.02 毛桃干茶 Maotaogan Cha

Ingredients:
毛桃干 Maotaogan, Immature Peach (Fructus Persicae Immaturus), 10 pieces
Directions: Decoct and drink the decoction.
Functions: To stop sweating.
Indications: Night sweating.
Source:《常见病验方研究参考资料》

38.03 白术叶茶 Baizhuye Cha

Ingredients:
白术叶 Baizhu Ye, Largehead Atractylodes Leaf (Folium Atractylodis Macrocephalae) 3-5g
Directions: Make as tea with boiling water.
Functions: To reinforce *qi*, strengthen defensive resistance.

Indications: Spontaneous sweating.
Source: 《普济方》

38.04 沙参蔗汁饮 Shashen Zhezhi Yin

Ingredients:
沙参 Shashen, Ladybell Root (Radix Adenophorae) 15g
甘蔗汁 Ganzhe Zhi, Sugarcane Stem Juice (Succus Saccharum Sinensis Caulis) 50ml

Directions: Decoct ladybell root, add sugarcane stem joice before drinking the decoction. Take while warm.

Functions: To nourish yin, clear *xu*-fire, produce body fluid.

Indications: Afternoon fever, night sweating, hot sensation in palms, malar flush, irritability, insomnia, dry throat, red and dry tongue with little coating, thready and rapid pulse.

Source: 《百病饮食自疗》

38.05 浮麦麻根茶 Fumai Magen Cha

Ingredients:
浮小麦 Fuxiaomai, Light Wheat (Fructus Tritici Levis) 30g
麻黄根 Mahuang Gen, Ephedra Root (Radix Ephedrae) 6g

Directions: Pestle into coarse powder, decoct and drink as tea.

Functions: To reinforce heart, control sweating.

Indications: Night sweating.

Source: 《常见病验方研究参考资料》

38.06 葡萄茶 Putao Cha

Ingredients:
葡萄 Putao, European Grape Fruit (Fructus Vitis Viniferae)

Directions: Decoct and drink.

Functions: To strengthen tendons and bones, replenish *qi* and blood.

Indications: Deficiency of *qi* and blood, irritability, night sweating.
Source:《患者保健食谱》

38.07 糯稻根茶 Nuodaogen Cha

Ingredients:
糯稻根 Nuodao Gen, Glutinous Rice Root (Radix Oryzae Glutinosae) 50g
红枣 Hongzao, Chinese Date (Fructus Jujubae) 50g

Directions: Decoct and drink. Use daily for four or five days.
Functions: To astringe yin, reduce sweating.
Indications: Spontaneous sweating and night sweating post partum.
Source:《民间验方》

39 便秘 For Constipation

39.01 生军茶 Shengjun Cha

Ingredients:
生军 Shengjun, Rhubarb (Radix et Rhizoma Rhei) 4g
白糖 Baitang, White Sugar, desired amount

Directions: Make as tea with boiling water.
Functions: To clear heat, relieve dryness, loosen the bowels, soften stools, purge.
Indications: Constipation.
Source:《黑龙江中医杂志》2:1985

39.02 芝麻核桃茶 Zhima Hetao Cha

Ingredients:
黑芝麻 Heizhima, Black Sesame (Semen Sesami Nigrum) 30g
核桃仁 Hetao Ren, English Walnut Seed (Semen Juglandis) 60g

Directions: Pestle ingredients. Take one spoonful a day in the morning with warm boiled water.

Functions: To replenish *yin*, moisten dryness and promote purgation.
Indications: Habitual constipation.
Source:《山东省中医验方汇编》第一辑

39.03 决明苁蓉茶 Jueming Congrong Cha

Ingredients:

决明子 Jueming Zi, Cassia Seed (Semen Cassiae) 10g (parched and ground)

肉苁蓉 Roucongrong, Desert-Living Cistanche (Herba Cistanches) 10g

Directions: Make as tea with boiling water, filter, add honey before drinking.
Functions: To loosen bowels, promote purgation.
Indications: Habitual constipation, senile constipation.
Source:《经验方》

39.04 连翘茶 Lianqiao Cha

Ingredients:

连翘 Lianqiao, Weeping Forsythia Capsule (Fructus Forsythiae) 30g

蜂蜜 Fengmi, Honey **or**

白糖 Baitang, White Sugar, desired amount

Directions: Make as tea with boiling water.
Functions: To clear heat, purge as laxative.
Indications: Constipation of shi-heat.
Source:《山东中医杂志》5:1985

39.05 黄豆皮饮 Huangdoupi Yin

Ingredients:

黄豆皮 Huangdou Pi, Yellow Soybean Testa (Testa Sojae) 120g

Directions: Decoct and drink three or four times a day. One dose is for one day.

Functions: To send *qi* downward, clear heat, moisten bowels and promote purgation.
Indications: Constipation.
Source:《中医验方汇选》内科第二集

39.06 番泻叶茶 Fanxieye Cha

Ingredients:
番泻叶 Fanxie Ye, Senna Leaf (Folium Sennae) 5-10g
白糖 Baitang, White Sugar, desired amount
Directions: Make as tea with boiling water. Take one dose each day.
Functions: To clear heat, remove retention, promote water metabolism, relieve swelling.
Indications: Constipation of *shi*-type (*shi* means excess).
Source:《中医大辞典·中药分册》

39.07 蜂蜜茶 II Fengmi Cha II

Ingredients:
茶叶 Chaye, Tea Leaf (Folium Camelliae Sinensis) 3g
蜂蜜 Fengmi, Honey 2 ml
Directions: Make one cup of tea with boiling water. Drink after meal.
Functions: To quench thirst, nourish blood, moisten lung and strengthen kidney.
Indications: Constipation, diseases due to disorders of the spleen and stomach.
Source:《烟酒茶俗》

39.08 蜂蜜饮 Fengmi Yin

Ingredients:
蜂蜜 Fengmi, Honey 15g
青盐 Qingyan, Halite (Halitum) 3g

Directions: Make as tea with warm boiled water. Drink everyday before breakfast.
Functions: To moisten bowels, promote purgation.
Indications: Habitual constipation.
Source: 《中国药膳学》

39.09 熟军苦丁茶 Shujun Kuding Cha

Ingredients:
熟军 Shujun, Rhubarb (Radix et Rhizoma Rhei) 3g
苦丁茶 Kudingcha, Holly Leaf (Folium Ilicis Cornutae) 10g
茜草 Qiancao, India Madder Root and Rhizome (Radix et Rhizoma Rubiae) 10g
Directions: Make as tea with boiling water. Take one dose every day.
Functions: To clear heat, reduce liver fire.
Indications: Hypertension, constipation and headache.
Source: 《常见病验方研究参考资料》

40 甲状腺肿大 For Thyroid Enlargement

40.01 五鲜茶 Wuxian Cha

Ingredients:
海带 Haidai, Laminaria (Thallus Laminariae) 15g
海藻 Haizao, Seaweed (Sargassum) 15g
昆布 Kunbu, Kelp (Thallus Laminariae seu Eckloniae) 15g
紫菜 Zicai, Lavar (Porphyra) 15g
龙须菜 Longxucai, Gracilaria Verrucosa (Gracilariae Verrucosae) 15g
Directions: Decoct and drink the decoction.
Functions: To clear heat, dissolve phlegm, soften masses.
Indications: Goiter.
Source: 《上海市蓬莱区验方一辑》

40.02 海藻茶 Haizao Cha

Ingredients:
海藻 Haizao, Seaweed (Sargassum) 60g
冰糖 Bingtang, Crystal Sugar, desired amount

Directions: Decoct seaweed, filter, add crystal sugar before drinking.
Functions: To clear heat, dissolve phlegm, soften and resolve masses.
Indications: Goiter.
Source:《常见病验方研究参考资料》

40.03 海带茶 Haidai Cha

Ingredients:
海带 Haidai, Laminaria (Thallus Laminariae) 30g

Directions: Decoct and drink as tea.
Functions: To dissolve phlegm, soften masses.
Indications: Goiter.
Source:《医学衷中参西录》

41 癌症 For Cancer

41.01 二菱茶 Erling Cha

Ingredients:
菱茎叶 Ling Jingye, Water Caltrop Petiole and Leaf (Petiolus et Folium Trapae) 30-60g
菱角壳 Lingjiao Ke, Water Caltrop Peel (Pericarpium Trapae) 30-60g
薏苡仁 Yiyi Ren, Coix Seed (Semen Coicis) 30g

Directions: Decoct and drink the decoction.
Functions: To strengthen the spleen and stomach, stop diarrhea, resist cancer. Used as an auxiliary treatment for the cancers of the digestive system.
Source:《全国中草药汇编》

41.02 玄参麦冬茶 Xunshen Maidong Cha

Ingredients:
玄参 Xuanshen, Figwort Root (Radix Scrophulariae) 15g
麦冬 Maidong, Dwarf Lilyturf Tuber (Radix Ophiopogonis) 15g
山豆根 Shandougen, Vietnamese Sophora Root (Radix Sophorae Tonkinensis) 15g
茅根 Maogen, Lalang Grass Rhizome (Rhizoma Imperatae) 15g
生地黄 Sheng Dihuang, Dried Rehmannia Root (Radix Rehmanniae) 9g
银花 Yinhua, Honeysuckle Flower (Flos Lonicerae) 9g
黄芩 Huangqin, Baical Skullcap Root (Radix Scutellariae) 9g
北沙参 Beishashen, Coastal Glehnia Root (Radix Glehniae) 9g
白毛藤 Baimaoteng, Lyrate Nightshade (Herba Solani Lyrati) 30g
藕 Ou, Lotus Rhizome (Nelumbinis Rhizomatis) 30g
白花蛇舌草 Baihuasheshecao, Spreading Hedyotis (Herba Hedyotis Diffusae) 30g

Directions: Decoct, drink. Use one dose daily.

Functions: To nourish *yin*, clear heat, resist cancer. It is used as an adjunct in cancer treatment.

Source: 《抗癌中草药制剂》

41.03 健胃防癌茶 Jianwei Fangai Cha

Ingredients:
向日葵杵蕊 Xiangrikui Churui, Sunflower Stamen (Stamen Helianthi) 30g

Directions: Decoct and drink.

Functions: To strengthen stomach, regulate *qi*, inhibit the influence of nitrosamine on the digestive tract.

Indications: Gastric cancer and infected gastric anastomosis.

Source: 《科学画报》 7:1985

41.04 麦冬地黄饮 Maidong Dihuang Yin

Ingredients:
麦冬 Maidong, Dwarf Lilyturf Tuber (Radix Ophiopogonis) 10g
生地黄 Sheng Dihuang, Dried Rehmannia Root (Radix Rehmanniae) 15g
鲜藕汁 Xian Ou Zhi, Fresh Lotus Juice (Succus Nelumbinis Rhizomatis)

Directions: Decoct the first two, add fresh lotus juice before drinking.
Functions: To replenish *yin*, clear heat, produce body fluid.
Indications: Difficulty swallowing (cancer of the esophagus) accompanied by emaciation. Irritability, dizziness, dream-disturbed sleep, tinnitus, and malar flush resulting from *yin* deficiency and fire hyperactivity.
Source:《百病饮食自疗》

41.05 葵髓茶 Kuisui Cha

Ingredients:
向日葵茎髓 Xiangrikui Jingsui, Sunflower Pith (Medulla Helianthi) 30g

Directions: Decoct and drink.
Functions: To resist cancers, induce diuresis and treat urination disturbances.
Indications: Gastric cancer.
Source:《常见病中医临床手册》

41.06 藕橘饮 Ouju Yin

Ingredients:
陈皮 Chenpi, Dried Tangerine Peel (Pericarpium Citri Reticulatae) 5-10g
藕粉 Ou Fen, Lotus Rhizome Starch (Amylum Nelumbinis Rhizomatis)
白糖 Baitang, White Sugar, desired amount

Directions: Decoct dried tangerine peel, filter, save fluid. Mix lotus rhizome starch and white sugar into it and drink.

Functions: To relax chest, regulate *qi*, dissolve phlegm, produce body fluid.
Indications: Difficulty swallowing (cancer of the esophogus) with fullness and pain in the chest, dry throat, emaciation, red tongue with sticky coating, wiry and thready pulse.
Source:《百病饮食自疗》

42 疝气 For Hernia

42.01 青果石榴茶 Qingguo Shiliu Cha

Ingredients:
青果 Qingguo, Chinese White Olive (Fructus Canarii) 5-10g
石榴皮 Shiliupi, Pomegranate Rind (Pericarpium Granati) 5-10g
Directions: Cut into slices and make as tea with boiling water.
Functions: To clear heat, astringe intestines.
Indications: Hernia.
Source:《辽宁中医验方》

42.02 茴香茶 Huixiang Cha

Ingredients:
小茴香 Xiaohuixiang, Fennel (Fructus Foeniculi) 9-15g (wrapped in a gauze-bag)
Directions: Make as tea with boiling water.
Functions: To warm kidney, dispel cold, circulate *qi* and relieve pain.
Indications: Hernia. Only for a newly diagnosed case of short duration. Not suggested for chronic case with possibility of necrosis.
Source:《安徽卫生》 2:1960

42.03 荔橄茶 Li Gan Cha

Ingredients:
荔枝核 Lizhi He, Lychee Seed (Semen Litchi) 10g

橄榄核 Ganlan He, White Canarytree Putamen (Putamen Canarii) 10g

Directions: Pestle, and make as tea with boiling water.
Functions: To regulate *qi*, dissolve masses, relieve pain.
Indications: Hernia.
Source:《经验方》

42.04 双核饮 Shuanghe Yin

Ingredients:
荔枝核 Lizhi He, Lychee Seed (Semen Litchi) 10g
橘核 Ju He, Tangerine Seed (Semen Citri Reticulatae) 10g

Directions: Decoct and drink.
Functions: To warm liver and kidney, relieve hernia pain.
Indications: Hernia pain due to cold stagnated in liver meridian.
Source:《民间验方》

43 寄生虫病 For Parasitosis

43.01 南瓜籽茶 Nanguazi Cha

Ingredients:
生南瓜子 Sheng Nangua Zi, Pumpkin Seed (Semen Cucurbitae) 60g

Directions: Decoct and drink.
Functions: To expel parasites, promote lactation.
Indications: Parasitosis.
Source:《湖北验方选集》

43.02 乌梅饮 Wumei Yin

Ingredients:
乌梅 Wumei, Smoked Plum (Fructus Mume) 30g

Directions: Decoct and add 30g white or brown sugar before drinking.
Functions: To dispel roundworms.

Indications: Ascariasis.
Source:《开卷有益》4:9, 1984

43.03 椒梅茶 Jiao Mei Cha

Ingredients:

花椒 Huajiao, Pricklyash Peel (Pericarpium Zanthoxyli), 50 pieces

乌梅 Wumei, Smoked Plum (Fructus Mume), 10 plums

Directions: Pestle pricklyash peel and with smoked plum make as tea with boiling water.

Functions: To warm middle *jiao*, discharge roundworms, relieve pain.

Indications: Abdominal pain of biliary ascariasis.

Source:《常见病验方研究参考资料》

43.04 榧子茶 Feizi Cha

Ingredients:

榧子 Fei Zi, Grand Torreya Seed (Semen Torreyae) 20g

Directions: Toast well. Make as tea with boiling water. Use daily for five or seven days.

Functions: To expel parasites, remove retention.

Indications: Ancylostomiasis, oxyuriasis.

Source:《经验方》

43.05 绿豆大蒜饮 Ludou Dasuan Yin

Ingredients:

绿豆 Ludou, Mung Bean (Semen Phaseoli Radiati) 360g

大蒜 Dasuan, Garlic Bulb (Bulbus Allii), 2 bulbs (peeled)

Directions: Soak mung beans in water for three hours, decoct together with garlic bulb over low heat. Add sugar to the decoction, drink three times a day. Use every day for seven days as one course of treatment. Try two courses. If not effective, stop. Avoid using salt during treatment.

Functions: To clear heat, remove toxins, induce diuresis, reduce swelling.
Indications: Ascites of late stage schistosomiasis.
Source: 《浙江中医杂志》2:1960

43.06 祛钩虫茶 Qugouchong Cha

Ingredients:
马齿苋 Machixian, Purslane Herb (Herba Portulacae) 2,000g
食醋 Shicu, Vinegar 1,000 ml
淀粉 Dianfen, Starch, a little

Directions: Grind purslane herb, screen, add vinegar and starch, mix well and divide into 30g pieces. Use one piece each day, make as tea with boiling water. Drink before sleep.
Functions: To remove toxins, expel parasites.
Indications: Ancylostomiasis.
Source: 《中草药制剂选编》

44 口腔疾患 For the diseases in Oral Cavity

44.01 竹叶茶 I Zhuye Cha I

Ingredients:
淡竹叶 Danzhuye, Lophatherum Herb (Herba Lophatheri) 10g
苦丁茶 Kudingcha, Holly Leaf (Folium Ilicis Cornutae) 6g
甘草 Gancao, Liquorice Root (Radix Glycyrrhizae) 3g

Directions: Decoct, add crystal sugar to taste before drinking.
Functions: To clear heat, remove toxin and promote appetite.
Indications: Pyorrhea alveolaris.
Source: 《百病饮食自疗》

44.02 灶心土竹叶茶 Zaoxintu Zhuye Cha

Ingredients:

灶心土 Zaoxintu, Furnace Soil (Terra Flava Usta)

竹叶 Zhuye, Bamboo Leaf (Folium Phyllostachys Nigra) in equal amounts

Directions: Decoct furnace soil and settle, use the clear fluid to decoct bamboo leaves. Drink.

Functions: To warm middle *jiao*, dry damp, induce diuresis, clear heat.

Indications: Mouth ulcer due to *yin* deficiency of heart and spleen with *xu*-fire flaring up.

Source:《常见病中医临床手册》

44.03 青刺尖茶 Qingcijian Cha

Ingredients:

青刺尖 Qingcijian, Himalayan Prinsepia Leaf (Folium Prinsepiae Utilis) 15g

Directions: Make as tea with boiling water.

Functions: To clear heat, activate blood circulation, relieve swelling.

Indications: Toothache, periodontitis.

Source:《全国中草药汇编》

44.04 茶树根茶 Chashugen Cha

Ingredients:

茶树根 Chashu Gen, Tea Tree Root (Radix Camelliae Sinensis) 30g

Directions: Pestle into coarse powder, decoct and drink.

Functions: To clear heat, dissolve phlegm-damp.

Indications: Mouth ulcer.

Source:《救生苦海》

44.05 绿茶 Lucha

Ingredients:
绿茶 Lucha, Green Tea

Directions: Make tea with boiling water.

Functions: To prevent dental caries, refresh mind, promote spleen. To prevent hypersensitive dentin and the loss of teeth in elderly.

Source:《退休生活百科全书》

44.06 银花柿霜饮 Yinhua Shishuang Yin

Ingredients:
银花 Yinhua, Honeysuckle Flower (Flos Lonicerae) 10g
柿霜 Shishuang, Persimmon Sugar (Mannosum Kaki) 10g

Directions: Decoct honeysuckle flower, use the decocted fluid to dissolve persimmon sugar and take the mixture as tea.

Functions: To clear fire, remove toxins.

Indications: Pyorrhea alveolaris with halitosis, tongue ulcers, irritability, hot sensation in palms and soles, scant and yellow urine.

Source:《百病饮食自疗》

45 流脑、乙脑 For Epidemic Encephalitis and Encephalitis B

45.01 牛筋草茶 Niujincao Cha

Ingredients:
牛筋草 Niujincao, Goosegrass Herb (Herba Eleusines Indicae) 60g

Directions: Decoct and drink the decoction.

Functions: To clear heat, remove toxins and dissolve damp and to prevent Japanese encephalitis.

Source:《福建中草药》

45.02 生石膏荸荠汤 Shengshigao Biqi Tang

Ingredients:

鲜荸荠 Xian Biqi, Fresh Waternut Corm (Cormus Eleocharis Dulcis) 250g (peeled)

生石膏 Sheng Shigao, Gypsum (Gypsum Fibrosum) 30g (crushed)

冰糖 Bingtang, Crystal Sugar, desired amount

Directions: Decoct, drink.

Functions: To clear the heat, cool blood and to prevent epidemic meningitis.

Source:《民间验方》

45.03 贯仲板蓝根茶 Guanzhong Banlangen Cha

Ingredients:

贯仲 Guanzhong, Thickrhizome Wood Fern (Rhizoma Dryopteris Crassirhizomae) 24g

板蓝根 Banlangen, Isatis Root (Radix Isatidis) 15g

Directions: Pestle, decoct and drink. Use daily for 3-5 days.

Functions: To clear heat, remove toxins. To prevent epidemic meningitis.

Source:《中药临床手册》

45.04 银花甘草茶 Yinhua Gancao Cha

Ingredients:

银花 Yinhua, Honeysuckle Flower (Flos Lonicerae) 30g

甘草 Gancao, Liquorice Root (Radix Glycyrrhizae) 3g

Directions: Make as tea with boiling water.

Functions: To clear heat, promote detoxification and to prevent epidemic encephalitis.

Source:《中药临床手册》

46 流行性腮腺炎 For Epidemic Parotitis

46.01 玄参三花饮 Xuanshen Sanhua Yin

Ingredients:
玄参 Xuanshen, Figwort Root (Radix Scrophulariae) 15g
银花 Yinhua, Honeysuckle Flower (Flos Lonicerae) 10g
菊花 Juhua, Chrysanthemum Flower (Flos Chrysanthemi) 10g
红花 Honghua, Safflower (Flos Carthami) 3g
冰糖 Bingtang, Crystal Sugar, desired amount

Directions: Decoct the first four and add crystal sugar to the decoction before taking it.
Functions: To clear heat, remove toxins.
Indications: Mumps with fever, pain and swelling, constipation, yellow and scanty urine, red tongue with yellow coating, rolling and rapid pulse.
Source:《百病饮食自疗》

46.02 忍冬夏枯草茶 Rendong Xiakucao Cha

Ingredients:
忍冬藤 Rendongteng, Honeysuckle Stem (Caulis Lonicerae) 30g
夏枯草 Xiakucao, Common Selfheal Fruit-spike (Spica Prunellae) 30g
蒲公英 Pugongying, Dandelion (Herba Taraxaci) 15g
玄参 Xuanshen, Figwort Root (Radix Scrophulariae) 15g

Directions: Grind, decoct and drink.
Functions: To clear heat, remove toxin, soften and resolve hard mass.
Indications: Mumps (epidemic parotitis).
Source:《常见病验方研究参考资料》

46.03 板蓝根花茶 Banlangenhua Cha

Ingredients:
板蓝根 Banlangen, Isatis Root (Radix Isatidis) 30g

银花　Yinhua, Honeysuckle Flower (Flos Lonicerae) 10g
薄荷　Bohe, Peppermint (Herba Menthae) 5g

Directions: Pestle into coarse powder. Decoct and drink.
Functions: To clear heat, remove toxins and dispel wind.
Indications: Fever and pain of parotitis
Source:《经验方》

46.04 荸藕茅根饮 Bi Ou Maogen Yin

Ingredients:
荸荠　Biqi, Waternut Corm (Cormus Eleocharis Dulcis) 250g
鲜藕　Xian Ou, Fresh Lotus Rhizome (Nelumbinis Rhizomatis) 250g (peeled and sliced)
鲜茅根　Xian Maogen, Fresh Lalang Grass Rhizome (Rhizoma Imperatae) 250g

Directions: Decoct over high heat and then low heat for 20 minutes. Filter, cool, and drink.
Functions: To clear heat, cool blood, remove toxins.
Indications: Infantile diseases such as mumps, fever, etc., caused by excessive heat.
Source:《民间验方》

46.05 绿豆菜心饮 Ludou Caixin Yin

Ingredients:
绿豆　Ludou, Mung Bean (Semen Phaseoli Radiati) 60g
白菜心　Baicai Xin, the midpart of Pakchoi (Plantula Brassicae Chinensis), 2-3 pieces

Directions: Decoct mung beans until almost cooked. Add pakchoi and continue decocting for 20 minutes. Drink. Take one or two times a day.
Functions: To clear heat, treat inflammation.
Indications: Mumps.

Source:《浙江中医》6:262, 1982

46.06 银花薄黄饮 Yinhua Bo Huang Yin

Ingredients:
银花 Yinhua, Honeysuckle Flower (Flos Lonicerae) 15g
薄荷 Bohe, Peppermint (Herba Menthae) 6g
黄芩 Huangqin, Baical Skullcap Root (Radix Scutellariae) 3g

Directions: Decoct, add crystal sugar 15g before drinking. Use one dose daily.
Functions: To clear heat, promote detoxification, reduce swelling.
Indications: Common cold, mumps.
Source:《百病饮食自疗》

47 麻疹、水痘 For Measles and Chickenpox

47.01 二根茶 Ergen Cha

Ingredients:
鲜芦根 Xian Lugen, Fresh Reed Rhizome (Rhizoma Phragmitis) 50g
鲜白茅根 Xian Baimao Gen, Fresh Lalang Grass Rhizome (Rhizoma Imperatae) 50g

Directions: Decoct and drink the decoction.
Functions: To clear heat, cool blood, produce body fluid.
Indications: Fever and dehydration associated with measles.
Source:《百病中医自我疗养丛书·麻疹》

47.02 牛蒡子芦根茶 Niubangzi Lugen Cha

Ingredients:
牛蒡子 Niubang Zi, Great Burdock Achene (Fructus Arctii) 10g (stir-baked)
樱桃核 Yingtao He, Cherry Stone (Nut Pseudocerasi) 10g

鲜芦根 Xian Lugen, Fresh Reed Rhizome (Rhizoma Phragmitis) 30g

Directions: Grind great burdock achene and cherry stone. Cut fresh reed rhizome. Decoct and drink the decoction.

Functions: To clear heat, quicken the eruptions of measles, remove toxins and treat sore throat.

Indications: Early stage of measles.

Source:《百病中医自我疗养丛书·麻疹》

47.03 生地青果茶 Shengdi Qingguo Cha

Ingredients:

生地黄 Sheng Dihuang, Dried Rehmannia Root (Radix Rehmanniae) 30g

青果 Qingguo, Chinese White Olive (Fructus Canarii), 5 pieces

Directions: Decoct, drink.

Functions: To clear heat, remove toxins, nourish *yin* and treat throat diseases.

Indications: Sore throat in measles.

Source:《百病中医自我疗养丛书·麻疹》

47.04 白头翁茶 Baitouweng Cha

Ingredients:

白头翁 Baitouweng, Chinese Pulsatilla Root (Radix Pulsatillae) 30g

Directions: Decoct, drink.

Functions: To clear heat, remove toxins, cool blood, stop dysentery.

Indications: Dysentery in measles with persistent fever post skin rash, abdominal pain, tenesmus, pus and blood in stools.

Source:《百病饮食自疗》

47.05 西河柳饮 Xiheliu Yin

Ingredients:

西河柳 Xiheliu, Chinese Tamarish Tops (Cacumen Tamaricis) 10g

银花 Yinhua, Honeysuckle Flower (Flos Lonicerae) 10g

Directions: Decoct and drink.
Functions: To clear heat, remove toxins and promote eruptions in measles.
Indications: The eruption stage of measles.
Source:《百病饮食自疗》

47.06 赤柽柳茶 Chichengliu Cha

Ingredients:
赤柽柳 Chichengliu, Chinese Tamarish Tops (Cacumen Tamaricis)

Directions: Cut and dry. Use 4-5g each time, decoct and drink.
Functions: To induce sweating in treating exterior syndromes, remove toxins, promote eruptions of measles.
Indications: Measles.
Source:《本草汇言》

47.07 车杏枇杷茶 Che Xing Pipa Cha

Ingredients:
车前子 Cheqian Zi, Plantain Seed (Semen Plantaginis) 10g
杏仁 Xing Ren, Apricot Seed (Semen Armeniacae Amarum) 3g
枇杷叶 Pipa Ye, Loquat Leaf (Folium Eriobotryae) 6g

Directions: Decoct and drink.
Functions: To clear heat, promote lung in dispersing, stop coughing.
Indications: Cough of measles.
Source:《百病中医自我疗养丛书·麻疹》

47.08 青果芦根茶 Qingguo Lugen Cha

Ingredients:
青果 Qingguo, Chinese White Olive (Fructus Canarii) 30g
芦根 Lugen, Reed Rhizome (Rhizoma Phragmitis) 60g

Directions: Decoct and drink.

Functions: To clear heat, remove toxins, produce body fluid and treat throat diseases.
Indications: Fever and sore throat in early chickenpox.
Source:《常见病中医临床手册》

47.09 杏仁麦冬饮 Xingren Maidong Yin

Ingredients:
杏仁 Xing Ren, Apricot Seed (Semen Armeniacae Amarum) 6g (peeled, tip removed, ground)
麦冬 Maidong, Dwarf Lilyturf Tuber (Radix Ophiopogonis) 10g
Directions: Decoct by bringing to the boil and then simmer for 15 minutes. Drink.
Functions: To promote the lung in dispersing, stop coughing, nourish *yin* and produce body fluid.
Indications: Cough and dry throat in the recovery stage of measles.
Source:《百病饮食自疗》

47.10 胡萝卜饮 Huluobo Yin

Ingredients:
胡萝卜 Huluobo, Carrot (Radix Dauci Sativae) 60g
Directions: Cut into small pieces, decoct and drink.
Functions: To clear heat, remove toxins, moisten intestines to promote purgation, strengthen stomach, expel parasites.
Indications: Fever of measles and chickenpox, dysentery, fullness in chest, constipation, tapeworm.
Source:《岭南草药志》

47.11 胡萝卜芫荽饮 Huluobo Yuansui Yin

Ingredients:
胡萝卜 Huluobo, Carrot (Radix Dauci Sativae) 120g

芫荽　Yuansui, Coriander (Herba Coriandri) 90g
荸荠　Biqi, Waternut Corm (Cormus Eleocharis Dulcis) 60g

Directions: Decoct and drink.

Functions: To clear heat, promote eruption of measles and remove toxins.

Indications: Measles.

Source:《岭南草药志》

47.12 茅根荠菜茶　Maogen Jicai Cha

Ingredients:
白茅根　Baimao Gen, Imperata Rhizome (Rhizoma Imperatae) 50-100g
荠菜　Jicai, Shepherds Purse (Herba Capsellae) 50-100g

Directions: Decoct and drink.

Functions: To clear heat, promote eruptions of measles.

Indications: Measles.

Source:《常用中草药》

47.13 浮萍茶　Fuping Cha

Ingredients:
紫背浮萍　Zibeifuping, Common Ducksmeat Herb (Herba Spirodelae)

Directions: Wash. Dry in the sun. Use 5-10g each time and make as tea with boiling water.

Functions: To induce diaphoresis, eliminate wind, clear heat, promote detoxification.

Indications: Measles.

Source:《常见病验方研究参考资料》

47.14 柴芦茶　Chai Lu Cha

Ingredients:
柴胡　Chaihu, Chinese Thorowax Root (Radix Bupleuri) 6g

芦根 Lugen, Reed Rhizome (Rhizoma Phragmitis) 15g

Directions: Pestle into coarse powder. Make as tea with boiling water.

Functions: To clear heat, treat exterior syndromes and to prevent epidemic measles.

Source:《常见病验方研究参考资料》

47.15 荸荠茅根茶 Biqi Maogen Cha

Ingredients:
荸荠 Biqi, Waternut Corm (Cormus Eleocharis Dulcis) 100g
白茅根 Baimao Gen, Imperata Rhizome (Rhizoma Imperatae) 100g

Directions: Decoct and drink.

Functions: To clear heat, cool blood, remove toxins.

Indications: Measles.

Source:《常用中草药》

47.16 甜菜茶 Tiancai Cha

Ingredients:
甜菜叶 Tiancai Ye, Common Beet Leaf (Folium Betae) 100g

Directions: Decoct and drink.

Functions: To dispel wind, clear heat, remove toxin and to prevent measles.

Source:《常见病验方研究参考资料》

47.17 梨皮茶 Lipi Cha

Ingredients:
梨皮 Li Pi, Pear Pericarp (Pericarpium Pyri) 30g (cut into thread-like pieces)
白糖 Baitang, White Sugar, desired amount

Directions: Make as tea with boiling water.

Functions: To produce body fluid, remove heart fire and moisten lung.

Indications: Measles with cough, loss of voice, and sore throat.
Source:《百病中医自我疗养丛书·麻疹》

47.18 紫草根茶 Zicaogen Cha

Ingredients:
紫草根 Zicao Gen, Gromwell Root (Radix Arnebiae seu Lithospermi) 15g
Directions: Pestle into coarse powder, make as tea with boiling water, add brown sugar to taste before drinking.
Functions: To moisten bowels, remove toxins, cool blood.
Indications: Measles with constipation.
Source:《常见病验方研究参考资料》

47.19 莲芯茶 Lianxin Cha

Ingredients:
连翘 Lianqiao, Weeping Forsythia Capsule (Fructus Forsythiae) 10g
莲子心 Lianzi Xin, Lotus Plumule (Plumula Nelumbinis) 2g
麦冬 Maidong, Dwarf Lilyturf Tuber (Radix Ophiopogonis) 10g
Directions: Pestle into coarse powder, make as tea with boiling water.
Functions: To clear heart fire, relieve irritability and nourish *yin*.
Indications: Mouth ulcer due to the excessive heart fire post measles.
Source:《百病中医自我疗养丛书·麻疹》

47.20 麦冬梅枝茶 Maidong Meizhi Cha

Ingredients:
麦冬 Maidong, Dwarf Lilyturf Tuber (Radix Ophiopogonis) 10g
梅枝 Mei Zhi, Plum Twig (Ramulus Mume) 10g
Directions: Decoct and drink. One dose is for a day.
Functions: To clear heat, remove toxins and to prevent measles.
Source:《绍兴中医验方单方集》

47.21 贯仲丝瓜络茶 Guanzhong Sigualuo Cha

Ingredients:
贯仲 Guanzhong, Thickrhizome Wood Fern (Rhizoma Dryopteris Crassirhizomae) 10g
丝瓜络 Sigua Luo, Luffa Vegetable Sponge (Retinervus Luffae Fructus) 15g

Directions: Pestle, decoct and drink.

Functions: To clear heat, remove toxins, cool blood and to prevent and treat measles.

Source:《实用中药学》

47.22 银蝉饮 Yin Chan Yin

Ingredients:
银花 Yinhua, Honeysuckle Flower (Flos Lonicerae) 6g
蝉蜕 Chantui, Cicada Slough (Periostracum Cicadae) 1.5g
前胡 Qianhu, Hogfennel Root (Radix Peucedani) 3g
冰糖 Bingtang, Crystal Sugar 15g

Directions: Decoct and drink.

Functions: To promote eruptions.

Indications: Eruptive stage of measles.

The eruptive stage is about three days, beginning with the appearance of eruptions and ending with the eruptions all over the body and on palms and soles, accompanied by high fever, irritability, thirst, cough, loose stools, red tongue with yellow coating, forceful and rapid pulse, purple venule of index finger.

Source:《百病饮食自疗》

47.23 鲜生地饮 Xianshengdi Yin

Ingredients:
鲜生地 Xian Sheng Dihuang, Fresh Rehmannia Root (Radix Rehmanniae)

Directions: Cut into small pieces, decoct and drink.
Functions: To clear heat, cool blood, replenish *yin*, produce body fluid.
Indications: The recovery stage of measles.
Source:《百病饮食自疗》

47.24 鲜萝卜饮 Xianluobo Yin

Ingredients:
鲜白萝卜　Xian Bailuobo, Fresh Radish Root (Radix Raphani)
Directions: Decoct and drink.
Functions: To clear heat, cool blood, replenish *yin*, produce body fluid.
Indications: Recovery stage measles.
Source:《百病饮食自疗》

47.25 腊梅绿豆饮 Lamei L(dou Yin

Ingredients:
腊梅花　Lamei Hua, Wintersweet Flower (Flos Chimonanthi Praecocis) 15g
银花　Yinhua, Honeysuckle Flower (Flos Lonicerae) 15g
绿豆　Ludou, Mung Bean (Semen Phaseoli Radiati) 30g
Directions: Decoct the first two. Save the fluid. Boil mung beans, when cooked, mix with the above fluid. Add crystal sugar before taking the mixture. Use two or three doses a day.
Functions: To clear heat, remove toxins, cool blood, produce body fluid.
Indications: Severe chickenpox with large crops of papules, high fever, irritability, thirst, flushed face, tongue ulcers, scant and dark yellow urine, dry yellow thin tongue coating, surging rapid pulse.
Source:《百病饮食自疗》

47.26 芦根茶 Lugen Cha

Ingredients:
芦根　Lugen, Reed Rhizome (Rhizoma Phragmitis) 50g

Directions: Decoct and drink.
Functions: To clear heat, remove toxins.
Indications: Dry throat in early stage measles.
Source: 《实用中药学》

47.27 芦菊茶 Lu Ju Cha

Ingredients:
芦根 Lugen, Reed Rhizome (Rhizoma Phragmitis) 60g
野菊花 Yejuhua, Wild Chrysanthemum Flower (Flos Chrysanthemi Indici) 10g
Directions: Decoct and drink.
Functions: To clear heat, promote detoxification, induce diuresis, dissolve damp and to prevent and treat chickenpox.
Source: 《常见病中医临床手册》

47.28 盐梅茶 Yan Mei Cha

Ingredients:
乌梅 Wumei, Smoked Plum (Fructus Mume), 5 plums
食盐 Shiyan, Salt, a little
白糖 Baitang, White Sugar, desired amount
Directions: Make as tea with boiling water.
Functions: To clear heat, nourish *yin* and stop sweating.
Indications: Profuse sweating in recovery stage of measles.
Source: 《百病中医自我疗养丛书·麻疹》

48 疟疾 For Malaria

48.01 水蜈蚣茶 Shuiwugong Cha

Ingredients:
水蜈蚣 Shuiwugong, Shortleaf Kyllinga Herb (Herba Kyllingae) 30g
Directions: Pestle. Decoct. Drink one or two hours before the attack. Use

20g, make as tea with boiling water.
Functions: Prevent recurrence of malaria, reduce swelling and remove toxins.
Indications: Malaria.
Source: 《常用中草药》

48.02 虎杖叶茶 Huzhangye Cha
Ingredients:
虎杖叶 Huzhang Ye, Giant Knotweed Leaf (Folium Polygoni Cuspidati) 50g
Directions: Decoct and drink.
Functions: To clear heat, dissolve damp, activate blood circulation and remove toxins.
Indications: Malaria.
Source: 《民间验方》

48.03 马兰糖饮 Malan Tang Yin
Ingredients:
马兰 Malan, Indian Kalimeris Herb (Herba Kalimeridis) 30g
白糖 Baitang, White Sugar 15g
Directions: Make as tea with boiling water.
Functions: To clear heat, remove toxins.
Indications: Intermittent chills and fever of malaria.
Source: 《圣济总录》

48.04 葵花茶 Kuihua Cha
Ingredients:
向日葵花瓣 Xiangrikui Huaban, Sunflower Flower (Flos Helianthi) 10g
Directions: Make as tea with boiling water.
Functions: To clear heat, treat malaria.
Indications: Summer diseases, malaria.

Source:《常见病验方研究参考资料》

48.05 杨桃速溶饮 Yangtao Surongyin

Ingredients:
鲜杨桃 Xian Yangtao, Common Averrhoa Fruit (Fructus Averrhoae Carambolae) 1,000g
白糖 Baitang, White Sugar 500g

Directions: Cut into small pieces. Wrap with gauze. Twist to get the juice. Concentrate the juice over a high heat and then simmer to a thick paste. Remove from heat, cool, mix white sugar into the paste. Dry, crush, and store in a bottle. Use 10g each time, melt with boiling water and drink it. Take three doses a day.

Functions: To inhibit malarial parasite, prevent malaria and relieve splenomegaly.

Indications: Splenomegaly.

Source:《福建民间草药》

49 小儿夜啼、夜尿 For Night Crying of Infants, Enuresis Nocturna in Children

49.01 竹叶茶 II Zhuye Cha II

Ingredients:
鲜竹叶 Xian Zhuye, Fresh Bamboo Leaf (Folium Phyllostachys Nigra) 15g

Directions: Make as tea with boiling water.

Functions: To induce diuresis, clear the heart fire, relieve irritability and remove the wind-heat of the upper *jiao*.

Indications: Scanty and dark yellow urine with pain in urination, irritability, thirst, ulcer on the tongue, infantile night crying caused by the heart fire. It can be used as a normal tea to promote digestion.

Source:《祝您健康》6:38, 1988

49.02 红枣茶 II Hongzao Cha II

Ingredients:
茶叶 Chaye, Tea Leaf (Folium Camelliae Sinensis) 5g
红枣 Hongzao, Chinese Date (Fructus Jujubae), 10 pieces
白糖 Baitang, White Sugar 10g

Directions: Make tea with boiling water. Decoct Chinese dates. Add the tea and white sugar to the decoction before drinking it.

Functions: To replenish blood and essence, strengthen spleen, harmonize stomach.

Indications: Pediatric enuresis.

Source: 《烟酒茶俗》

49.03 灯心草茶 Dengxincao Cha

Ingredients:
灯心草 Dengxincao, Common Rush (Medulla Junci) 2g
淡竹叶 Danzhuye, Lophatherum Herb (Herba Lophatheri), 10 leaves

Directions: Make as tea with boiling water. Feed tea to baby.

Functions: To clear heart fire, relieve irritability.

Indications: Baby night crying due to heart fire.

Source: 《实用中药学》

49.04 苏连茶 Su Lian Cha

Ingredients:
紫苏叶 Zisu Ye, Perilla Leaf (Folium Perillae) 3g
黄连 Huanglian, Coptis Root (Rhizoma Coptidis) 1g

Directions: Make as tea with boiling water.

Functions: To reduce heart fire, calm mind.

Indications: Baby crying at night due to heart fire.

Source: 《民间验方》

50 缺乳、回乳 For Lack of Lactation and Delactation

50.01 山楂麦芽茶 Shanzha Maiya Cha

Ingredients:
山楂 Shanzha, Hawthorn Fruit (Fructus Crataegi) 20g
炒麦芽 Chao Mai Ya, Parched Germinated Barley (Fructus Hordei Germinatus) 60g

Directions: Decoct and drink the decoction.

Functions: To promote digestion, stop lactation. It is applicable to the mother who wishes to stop lactation.

Source:《百病中医自我疗养丛书》

50.02 赤小豆饮 Chixiaodou Yin

Ingredients:
赤小豆 Chixiaodou, Rice Bean (Semen Phaseoli) 250g

Directions: Decoct and drink. Take two doses morning and evening, Use everyday for three or five days.

Functions: To alleviate milk retention, regulate *qi* and remove toxins.

Indications: Lactation deficiency caused by *qi* and blood deficiency, *qi* stagnation or milk retention.

Source:《赤脚医生杂志》 12:1957

50.03 丝瓜芝麻核桃饮 Sigua Zhima Hetao Yin

Ingredients:
丝瓜 Sigua, Towel Gourd (Luffae Cylindricae), 10 pieces
黑芝麻 Heizhima, Black Sesame (Semen Sesami Nigrum) 120g
红糖 Hongtang, Brown Sugar 60g
核桃仁 Hetao Ren, English Walnut Seed (Semen Juglandis) 60g

Directions: Pestle into powder. Use 6g each day. Decoct and drink.

Functions: To remove obstruction of meridian, promote lactation.

Indications: Lactation insufficiency post partum.
Source:《山西省中医验方秘方汇集》第一辑

51 月经不调 For Irregular Menses

51.01 山楂向日葵饮 Shanzha Xiangrikui Yin
Ingredients:
山楂 Shanzha, Hawthorn Fruit (Fructus Crataegi) 30g
向日葵籽 Xiangrikui Zi, Sunflower Seed (Semen Helianthi) 15g
Directions: Bake, pestle, decoct, and add 30g brown sugar before drinking the decoction.
Functions: To activate blood circulation, and as an analgesic.
Indications: Dysmenorrhea. (Before the menstruation starts, take once a day for two days in succession.)
Source:《常见病验方研究参考资料》

51.02 月季花汤 Yuejihua Tang
Ingredients:
月季花 Yueji Hua, Chinese Rose Flower (Flos Rosae Chinensis), 3-5 Flowers (blossomed)
Directions: Decoct over low heat. Add crystal sugar to taste before drinking the decoction.
Functions: To activate blood circulation, regulate menstruation, reduce swelling.
Indications: Amenorrhea and dysmenorrhea due to blood stasis and swelling and pain due to carbuncles, boils, ulcers and traumatic injury.
Source:《本草纲目》

51.03 四炭止漏茶 Sitan Zhilou Cha

Ingredients:
乌梅炭 Wumei Tan, Tharred Smoked Plum (Fructus Mume) 500g
棕榈炭 Zonglu Tan, Carbinized Fortune Windmillpalm Petiole (Petiolus Trachycarpi Carbonisatus) 500g
地榆炭 Diyu Tan, Carbonized Burnet Root (Radix Sanguisorbae Carbonisatus) 500g
干姜炭 Gan Jiang Tan, Charred Ginger (Rhizoma Zingiberis) 750g

Directions: Grind the first three into powder and sift. Decoct ginger for 30 minutes and filter. Add water to decoct again for 20 minutes, filter, squeeze the decocted charred ginger to get juice, mix the juice with the previously prepared decoctions. Make a paste with the powder and the decoction. Dry and cut into 9g pieces. Use one piece each time, make as tea with boiling water. Take twice a day.

Functions: To cool blood, stop bleeding, warm the middle *jiao*, regulate *qi* circulation.

Indications: Menorrhagia.

Source:《中草药制剂选编》

51.04 苎麻根饮 Zhumagen Yin

Ingredients:
鲜苎麻根 Xian Zhuma Gen, Root of Ramie (Radix Boehmeriae) 250g
黄砂糖 Huangshatang, Brown Granulated Sugar 30g

Directions: Pestle the root of ramie and use the juice to make as tea with boiling water. Add brown granulated sugar before drinking.

Functions: To clear heat, stop bleeding.

Indications: Functional uterine bleeding due to pathogenic heat.

Source: 重庆《祖国医学采风录》第一集

51.05 卷柏茶 Juanbai Cha

Ingredients:
卷柏 Huanbai, Spikemoss (Herba Selaginellae) 15g

Directions: Pestle into coarse powder. Make as tea with boiling water.
Functions: To activate blood circulation, stop bleeding.
Indications: Functional uterine bleeding.
Source:《常见病验方研究参考资料》

51.06 芹菜大戟饮 Qincai Daji Yin

Ingredients:
干芹菜 Gan Qincai, Dried Celery (Herba Apii) 30g
大戟 Daji, Knoxia Root (Radix Knoxiae) 15g

Directions: Decoct and drink.
Functions: To dissolve blood stasis.
Indications: Premenstrual pain. (Begin to take four or five days before menstruation.)
Source:《民间灵验便方》

51.07 松树皮茶 Songshupi Cha

Ingredients:
油松树树皮 Yousongshu Shupi, Chinese Pine Bark (Cortex Pini Tabulaeformis) 20-30g

Directions: Decoct and drink.
Functions: To dispel wind, dissolve damp, remove blood stasis.
Indications: Amenorrhea due to blood stasis.
Source:《本草纲目拾遗》

51.08 青蒿丹皮茶 Qinghao Danpi Cha

Ingredients:
青蒿 Qinghao, Sweet Wormwood Herb (Herba Artemisiae Chinghao) 6g

丹皮 Danpi, Tree Peony Bark (Cortex Moutan Radicis) 6g
茶叶 Chaye, Tea Leaf (Folium Camelliae Sinensis) 3g

Directions: Make as tea with boiling water. Add 15g crystal sugar before drinking.

Functions: To clear damp-heat.

Indications: Menstruation to early due to *shi*-heat (*shi* means excess) with copious dark, thick flow. Irritability, oliguria, morbid leukorrhea with foul smell, red tongue with a thick yellow coating, rapid and forceful pulse.

Source: 《百病饮食自疗》

51.09 刺玫根茶 Cimeigen Cha

Ingredients:
刺玫根 Cimei Gen, Dahurian Rosa Root (Radix Rosae Davuricae) 30g

Directions: Decoct and drink.

Functions: To clear heat, remove stasis, cool blood, promote hemostasis.

Indications: Functional uterine bleeding.

Source: 《中国医药报》225:1987

51.10 柿霜桑椹饮 Shishuang Sangshen Yin

Ingredients:
桑椹 Sangshen, Mulberry Fruit (Fructus Mori) 20g
柿霜 Shishuang, Persimmon Sugar (Mannosum Kaki) 10g

Directions: Decoct mulberry fruit, add persimmon sugar before drinking the decoction. Take three doses a day.

Functions: To reinforce *yin*, moisten dryness.

Indications: Hematemesis and epistaxis before or during menstruation, dizziness, tinnitus, afternoon fever, cough, hot sensation in palms and soles, irregular menstruation with little flow, red tongue, thready and rapid pulse.

Source:《百病饮食自疗》

51.11 红高粱花茶 Honggaolianghua Cha

Ingredients:

红高粱花 Honggaoliang Hua, Sorghum Flower (Flos Sorghi Vulgaris)

Directions: Decoct and add brown sugar to taste before drinking the decoction.

Functions: To replenish blood, dispel cold, regulate menstruation.

Indications: Amenorrhea due to blood deficiency and effects of cold.

Source:《常见病验方研究参考资料》

51.12 红糖姜枣茶 Hongtang Jiang Zao Cha

Ingredients:

红糖 Hongtang, Brown Sugar 60g

大枣 Dazao, Chinese Date (Fructus Jujubae) 60g

生姜 Sheng Jiang, Fresh Ginger (Rhizoma Zingiberis Recens) 20g

Directions: Decoct and drink.

Functions: To warm the meridians, activate blood circulation.

Indications: Amenorrhea due to blood deficiency and affection of cold.

Source:《中国药膳学》

51.13 香附茶 Xiangfu Cha

Ingredients:

生香附子 Sheng Xiangfuzi, Nutgrass Galingale Rhizome (Rhizoma Cyperi) 6g

炒香附子 Chao Xiangfuzi, Parched Nutgrass Galingale Rhizome (Rhizoma Cyperi) 6g

Directions: Pestle into coarse powder, decoct and add brown sugar to taste before drinking.

Functions: To activate *qi* and blood circulation, regulate menstruation.

Indications: Amenorrhea due to *qi* stagnation and blood stasis.
Source:《常见病验方研究参考资料》

51.14 姜艾红糖饮 Jiang Ai Hongtang Yin

Ingredients:
生姜 Sheng Jiang, Fresh Ginger (Rhizoma Zingiberis Recens) 6g
艾叶 Aiye, Argyi Wormwood Leaf (Folium Artemisiae Argyi) 6g
红糖 Hongtang, Brown Sugar 15g

Directions: Decoct and drink. Or make as tea with boiling water.
Functions: To regulate menstruation, relieve pain.
Indications: Delayed menstruation caused by *shi*-cold manifested as scant dark flow, cold pain in lower abdomen, cold extremities, sensitivity to cold, blue-white complexion, thin white tongue coating, deep and slow pulse.
Source:《百病饮食自疗》

51.15 桑叶苦丁茶 Sangye Kuding Cha

Ingredients:
冬桑叶 Dongsangye, Mulberry Leaf (Folium Mori) 15g
苦丁茶 Kudingcha, Holly Leaf (Folium Ilicis Cornutae) 15g

Directions: Decoct and add crystal sugar to taste before drinking.
Functions: To pacify liver fire.
Indications: Hematemesis and epistaxis before or during menstruation accompanied with dizziness, tinnitus, irritability, distending pain in hypochondrium, bitter taste in mouth, red tongue with a yellow coating.
Source:《百病饮食自疗》

51.16 桂姜红糖饮 Gui Jiang Hongtang Cha

Ingredients:
生姜 Sheng Jiang, Fresh Ginger (Rhizoma Zingiberis Recens) 10g

桂枝 Guizhi, Cassia Twig (Ramulus Cinnamomi) 10g
红糖 Hongtang, Brown Sugar 15g

Directions: Decoct and drink. Take two doses a day.
Functions: To dispel cold, stop pain.
Indications: Delayed menstruation caused by *shi*-cold with dark scant flow, cold pain in abdomen, cold extremities, blue white complexion, thin white tongue coating, deep slow and tight pulse.
Source:《百病饮食自疗》

51.17 清心止血饮 Qingxin Zhixue Yin

Ingredients:
生地黄 Sheng Dihuang, Dried Rehmannia Root (Radix Rehmanniae) 60g
藕节 Ou Jie, Lotus Node (Nodus Nelumbinis Rhizomatis) 60g
白茅根 Baimao Gen, Imperata Rhizome (Rhizoma Imperatae) 60g

Directions: Decoct and add crystal sugar to taste before drinking.
Functions: To clear heat, cool blood.
Indications: Functional uterine bleeding due to heat in blood.
Source:《百病饮食自疗》

51.18 黑白茶 Hei Bai Cha

Ingredients:
墨旱莲 Mohanlian, Eclipta (Herba Ecliptae) 30g
白茅根 Baimao Gen, Imperata Rhizome (Rhizoma Imperatae) 30g
苦瓜根 Kugua Gen, Momordica Charantia Root (Radix Momordicae Charantiae) 15g

Directions: Decoct and add some crystal sugar before drinking.
Functions: To cool blood, stop bleeding.
Indications: Menorrhagia due to heat in blood, accompanied by irritability, thirst, red face, dry lips, scant urine, red tongue with yellow

coating, rolling and rapid pulse.
Source:《百病饮食自疗》

51.19 黑豆红花饮 Heidou Honghua Yin
Ingredients:
黑豆 Heidou, Black Soybean (Semen Sojae Nigrum) 30g
红花 Honghua, Safflower (Flos Carthami) 6g
红糖 Hongtang, Brown Sugar 30g
Directions: Decoct for 30-40 minutes and drink.
Functions: To activate blood circulation, normalize menstruation.
Indications: Amenorrhea with cold pain and distention in lower abdomen.
Source:《食物与治疗》

51.20 枣树根皮茶 Zaoshugenpi Cha
Ingredients:
红枣树根皮 Hongzaoshu Genpi, Root-Bark of Chinese Date (Cortex Jujuba)
Directions: Decoct and drink.
Functions: To warm middle *jiao*, replenish blood.
Indications: Amenorrhea.
Source:《广西中医验方秘方汇集》

51.21 莲蓬茶 Lianpeng Cha
Ingredients:
莲蓬壳 Lianpengke, Lotus Receptacle (Receptaculum Nelumbinis) 20g
Directions: Place in a well-sealed double boiler. Cover with a sheet of white paper. Use mud to seal again. Calcine until the white paper becomes burnt yellow. Remove from the boiler. Cool. Pestle the calcined material into coarse powder. Wrap in a gauze bag, add brown sugar to taste and make as tea with boiling water.

Functions: To remove stasis, stop bleeding.
Indications: Functional uterine bleeding, menorrhagia.
Source:《常见病验方研究参考资料》

51.22 橘叶荔梗茶 Juye Ligeng Cha

Ingredients:
鲜橘叶 Xian Juye, Fresh Tangerine Leaf (Folium Citri Reticulatae) 20g
荔梗 Ligeng, Litchi Branch (Ramusculus Litchi) 10g
红糖 Hongtang, Brown Sugar 15g

Directions: Make as tea with boiling water, cover and let sit for 15 minutes. Drink the tea.
Functions: To promote circulation of liver *qi*, regulate menstruation.
Indications: Irregular menstruation due to liver *qi* stagnation, manifested as early or late period with a non-smooth flow and painful breasts, lower abdomen and hypochondrium pain, sighing, and wiry pulse.
Source:《百病饮食自疗》

51.23 薏苡根饮 Yiyigen Yin

Ingredients:
薏苡根 Yiyi Gen, Coix Root (Radix Coicis) 30g

Directions: Decoct and drink.
Functions: To clear heat, dissolve damp.
Indications: Amenorrhea, liver pain, hematuria.
Source:《海上方》

52 阴道炎、带下 For Vaginitis and Abnormal Leukorrhagia

52.01 向日葵茎饮 Xiangrikuijing Yin

Ingredients:
向日葵茎 Xiangrikui Jing, Sunflower Stem (Caulis Helianthi) 30g (peeled)

Directions: Decoct, add white sugar to taste before drinking.
Functions: To strengthen the spleen by reinforcing its *yang*.
Indications: Profuse leukorrhea, pale complexion, cold extremities, listlessness, poor appetite, loose stools, pedal edema, pale tongue with white and sticky coating, weak pulse due to the spleen *yang* deficiency.
Source:《全国中草药汇编》

52.02 扁豆山药茶 Biandou Shanyao Cha

Ingredients:

白扁豆 Baibiandou, White Hyacinth Bean (Semen Lablab Album) 20g
山药 Shanyao, Common Yam Rhizome (Rhizoma Dioscoreae) 20g

Directions: Toast beans until they are slightly burnt and pestle into coarse powder. Slice yam and decoct both ingredients. Add white sugar to taste before drinking.
Functions: To strengthen spleen, dry damp.
Indications: Morbid leukorrhea due to spleen deficiency.
Source:《常见病验方选编》

52.03 马兰茶 Malan Cha

Ingredients:

马兰根 Malangen, Indian Kalimeris Root (Radix Kalimeridis) 20g
红枣 Hongzao, Chinese Date (Fructus Jujubae) 10g

Directions: Decoct and drink.
Functions: To clear heat, dissolve damp, cool blood, remove toxins.
Indications: Morbid leukorrhea due to damp-heat.
Source:《常见病验方研究参考资料》

52.04 鸡冠花茶 Jiguanhua Cha

Ingredients:

鸡冠花 Jiguanhua, Cockscomb Flower (Flos Celosiae Cristatae) 30g

Directions: Decoct and drink.
Functions: To clear heat, dissolve damp, stop morbid leukorrhea.
Indications: Morbid leukorrhea.
Source:《常见病验方研究参考资料》

52.05 鸡冠花藕汁速溶饮 Jiguanhua Ouzhi Surongyin

Ingredients:
鲜鸡冠花 Xian Jiguanhua, Fresh Cockscomb Flower (Flos Celosiae Cristatae) 500g
鲜藕汁 Xian Ou Zhi, Fresh Lotus Juice (Succus Nelumbinis Rhizomatis) 500 ml
白糖 Baitang, White Sugar 500g

Directions: Decoct cockscomb flower three times. Pour the decoction fluid into a bowl every 20 minutes. Add fresh lotus juice and boil again. Remove from heat when slightly thickened. Cool and add white sugar to make a thick paste. Dry, crush, and store in a bottle. Use 10g each time, melt with boiling water and drink. Take three times a day.
Functions: To clear heat, treat inflammation, dissolve damp, stop morbid leukorrhea.
Indications: Trichomoniasis, vaginitis, leukorrhagia.
Source:《民间验方》

53 乳腺炎 For Mastitis

53.01 牛蒡叶茶 Niubangye Cha

Ingredients:
牛蒡叶 Niubang Ye, Great Burdock Leaf (Folium Arctii) 10g

Directions: Pestle and make as tea with boiling water.
Functions: To expel wind-heat, remove toxins.
Indications: Acute mastitis.

Source: 《全国中草药汇编》

53.02 野菊花茶 Yejuhua Cha

Ingredients:
野菊花 Yejuhua, Wild Chrysanthemum Flower (Flos Chrysanthemi Indici) 15g

Directions: Make as tea with boiling water.
Functions: To clear heat, remove toxins, relieve swelling.
Indications: Early stage of mastitis.
Source: 《百病中医自我疗养丛书·乳房疾患》

53.03 银花地丁茶 Yinhua Diding Cha

Ingredients:
银花 Yinhua, Honeysuckle Flower (Flos Lonicerae) 30g
紫花地丁 Zihuadiding, Tokyo Violet Herb (Herba Violae) 30g

Directions: Decoct and drink.
Functions: To clear heat, promote detoxification, reduce swelling.
Indications: Early onset of mastitis.
Source: 《百病中医自我疗养丛书·乳房疾患》

54 妊娠期疾患 For Diseases in the Duration of Pregnancy

54.01 止呕茶 Zhiou Cha

Ingredients:
韭菜 Jiucai, Tuber Onion (Folium Allii Tuberosi)
生姜 Sheng Jiang, Fresh Ginger (Rhizoma Zingiberis Recens)

Directions: Crush into liquid, add white sugar to taste, make as tea with boiling water.
Functions: To nourish liver blood, reinforce kidney essence, warm middle *jiao*, regulate *qi*.

Indications: Morning sickness.
Source:《河南省中医秘方验方汇编》

54.02 玉米嫩衣茶 Yuminenyi Cha

Ingredients:
玉米嫩衣 Yumi Nenyi, Young Coating Leaves of Corn (Folium Tunicae Maydis) 10g
Directions: Decoct. Drink.
Functions: To prevent miscarriage.
Indications: Habitual abortion. Drink everyday from the beginning of pregnancy. Double the dosage when the month of previous abortion comes. Continue the treatment till term birth.
Source:《浙江中医杂志》10:1959

54.03 玉米须赤小豆饮 Yumixu Chixiaodou Yin

Ingredients:
鲜玉米须 Xian Yumi Xu, Fresh Corn Stigma (Stigma Maydis) 100g
赤小豆 Chixiaodou, Rice Bean (Semen Phaseoli) 30g
Directions: Wrap fresh corn stigma in a gauze bag. Decoct till rice beans are ready to eat. Remove the bag. Drink the decoction and eat the beans. Take one dose every day, continue for one week.
Functions: To strengthen the spleen, relieve water retention, soothe the liver.
Indications: Hypertension of pregnancy, edema in the third trimester of pregnancy, eclampsia of pregnancy.
Source:《百病饮食自疗》

54.04 竹沥茶 Zhuli Cha

Ingredients:
竹沥 Zhuli, Bamboo Juice (Succus Bambosae) 10-20 ml
Directions: Make as tea with warm boiled water.

Functions: To clear heat, dissolve phlegm, relieve irritability, ease the mind and stop palpitation.
Indications: Irritability and palpitation caused by heart fire.
Source:《本草纲目》

54.05 灶心土茶 Zaoxintu Cha

Ingredients:
灶心土 Zaoxintu, Furnace Soil (Terra Flava Usta) 100g
Directions: Decoct, settle, save clear fluid for use. Add brown sugar to taste before drinking.
Functions: To warm middle *jiao*, stop vomiting.
Indications: Pernicious vomiting, abdominal pain, diarrhea, uterine bleeding, morbid leukorrhea.
Source:《常见病中医临床手册》

54.06 阿胶奶饮 Ejiao Nai Yin

Ingredients:
牛奶 Niunai, Milk 200 ml
阿胶 Ajiao, Ass-Hide Glue (Colla Corii Asini) 10g
Directions: Dissolve ass-hide glue into the boiling milk. Take two doses a day.
Functions: To replenish blood.
Indications: Abdominal pain during pregnancy due to blood deficiency.
Source:《百病饮食自疗》

54.07 南瓜蒂茶 Nanguadi Cha

Ingredients:
南瓜蒂 Nangua Di, Pumpkin Base (Pedicellus Cucurbitae), 3 bases
Directions: Decoct and drink. Begin during the first month and continue until the fifth month of pregnancy, once a month, five times in total.

Functions: To replenish blood, prevent miscarriage.
Indications: Threatened abortion.
Source:《常见病验方研究参考资料》

54.08 红茶叶茶 Hongchaye Cha

Ingredients:

红茶 Hongcha, Black Tea, desired amount

Directions: Make tea and drink. Begin three months before delivery.
Functions: To induce diuresis, relieve irritability and quench thirst.
Indications: Hydramnion.
Source:《食物疗法精萃》

54.09 建兰茶 Jianlan Cha

Ingredients:

建兰叶 Jianlan Ye, Swordleaf Cymbidium Leaf (Folium Cymbidium Ensifolium), 3-4 leaves

Directions: Make as tea with boiling water.
Functions: To clear heat, dissolve damp, regulate *qi*.
Indications: Morning sickness.
Source:《常见病验方研究参考资料》

54.10 桑菊茶 II Sang Ju Cha II

Ingredients:

冬桑叶 Dongsangye, Mulberry Leaf (Folium Mori) 3g

菊花 Juhua, Chrysanthemum Flower (Flos Chrysanthemi) 3g

老茶叶 Laochaye, Tea Leaf (Folium Camelliae Sinensis) 3g

Directions: Make as tea with boiling water.
Functions: To replenish *yin*, pacify liver *yang*.
Indications: Hypertension during pregnancy.
Source:《百病饮食自疗》

54.11 荷叶饮 II Heye Yin II

Ingredients:
鲜荷叶 Xian Heye, Fresh Lotus Leaf (Folium Nelumbinis), 2 leaves (cut into thread-like pieces)
红糖 Hongtang, Brown Sugar 30g

Directions: Decoct over high heat and then low heat for 30 minutes. Filter, and drink.

Functions: To stop bleeding, ease mind.

Indications: Vaginal bleeding in the first trimester of pregnancy.

Source:《食物与食治》

54.12 紫苏姜橘饮 Zisu Jiang Ju Yin

Ingredients:
苏梗 Sugeng, Perilla Stem (Caulis Perillae) 9g
生姜 Sheng Jiang, Fresh Ginger (Rhizoma Zingiberis Recens) 6g
大枣 Dazao, Chinese Date (Fructus Jujubae), 10 dates
陈皮 Chenpi, Dried Tangerine Peel (Pericarpium Citri Reticulatae) 6g
红糖 Hongtang, Brown Sugar 15g

Directions: Decoct and drink. Take three doses a day.

Functions: To strengthen spleen and stomach, stop vomiting.

Indications: Morning sickness, accompanied by fullness and distention in epigastric region, poor appetite, tiredness, pale tongue with white coating, soft rolling and forceless pulse.

Source:《百病饮食自疗》

54.13 葡萄须饮 Putaoxu Yin

Ingredients:
葡萄须 Putao Xu, European Grape Tendril (Cirrus Vitis Viniferae) 30g

Directions: Decoct and drink.

Functions: To ease the fetus.

Indications: Upward flow of the fetus-*qi* to the chest, i.e., a morbid condition during pregnancy marked by dyspnea, fullness in the chest, and even hypochondriac pain and restlessness due to deficiency of kidney *yin* and excess liver *qi*.
Source: 《山东省中医验方汇编》第一辑

54.14 橘皮竹茹茶 Jupi Zhuru Cha

Ingredients:
橘皮 Jupi, Dried Tangerine Peel (Pericarpium Citri Reticulatae) 5g
竹茹 Zhuru, Bamboo Shavings (Caulis Bambusae in Taeniam) 10g
Directions: Cut into small pieces and make as tea with boiling water.
Functions: To regulate *qi*, harmonize stomach, stop vomiting.
Indications: Morning sickness.
Source: 《常见病验方研究参考资料》

54.15 苏叶生姜茶 Suye Shengjiang Cha

Ingredients:
紫苏叶 Zisu Ye, Perilla Leaf (Folium Perillae) 4.5g
生姜汁 Sheng Jiang Zhi, Fresh Ginger Juice (Succus Zingiberis Rhizoma Recens)
Directions: Make as tea with boiling water.
Functions: To regulate *qi*, harmonize stomach, ease fetus.
Indications: Morning sickness.
Source: 《常见病验方研究参考资料》

55 产后疾患 For the Diseases of Post Partum

55.01 四乳饮 Siru Yin

Ingredients:
生麦芽 Sheng Mai Ya, Germinated Barley (Fructus Hordei Germinatus) 120g (toasted until yellow)

Directions: Decoct with 800ml water until reduced to 400ml, filter. Save the decoction. Add 600ml water to decoct until reduced to 400ml, filter. Mix the decoctions. Take all within one day.

Functions: To circulate *qi*, remove retention of milk.

Indications: Distending pain in the breasts after delactation.

Source: 《中医杂志》 2:1964

55.02 红糖胡椒茶 Hongtang Hujiao Cha

Ingredients:

红糖　Hongtang, Brown Sugar 15g

胡椒　Hujiao, Pepper Fruit (Fructus Piperis) 1.5g

茶叶　Chaye, Tea Leaf (Folium Camelliae Sinensis) 3g

Directions: Bake brown sugar, grind pepper fruit, make all ingredients as tea with boiling water.

Functions: To warm middle *jiao*, remove stasis and stop dysentery.

Indications: Abdominal pain of dysentery post partum.

Source: 《常见病验方研究参考资料》

55.03 柚皮茶 II　Youpi Cha II

Ingredients:

柚皮　You Pi, Pummelo Peel (Exocarpium Citri Grandis)

Directions: Decoct and drink.

Functions: To activate blood circulation, relieve pain.

Indications: After-pains.

Source: 《续名家方选》

55.04 胡萝卜缨饮　Huluoboying Yin

Ingredients:

胡萝卜缨　Huluobo Ying, Carrot Leaf (Folium Dauci sativae)

Directions: Decoct and drink.

Functions: To remove toxins, induce diuresis and dispel wind-cold.
Indications: Sensitivity to cold after delivery manifested by chills.
Source: 《黑龙江秘方验方》第二集

55.05 南瓜须茶 Nanguaxu Cha

Ingredients:
南瓜须 Nangua Xu, Pumpkin Tendril (Cirrus Cucurbitae), a handful

Directions: Make as tea with boiling water. Add salt to taste before drinking.
Functions: To clear heat, relieve swelling.
Indications: Mammillary pain due to swelling of the breast.
Source: 《中医大辞典·中药分册》

55.06 益母糖茶 Yimu Tang Cha

Ingredients:
益母草 Yimucao, Motherwort Herb (Herba Leonuri) 6g
红糖 Hongtang, Brown Sugar 15g
茶叶 Chaye, Tea Leaf (Folium Camelliae Sinensis) 3g

Directions: Make as tea with boiling water.
Functions: To activate blood circulation, remove blood stasis, relieve pain.
Indications: After-pains of blood-stasis type manifested by aggravation of pain on pressure, small quantity of lochia with dark purple clots, dark purple complexion, dark purple tongue with blood spots, wiry and hesitant pulse.
Source: 《百病饮食自疗》

55.07 菊花根茶 Juhuagen Cha

Ingredients:
白菊花根 Baijuhua Gen, White Chrysanthemum Root (Radix Chrysanthemi Flos), 3 roots

Directions: Cut into small pieces. Make as tea with boiling water.
Functions: To induce diuresis, dissolve stasis, remove toxins.
Indications: Abdominal pain resulting from *qi* and blood deficiency after delivery or from invasion of damp-heat.
Source:《常见病验方研究参考资料》

55.08 黄瓜花茶 Huangguahua Cha

Ingredients:
黄瓜花 Huanggua Hua, Cucumber Flower (Flos Cucumeris sativi)
Directions: Dry in shade. Use 10g each time and make as tea with boiling water.
Functions: To clear heat, nourish blood and soothe liver.
Indications: Muscular contracture resulting from blood deficiency after delivery.
Source:《常见病验方研究参考资料》

Index (Chinese)

一画
一味生姜饮 Yiwei Shengjiang Yin   (10.01)
一味薯蓣饮 Yiwei Shuyu Yin   (30.01)

二画
丁香茶 Dingxiang Cha   (10.02)
丁香酸梅汤 Dingxiang Suanmei Tang   (18.02)
七叶芦根饮 Qiye Lugen Yin   (18.05)
七鲜汤 Qixian Tang   (18.03)
七鲜茶 Qixian Cha   (18.04)
二花参麦茶 Erhua Shen Mai Cha   (12.01)
二花茶 Erhua Cha   (35.02)
二花桔萸茶 Erhua Ju Yu Cha   (12.02)
二陈竹叶茶 Erchen Zhuye Cha   (37.01)
二根麦萝茶 Ergen Mai Luo Cha   (13.01)
二根茶 Ergen Cha   (47.01)
二绿女贞茶 Erlu Nuzhen Cha   (12.04)
二绿玉冰茶 Erlu Yu Bing Cha   (08.01)
二绿合欢茶 Erlu Hehuan Cha   (12.03)
二菱茶 Erling Cha   (41.01)
二鲜三花饮 Erxian Sanhua Cha   (18.01)
二鲜饮 Erxian Yin   (35.01)
人字草茶 Renzicao Cha   (35.03)
人参大枣茶 Renshen Dazao Cha   (01.02)

人参乌梅茶 Renshen Wumei Cha (09.01)
人参双花茶 Renshen Shuanghua Cha (21.01)
人参汤 Renshen Tang (06.01)
人参枣仁汤 Renshen Zaoren Tang (06.02)
人参枸杞饮 Renshen Gouqi Yin (11.01)
人参茶 Renshen Cha (01.01)
人参核桃饮 Renshen Hetao Yin (05.02)
八仙茶 Baxian Cha (05.01)
刀豆饮 Daodou Yin (10.03)
刀豆茶Ⅰ Daodou Cha Ⅰ (10.04)
刀豆茶Ⅱ Daodou Cha Ⅱ (14.01)

三画

三七花茶 Sanqihua Cha (23.03)
三子饮 Sanzi Yin (21.02)
三子茶 Sanzi Cha (23.01)
三分茶 Sanfen Cha (21.03)
三叶茶 Sanye Cha (18.06)
三汁饮 Sanzhi Yin (09.02)
三白茶 Sanbai Cha (21.04)
三花减肥茶 Sanhua Jianfei Cha (02.01)
三宝茶 Sanbao Cha (23.02)
三金茶 Sanjin Cha (36.01)
三鲜饮 Sanxian Yin (32.01)
三鲜茶Ⅰ Sanxian Cha Ⅰ (09.03) (18.07)
三鲜茶Ⅱ Sanxian Cha Ⅱ (15.01)
三鲜茶Ⅲ Sanxian Cha Ⅲ (17.01)
土牛膝茶 Tuniuxi Cha (20.03)
大小蓟速溶饮 Daxiaoji Surongyin (35.04)

大麦秸茶 Damaijie Cha （37.02）
大青叶茶 Daqingye Cha （16.01）
大海瓜子茶 Dahai Guazi Cha （20.02）
大海茶 Dahai Cha （20.01）
大蒜冰糖茶 Dasuan Bingtang Cha （21.05）
小儿七星茶 Xiaoer Qixing Cha （13.05）
小麦大枣饮 Xiaomai Dazao Yin （21.06）
小蓟根茶 Xiaojigen Cha （33.01）
山扁豆草茶 Shanbiandoucao Cha （37.03）
山药茶 Shanyao Cha （26.01）
山楂叶(花)茶 Shanzhaye (hua) Cha （23.04）
山楂决明茶 Shanzha Jueming Cha （23.05）
山楂向日葵饮 Shanzha Xiangrikui Yin （51.01）
山楂红白糖茶 Shanzha Hongbaitang Cha （30.02）
山楂麦芽茶 Shanzha Maiya Cha （50.01）
山楂神曲汤 Shanzha Shenqu Tang （13.04）
山楂茶 Shanzha Cha （13.02）
山楂核桃茶 Shanzha Hetao Cha （05.03）
山楂根茶 Shanzhagen Cha （02.02）
山楂荷叶茶 Shanzha Heye Cha （18.08）
山楂银菊茶 Shanzha Yin Ju Cha （02.03）
山楂橘皮茶 Shanzha Jupi Cha （13.03）
川贝杏仁饮 Chuanbei Xingren Yin （21.08）
川贝莱菔茶 Chuanbei Laifu Cha （21.07）
川芎糖茶 Chuanxiong Tang Cha （14.02）
干姜饮 Ganjiang Yin （10.07）
马兰茶 Malan Cha （52.03）
马兰糖饮 Malan Tang Yin （48.03）
马齿苋红糖茶 Machixian Hongtang Cha （35.19）

马齿苋饮 Machixian Yin (35.18)
马齿苋绿豆汤 Machixian Ludou Tang (30.15)
马齿苋槟榔茶 Machixian Binglang Cha (30.16)
马鞭草茶 Mabiancao Cha (27.11)

四画

丹皮京菖茶 Danpi Jingchang Cha (11.02)
丹参茶 Danshen Cha (25.01)
乌梅饮 Wumei Yin (43.02)
乌梅清暑饮 Wumei Qingshu Yin (18.27)
五叶芦根茶 Wuye Lugen Cha (18.10)
五皮饮 Wupi Yin (37.04)
五君子饮 Wujunzi Yin (33.02)
五味子饮 Wuweizi Yin (09.04)
五味枸杞饮 Wuwei Gouqi Yin (18.09)
五神汤 Wushen Tang (14.04)
五鲜茶 Wuxian Cha (40.01)
六叶茶 (感冒茶) Liuye Cha (Ganmao Cha) (15.03)
六和茶 Liuhe Cha (30.06)
凤衣冬蜜饮 Fengyi Dong Mi Yin (20.24)
凤眼草茶 Fengyancao Cha (35.27)
午时茶 Wushi Cha (14.05)
化橘红茶 Huajuhong Cha (21.38)
双皮茶 Shuangpi Cha (18.47)
双花杏蜜饮 Shuanghua Xing Mi Yin (21.60)
双花饮 Shuanghua Yin (09.14)
双核饮 Shuanghe Yin (42.04)
双荷汤 Shuanghe Tang (33.11)
天中茶 Tianzhong Cha (14.03)

天麻菊花饮 Tianma Juhua Yin (23.06)
太子乌梅饮 Taizi Wumei Yin (18.11)
太子奶饮 Taizinai Yin (05.04)
巴豆茶 Badou Cha (24.01)
无花果叶茶 Wuhuaguoye Cha (27.16)
无花果茶 Wuhuaguo Cha (21.50)
无花果糖饮 Wuhuaguo Tang Yin (30.20)
月季花汤 Yuejihua Tang (51.02)
木耳芝麻茶 Muer Zhima Cha (34.01)
木槿花速溶饮 Mujinhua Surongyin (30.05)
止汗饮 Zhihan Yin (38.01)
止血茶 Zhixue Cha (33.03)
止呕茶 Zhiou Cha (54.01)
止泻茶 I Zhixie Cha I (30.03)
止泻茶 II Zhixie Cha II (30.04)
止咳茶 Zhike Cha (21.09)
止消渴速溶饮 Zhixiaoke Surongyin (26.02)
毛山茶(香风茶) Maoshancha (Xiangfengcha) (21.10)
毛桃干茶 Maotaogan Cha (38.02)
水翁花茶 Shuiwenghua Cha (17.02)
水蜈蚣茶 Shuiwugong Cha (48.01)
牛奶茶 Niunai Cha (02.04)
牛乳饮 Niuru Yin (06.03)
牛筋草茶 Niujincao Cha (45.01)
牛蒡子芦根茶 Niubangzi Lugen Cha (47.02)
牛蒡子茶 Niubangzi Cha (15.02)
牛蒡叶茶 Niubangye Cha (53.01)
车杏枇杷茶 Che Xing Pipa Cha (47.07)
车前子茶 Cheqianzi Cha (17.05)

车前草茶 Cheqiancao Cha (37.09)
车前根茶 Cheqiangen Cha (21.24)
车前海金饮 Cheqian Haijin Yin (35.14)
车前蜂蜜饮 Cheqian Fengmi Yin (30.12)

五画

丝瓜芝麻核桃饮 Sigua Zhima Hetao Yin (50.03)
丝瓜花蜜饮 Siguahua Mi Yin (21.48)
丝瓜饮Ⅰ Sigua Yin Ⅰ (07.04)
丝瓜饮Ⅱ Sigua Yin Ⅱ (08.09)
丝瓜茶 Sigua Cha (09.13)
丝瓜速溶饮 Sigua Surongyin (20.18)
仙鹤草茶 Xianhecao Cha (33.07)
冬瓜子芦根饮 Dongguazi Lugen Yin (22.02)
冬瓜叶饮 Dongguaye Yin (30.09)
冬瓜麦冬饮 Donggua Maidong Yin (21.14)
冬瓜藤饮 Dongguateng Yin (22.01)
冬瓜瓤汤 Dongguarang Tang (26.04)
加味三七饮 Jiawei Sanqi Yin (33.06)
加味菊花茶 Jiawei Juhua Cha (15.04)
加味槐花饮 Jiawei Huaihua Yin (34.02)
加减人参乌梅汤 Jiajian Renshen Wumei Tang (28.02)
加减三花饮 Jiajian Sanhua Yin (26.06)
加减小蓟饮 Jiajian Xiaoji Yin (35.08)
加减石膏饮 Jiajian Shigao Yin (17.03)
加减香薷饮 Jiajian Xiangru Yin (17.04)
加减清燥润肺饮 Jiajian Qingzao Runfei Yin (20.07)
半边钱茶 Banbianqian Cha (35.07)
四花饮 Sihua Yin (33.05)

四乳饮 Siru Yin (55.01)
四味茶 Siwei Cha (18.12)
四炭止漏茶 Sitan Zhilou Cha (51.03)
平肝清热茶 Pinggan Qingre Cha (11.03)
玄麦甘桔汤 Xuanmai Gan Jie Tang (20.06)
玄参三花饮 Xuanshen Sanhua Yin (46.01)
玄参麦冬茶 Xunshen Maidong Cha (41.02)
玄参青果茶 Xuanshen Qingguo Cha (20.05)
玉竹乌梅饮 Yuzhu Wumei Yin (09.06)
玉竹茶 Yuzhu Cha (09.05)
玉竹速溶饮 Yuzhu Surongyin (25.02)
玉竹薄荷饮 Yuzhu Bohe Yin (03.01)
玉米芯茶 Yumixin Cha (37.05)
玉米花茶 Yumihua Cha (32.02)
玉米须冰糖茶 Yumixu Bingtang Cha (33.04)
玉米须赤小豆饮 Yumixu Chixiaodou Yin (54.03)
玉米须茶 Yumixu Cha (37.06)
玉米须桔皮茶 Yumixu Jupi Cha (21.11)
玉米须速溶饮 Yumixu Surongyin (37.07)
玉米根叶茶 Yumigenye Cha (36.02)
玉米嫩衣茶 Yuminenyi Cha (54.02)
瓜蒌茶 Gualou Cha (22.03)
甘竹茶 Gan Zhu Cha (35.05)
甘草生姜汤 Gancao Shengjiang Tang (21.13)
甘草醋茶 Gancao Cu Cha (21.12)
甘桔速溶饮 Gan Jie Surongyin (20.04)
甘蔗茶 Ganzhe Cha (09.07)
甘露茶 Ganlu Cha (13.06)
生石膏荸荠汤 Shengshigao Biqi Tang (45.02)

生军茶 Shengjun Cha (39.01)
生地石膏茶 Shengdi Shigao Cha (26.05)
生地青果茶 Shengdi Qingguo Cha (47.03)
生姜茶 Shengjiang Cha (16.02)
生姜蔻仁汤 Shengjiang Kouren Tang (31.01)
生津茶 Shengjin Cha (09.10)
生脉饮 Shengmai Yin (18.13)
田螺茶 Tianluo Cha (26.03)
白头翁茶 Baitouweng Cha (47.04)
白术叶茶 Baizhuye Cha (38.03)
白杨树皮茶 Baiyangshupi Cha (16.04)
白果冬瓜子饮 Baiguo Dongguazi Yin (35.06)
白茅花茶 Baimaohua Cha (32.03)
白茅根茶 Baimaogen Cha (32.04)
白菜根饮 Baicaigen Yin (16.03)
白菜绿豆芽饮 Baicai Ludouya Yin (14.06)
白蔻茶 Baikou Cha (13.07)
白糖茶 Baitang Cha (29.01)
石花茶 Shihua Cha (27.01)
石苇车前茶 Shiwei Cheqian Cha (36.03)
石斛甘蔗饮 Shihu Ganzhe Yin (09.09)
石斛冰糖茶 Shihu Bingtang Cha (09.08)
石斛茶 Shihu Cha (28.01)
石榴叶茶 Shiliuye Cha (30.07)
石榴皮茶 Shiliupi Cha (30.08)
艾叶茶 Aiye Cha (10.05)
龙眼枣仁饮 Longyan Zaoren Yin (06.08)
龙眼洋参饮 Longyan Yangshen Yin (01.04)
龙眼茶 Longyan Cha (06.07)

六画

冰糖木蝴蝶饮 Bingtang Muhudie Yin (20.09)
决明子茶 Juemingzi Cha (03.02)
决明苁蓉茶 Jueming Congrong Cha (39.03)
决明菊花茶 Jueming Juhua Cha (23.10)
向日葵叶饮 Xiangrikuiye Yin (23.09)
向日葵花茶 Xiangrikuihua Cha (37.08)
向日葵茎饮 Xiangrikuijing Yin (52.01)
向日葵根茶 Xiangrikuigen Cha (35.10)
地骨皮茶 Digupi Cha (32.05)
地榆叶茶 Diyuye Cha (18.14)
地锦草茶 Dijincao Cha (30.10)
安神茶 Anshen Cha (07.01)
当归补血饮 Danggui Buxue Yin (05.12)
灯心竹叶茶 Dengxin Zhuye Cha (07.05)
灯心柿饼汤 Dengxin Shibing Tang (35.29)
灯心草茶 Dengxincao Cha (49.03)
百合茶 Baihe Cha (08.03)
百两金茶 Bailiangjin Cha (20.08)
百药煎茶 Baiyaojian Cha (21.15)
百部四味饮 Baibu Siwei Yin (21.16)
百解茶 Baijie Cha (18.15)
竹叶茶 I Zhuye Cha I (44.01)
竹叶茶 II Zhuye Cha II (49.01)
竹沥茶 Zhuli Cha (54.04)
竹茅饮 Zhu Mao Yin (35.09)
竹茹芦根茶 Zhuru Lugen Cha (28.03)
红枣茶 I Hongzao Cha I (05.10)
红枣茶 II Hongzao Cha II (49.02)

红茶叶茶 Hongchaye Cha　(54.08)
红高粱花茶 Honggaolianghua Cha　(51.11)
红糖姜枣茶 Hongtang Jiang Zao Cha　(51.12)
红糖胡椒茶 Hongtang Hujiao Cha　(55.02)
羊乳饮 Yangru Yin　(28.04)
芝麻枸杞饮 Zhima Gouqi Yin　(04.02)
芝麻茶 Zhima Cha　(30.11)
芝麻核桃茶 Zhima Hetao Cha　(39.02)
西瓜决明茶 Xigua Jueming Cha　(23.07)
西瓜翠衣茶 Xiguacuiyi Cha　(23.08)
西河柳饮 Xiheliu Yin　(47.05)
西青果茶 Xiqingguo Cha　(08.02)
西洋参茶 Xiyangshen Cha　(05.05)
防风甘草茶 Fangfeng Gancao Cha　(15.05)
防疫清咽茶 Fangyi Qingyan Cha　(20.11)
防暑茶 Fangshu Cha　(18.16)

七画

何首乌茶 Heshouwu Cha　(04.01)
佛手枣汤 Foshou Zao Tang　(12.06)
佛手茶 Foshou Cha　(12.05)
佛耳草茶 Foercao Cha　(36.04)
利咽茶 Liyan Cha　(20.10)
尿利清茶 Niaoliqing Cha　(35.13)
尿感茶 Niaogan Cha　(37.10)
忍冬夏枯草茶 Rendong Xiakucao Cha　(46.02)
忍冬藤茶 Rendongteng Cha　(19.01)
旱芹车前茶 Hanqin Cheqian Cha　(23.11)
旱莲草红枣汤 Hanliancao Hongzao Tang　(34.03)

旱莲草茶 Hanliancao Cha (35.12)
杏仁奶茶 Xingren Nai Cha (21.19)
杏仁冰糖饮 Xingren Bingtang Yin (21.18)
杏仁麦冬饮 Xingren Maidong Yin (47.09)
杏梨饮 Xing Li Yin (21.17)
杏菊饮 I Xing Ju Yin I (24.02)
杏菊饮 II Xing Ju Yin II (24.03)
杜仲茶 Duzhong Cha (23.12)
杞叶长寿茶 Qiye Changshou Cha (05.06)
杞菊茶 Qi Ju Cha (03.03)
杨桃速溶饮 Yangtao Surongyin (48.05)
沙母二草茶 Sha Mu Ercao Cha (18.20)
沙参百合饮 Shashen Baihe Yin (21.21)
沙参麦冬饮 Shashen Maidong Yin (21.23)
沙参梨皮饮 Shashen Lipi Yin (21.22)
沙参蔗汁饮 Shashen Zhezhi Yin (38.04)
沙苑子茶 Shayuanzi Cha (05.07)
灵芝茶 Lingzhi Cha (05.17)
灵芝薄荷饮 Lingzhi Bohe Yin (01.05)
灶心土竹叶茶 Zaoxintu Zhuye Cha (44.02)
灶心土茶 Zaoxintu Cha (54.05)
皂荚芽茶 Zaojiaya Cha (21.20)
芥菜茶 Jiecai Cha (15.06)
芦根冰糖饮 Lugen Bingtang Yin (17.18)
芦根苡仁饮 Lugen Yiren Yin (17.17)
芦根饮 I Lugen Yin (13.27)
芦根饮 II Lugen Yin (13.28)
芦根茶 Lugen Cha (47.26)
芦菊茶 Lu Ju Cha (47.27)

芫荽茶 Yuansui Cha (14.07)
花生全草茶 Huashengquancao Cha (23.14)
花生红枣茶 Huasheng Hongzao Cha (06.04)
花粉茶 Huafen Cha (09.11)
芳香化浊饮 Fangxiang Huazhuo Yin (17.06)
芹菜大戟饮 Qincai Daji Yin (51.06)
芹菜根陈皮茶 Qincaigen Chenpi Cha (21.25)
芹菜根茶 Qincaigen Cha (23.13)
苋菜茶 Xiancai Cha (30.17)
苍术贯仲茶 Cangzhu Guanzhong Cha (16.10)
苍耳子茶 Cangerzi Cha (15.11)
苎麻根饮 Zhumagen Yin (51.04)
苏叶生姜茶 Suye Shengjiang Cha (54.15)
苏叶茶 Suye Cha (08.14)
苏叶薄荷茶 Suye Bohe Cha (18.50)
苏杏汤 Su Xing Tang (14.18)
苏羌茶 Su Qiang Cha (14.19)
苏连茶 Su Lian Cha (49.04)
苡仁竹叶饮 Yiren Zhuye Yin (17.07)
诃玉茶 He Yu Cha (20.19)
谷皮藤茶 Gupiteng Cha (36.05)
谷芽露茶 Guyalu Cha (13.08)
谷精菊花饮 Gujing Juhua Yin (03.04)
豆豉茶 Douchi Cha (35.11)
赤小豆饮 Chixiaodou Yin (50.02)
赤柽柳茶 Chichengliu Cha (47.06)
辛夷花茶 Xinyihua Cha (24.04)
连翘茶 Lianqiao Cha (39.04)
阿胶奶饮 Ejiao Nai Yin (54.06)

陈仓米柿饼霜茶 Chencangmi Shibingshuang Cha (13.18)
陈皮饮 Chenpi Yin (21.45)
陈茗饮 Chenming Yin (13.16)
陈醋茶 Chencu Cha (30.18)
鸡苏饮 Jisu Yin (17.14)
鸡冠花茶 Jiguanhua Cha (52.04)
鸡冠花藕汁速溶饮 Jiguanhua Ouzhi Surongyin (52.05)
鸡骨草茶 Jigucao Cha (18.45)
鸡蛋花茶 Jidanhua Cha (18.46)
鸡蛋清白糖饮 Jidanqing Baitang Yin (32.06)
麦冬乌梅饮 Maidong Wumei Yin (26.11)
麦冬地黄饮 Maidong Dihuang Yin (41.04)
麦冬茅根饮 Maidong Maogen Yin (33.09)
麦冬梅枝茶 Maidong Meizhi Cha (47.20)
麦芽山楂饮 Maiya shanzha Yin (13.20)
麦芽茶 Maiya Cha (13.19)

八画

佩香茶 Pei Xiang Cha (13.09)
侧柏叶茶 Cebaiye Cha (23.25)
刺五加茶 Ciwujia Cha (05.08)
刺玫根茶 Cimeigen Cha (51.09)
卷柏茶 Juanbai Cha (51.05)
参叶青果茶 Shenye Qingguo Cha (08.08)
参味茶 Shen Wei Cha (07.03)
参须京菖茶 Shenxu Jingchang Cha (11.04)
参芪精 Shen Qi Jing (06.05)
定嗽定喘饮 Dingsou Dingchuan Yin (21.26)
建兰茶 Jianlan Cha (54.09)

建曲茶 Jianqu Cha (18.24)
明目茶 I Mingmu Cha (03.05)
明目茶 II Mingmu Cha (03.06)
松树皮茶 Songshupi Cha (51.07)
板蓝根花茶 Banlangenhua Cha (46.03)
板蓝根茶 Banlangen Cha (16.05)
枇杷饮 Pipa Yin (28.05)
枣树根皮茶 Zaoshugenpi Cha (51.20)
玫瑰花灯心茶 Meiguihua Dengxin Cha (35.15)
玫瑰花茶 Meiguihua Cha (12.07)
盲肠草茶 Mangchangcao Cha (16.06)
罗布麻叶茶 Luobumaye Cha (23.46)
罗布麻平喘茶 Luobuma Pingchuancha (21.61)
罗布麻降压茶 Luobuma Jiangyacha (23.44)
罗布麻速溶饮 Luobuma Surongyin (23.45)
罗布麻减肥茶 Luobuma Jianfeicha (02.10)
罗汉果柿饼饮 Luohanguo Shibing Yin (21.62)
罗汉果速溶饮 Luohanguo Surongyin (08.13)
苦丁茶 Kuding Cha (23.16)
苦瓜茶 Kugua Cha (18.21)
苦瓜根茶 Kuguagen Cha (30.14)
苦竹叶速溶饮 Kuzhuye Surongyin (09.12)
苦刺花茶 Kucihua Cha (18.22)
茅根车前饮 Maogen Cheqian Yin (35.16)
茅根竹蔗饮 Maogen Zhuzhe Yin (35.17)
茅根荠菜茶 Maogen Jicai Cha (47.12)
茅根菠萝速溶饮 Maogen Boluo Surongyin (37.11)
茉莉花茶 Molihua Cha (18.23)
虎杖叶茶 Huzhangye Cha (48.02)

贯仲丝瓜络茶 Guanzhong Sigualuo Cha (47.21)
贯仲板兰根茶 Guanzhong Banlangen Cha (45.03)
贯仲茶 Guanzhong Cha (16.08)
金花牡荆茶 Jinhua Mujing Cha (18.18)
金鸡饮 Jin Ji Yin (27.02)
金鸡脚草茶 Jinjijiaocao Cha (18.19)
金钱草茶 Jinqiancao Cha (36.06)
金银花茶 Jinyinhua Cha (18.17)
金锁茶 Jinsuo Cha (20.12)
金橘茶 Jinju Cha (13.10)
降压茶Ⅰ Jiangya Cha (23.17)
降压茶Ⅱ Jiangya Cha (23.18)
降脂茶 Jiangzhi Cha (25.04)
青皮麦芽饮 Qingpi Maiya Yin (12.08)
青刺尖茶 Qingcijian Cha (44.03)
青果石榴茶 Qingguo Shiliu Cha (42.01)
青果芦根茶 Qingguo Lugen Cha (47.08)
青葙子速溶饮 Qingxiangzi Surongyin (24.05)
青蒿丹皮茶 Qinghao Danpi Cha (51.08)
鱼腥草饮 Yuxingcao Yin (21.46)

九画

南瓜籽茶 Nanguazi Cha (43.01)
南瓜须茶 Nanguaxu Cha (55.05)
南瓜蒂茶 Nanguadi Cha (54.07)
厚朴花茶 Houpuhua Cha (12.09)
咽喉茶 Yanhou Cha (20.14)
复方贯仲茶 Fufang Guanzhong Cha (16.09)
复盆子茶 Fupenzi Cha (05.15)

姜艾红糖饮 Jiang Ai Hongtang Yin (51.14)
姜枣饮Ⅰ Jiang Zao Yin Ⅰ (21.31)
姜枣饮Ⅱ Jiang Zao Yin Ⅱ (30.23)
姜茶乌梅饮 Jiang Cha Wumei Yin (30.27)
姜茶饮 Jiang Cha Yin (30.25)
姜茶速溶饮 Jiang Cha Surongyin (30.26)
姜糖苏叶饮 Jiang Tang Suye Yin (14.10)
姜糖饮Ⅰ Jiang Tang Yin Ⅰ (14.08)
姜糖饮Ⅱ Jiang Tang Yin Ⅱ (21.32)
姜糖茶Ⅰ Jiang Tang Cha Ⅰ (14.09)
姜糖茶Ⅱ Jiang Tang Cha Ⅱ (30.24)
威灵仙茶 Weilingxian Cha (20.13)
宣肺饮 Xuanfei Yin (21.30)
扁豆山药茶 Biandou Shanyao Cha (52.02)
扁豆益胃饮 Biandou Yiwei Yin (28.08)
扁柏叶茶 Bianbaiye Cha (21.33)
扁蓄茶 Bianxu Cha (35.24)
枸杞五味子茶 Gouqi Wuweizi Cha (05.09)
枸杞茶 Gouqi Cha (03.07)
柏子仁茶 Baiziren Cha (07.02)
柚子壳荷叶饮 Youzike Heye Yin (21.27)
柚子鸡蛋饮 Youzi Jidan Yin (28.06)
柚皮茶Ⅰ Youpi Cha Ⅰ (30.13)
柚皮茶Ⅱ Youpi Cha Ⅱ (55.03)
柠檬速溶饮 Ningmeng Surongyin (18.44)
柿叶降脂茶 Shiye Jiangzhi Cha (25.03)
柿蒂茶 Shidi Cha (21.28)
柿霜桑椹饮 Shishuang Sangshen Yin (51.10)
点地梅茶 Diandimei Cha (08.12)

玳玳花茶 Daidaihua Cha (13.11)
砂仁甘草茶 Sharen Gancao Cha (13.12)
祛钩虫茶 Qugouchong Cha (43.06)
祛暑清心茶 Qushu Qingxin Cha (18.26)
神曲饮 Shenqu Yin (13.15)
秋梨椿根皮茶 Qiuli Chungenpi Cha (34.04)
胃乐茶 Weile Cha (12.10)
胃溃疡茶 Weikuiyang Cha (29.02)
胖大海冰糖茶 Pangdahai Bingtang Cha (08.04)
胡桐叶茶 Hutongye Cha (23.15)
胡萝卜大枣饮 Huluobo Dazao Yin (21.29)
胡萝卜芫荽饮 Huluobo Yuansui Yin (47.11)
胡萝卜饮 Huluobo Yin (47.10)
胡萝卜缨饮 Huluoboying Yin (55.04)
茴香茶 Huixiang Cha (42.02)
茵地茶 Yin Di Cha (35.20)
茵陈红糖饮 Yinchen Hongtang Yin (27.08)
茵陈陈皮茶 Yinchen Chenpi Cha (27.07)
茵陈茶 Yinchen Cha (27.05)
茵陈香芦茶 Yinchen Xiang Lu Cha (27.06)
茵陈银花饮 Yinchen Yinhua Yin (27.09)
茶树根茶 Chashugen Cha (44.04)
茶榄海蜜饮 Cha Lan Hai Mi Yin (08.05)
草决明茶 Caojueming Cha (03.09)
荔橄茶 Li Gan Cha (42.03)
荠菜茶 Jicai Cha (23.43)
药王茶 Yaowangcha (18.48)
退黄饮 Tuihuang Yin (27.10)
钩藤茶 Gouteng Cha (23.34)

香附川芎茶 Xiangfu Chuanxiong Cha (24.06)
香附茶 Xiangfu Cha (51.13)
香蕉根茶 Xiangjiaogen Cha (23.19)
香橼茶 Xiangyuan Cha (28.07)
香薷饮 Xiangru Yin (17.08)
骨碎补茶 Gusuibu Cha (21.40)
健胃防癌茶 Jianwei Fangai Cha (41.03)

十画

健胃茶 I Jianwei Cha I (10.09)
健胃茶 II Jianwei Cha II (10.10)
健胃茶 III Jianwei Cha III (28.10)
健胃茶 IV Jianwei Cha IV (28.11)
健脾饮 Jianpi Yin (30.19)
党参红枣茶 Dangshen Hongzao Cha (07.06)
党参黄米茶 Dangshen Huangmi Cha (05.16)
夏枯瓜络饮 Xiaku Gualuo Yin (12.14)
夏枯草茶 Xiakucao Cha (23.23)
夏枯草荷叶茶 Xiakucao Heye Cha (23.24)
夏菊茶 Xia Ju Cha (16.07)
柴甘茅根茶 Chai Gan Maogen Cha (27.04)
柴芦茶 Chai Lu Cha (47.14)
桂皮山楂饮 Guipi Shanzha Yin (10.06)
桂姜红糖饮 Gui Jiang Hongtang Cha (51.16)
桑叶枇杷茶 Sangye Pipa Cha (21.34)
桑叶苦丁茶 Sangye Kuding Cha (51.15)
桑叶茶 Sangye Cha (15.07)
桑杏豆豉饮 Sang Xing Douchi Yin (21.36)
桑杏饮 Sang Xing Yin (21.35)

桑枝茶　Sangzhi Cha　　(02.05)
桑树根茶　Sangshugen Cha　　(23.20)
桑根白皮茶　Sanggenbaipi Cha　　(23.21)
桑菊杏仁饮　Sang Ju Xingren Cha　　(21.37)
桑菊豆豉饮　Sang Ju Douchi Yin　　(15.09)
桑菊枸杞饮　Sang Ju Gouqi Yin　　(23.22)
桑菊茶Ⅰ　Sang Ju Cha Ⅰ　　(15.08)
桑菊茶Ⅱ　Sang Ju Cha Ⅱ　　(54.10)
桑菊香豉梨皮饮　Sang Ju Xiangchi Lipi Yin　(17.09)
桑菊薄竹饮　Sang Ju Bo Zhu Yin (15.10)
桑银茶　Sang Yin Cha　　(03.08)
桑蜜茶　Sang Mi Cha　　(18.25)
桑薄花蜜饮　Sang Bo Hua Mi Yin (17.10)
桔姜茶　Ju Jiang Cha　　(14.11)
桔梗甘草茶　Jiegeng Gancao Cha　　(21.39)
梧桐茶　Wutong Cha　　(23.26)
梨皮茶　Lipi Cha　　(47.17)
浮麦麻根茶　Fumai Magen Cha　　(38.05)
浮萍茶　Fuping Cha　　(47.13)
海金砂草茶　Haijinshacao Cha　　(37.12)
海带茶　Haidai Cha　　(40.03)
海藻茶　Haizao Cha　　(40.02)
消炎茶　Xiaoyan Cha　　(20.15)
消食茶　Xiaoshi Cha　　(13.14)
消黄茶　Xiaohuang Cha　　(27.03)
消渴茶　Xiaoke Cha　　(26.07)
消滞茶　Xiaozhi Cha　　(13.13)
润肺止咳茶　Runfei Zhike Cha　　(21.56)
皋芦叶茶　Gaoluye Cha　　(26.08)

益母糖茶　Yimu Tang Cha　(55.06)
益胃茶Ⅰ　Yiwei Cha Ⅰ　(10.08)
益胃茶Ⅱ　Yiwei Cha Ⅱ　(26.09)
盐柠檬茶　Yan Ningmeng Cha　(17.19)
盐茶　Yan Cha　(17.20)
盐梅茶　Yan Mei Cha　(47.28)
积雪草茶　Jixuecao Cha　(18.43)
脑清茶　Naoqing Cha　(01.03)
荷叶饮Ⅰ　Heye Yin Ⅰ　(33.08)
荷叶饮Ⅱ　Heye Yin Ⅱ　(54.11)
荷叶茶　Heye Cha　(02.06)
荷叶减肥茶　Heye Jianfei Cha　(02.07)
荸荠内金饮　Biqi Neijin Yin　(36.07)
荸荠茅根茶　Biqi Maogen Cha　(47.15)
荸荠茶　Biqi Cha　(27.13)
荸藕茅根饮　Bi Ou Maogen Yin　(46.04)
莱菔子饮　Laifuzi Yin　(13.17)
莲芯茶　Lianxin Cha　(47.19)
莲花茶叶茶　Lianhua Chaye Cha　(20.25)
莲蓬茶　Lianpeng Cha　(51.21)
蚕豆壳茶　Candouke Cha　(37.18)
蚕豆花冰糖茶　Candouhua Bingtang Cha　(33.14)
蚕豆花茶　Candouhua Cha　(23.47)
蚕豆饮　Candou Yin　(37.17)
蚕茧茶　Canjian Cha　(26.13)
都梁茶　Duliang Cha　(17.12)
高粱叶茶　Gaoliangye Cha　(28.09)

十一画

减肥茶 I　Jianfei Cha I　(02.08)
减肥茶 II　Jianfei Cha II　(02.09)
望江南茶　Wangjiangnan Cha　(23.28)
淡竹叶灯心茶　Danzhuye Dengxin Cha　(35.23)
淡盐糖水　Danyan Tangshui　(18.35)
淮山药茶　Huaishanyao Cha　(26.10)
清心止血饮　Qingxin Zhixue Yin　(51.17)
清心止嗽茶　Qingxin Zhisou Cha　(21.41)
清肝利黄茶　Qinggan Lihuang Cha　(27.12)
清明柳叶速溶饮　Qingming Liuye Surongyin　(35.22)
清咽四味茶　Qingyan Siwei Cha　(20.17)
清咽饮 I　Qingyan Yin I　(08.06)
清咽饮 II　Qingyan Yin II　(20.16)
清络饮　Qingluo Yin　(18.28)
清热理气茶　Qingre Liqi Cha　(23.27)
清眩饮　Qingxuan Yin　(31.02)
清淋茶　Qinglin Cha　(35.21)
清喉茶　Qinghou Cha　(08.07)
清暑明目茶　Qingshu Mingmu Cha　(18.32)
清暑茶 I　Qingshu Cha I　(18.29)
清暑茶 II　Qingshu Cha II　(18.30)
清暑茶 III　Qingshu Cha III　(18.31)
清暑益气饮　Qingshu Yiqi Yin　(18.34)
清暑解毒茶　Qingshu Jiedu Cha　(18.33)
清燥润肺饮 I　Qingzao Runfei Yin I　(21.42)
清燥润肺饮 II　Qingzao Runfei Yin II　(21.43)
猪毛菜茶　Zhumaocai Cha　(23.41)
甜菜茶　Tiancai Cha　(47.16)

绿合海糖茶 Lu He Hai Tang Cha (20.22)
绿豆大蒜饮 Ludou Dasuan Yin (43.05)
绿豆芽白皮饮 Ludouya Baipi Yin (34.11)
绿豆芽白糖饮 Ludouya Baitang Yin (35.28)
绿豆饮 Ludou Yin (28.14)
绿豆菜心饮 Ludou Caixin Yin (46.05)
绿豆蜂蜜饮 Ludou Fengmi Yin (18.40)
绿豆酸梅茶 Ludou Suanmei Cha (18.39)
绿茶 Lucha (44.05)
绿茶合欢饮 Lucha Hehuan Yin (08.11)
绿茶梅花饮 Lucha Meihua Yin (20.21)
绿茶蜜饮 Lucha Mi Yin (30.22)
绿萼梅茶 Luemei Cha (12.11)
羚羊菊花茶 Lingyang Juhua Cha (03.10)
菊花龙井茶 Juhua Longjing Cha (24.08)
菊花茶 Juhua Cha (24.07)
菊花钩藤饮 I Juhua Gouteng Yin (23.29)
菊花钩藤饮 II Juhua Gouteng Yin (23.30)
菊花根茶 Juhuagen Cha (55.07)
菊楂决明饮 Ju Zha Jueming Yin (25.05)
菊槐绿茶饮 Ju Huai Lucha Yin (23.31)
菊藤茶 Ju Teng Cha (23.32)
菖蒲茶 Changpu Cha (06.06)
菝葜叶茶 Baqiaye Cha (26.12)
菟丝子茶 Tusizi Cha (11.05)
菟丝草茶 Tusicao Cha (27.17)
菩提树根茶 Putishugen Cha (37.13)
萝卜叶鸡蛋饮 Luoboye Jidan Yin (13.30)
萝卜叶茶 I Luoboye Cha I (13.29)

萝卜叶茶 II Luoboye Cha II   (32.07)
萝卜饴糖饮 Luobo Yitang Yin   (21.64)
萝卜姜蜜茶 Luobo Jiang Mi Cha   (30.29)
萝卜茶 I Luobo Cha I   (21.63)
萝卜茶 II Luobo Cha II   (30.28)
萝卜糖姜饮 Luobo Tang Jiang Yin   (20.29)
萝芙木根茶 Luofumugen Cha   (23.42)
野秋根茶 Yeshugen Cha   (18.36)
野菊花茶 Yejuhua Cha   (53.02)
银杏叶茶 Yinxingye Cha   (25.06)
银花甘草茶 Yinhua Gancao Cha   (45.04)
银花地丁茶 Yinhua Diding Cha   (53.03)
银花芦根饮 Yinhua Lugen Cha   (21.55)
银花柿霜饮 Yinhua Shishuang Yin   (44.06)
银花绿豆茶 Yinhua L(dou Cha   (19.03)
银花薄黄饮 Yinhua Bo Huang Yin   (46.06)
银花露茶 Yinhualu Cha   (19.02)
银麦甘桔饮 Yin Mai Gan Jie Yin (08.10)
银菊茶 Yin Ju Cha   (23.37)
银蝉饮 Yin Chan Yin   (47.22)
雪梨饮 Xueli Yin   (18.37)
雪羹汤 Xuegeng Tang   (21.44)
黄瓜叶速溶饮 Huangguaye Surongyin   (17.11)
黄瓜花茶 Huangguahua Cha   (55.08)
黄瓜藤茶 Huangguateng Cha   (23.33)
黄芩茶 Huangqin Cha   (03.11)
黄花菜马齿苋饮 Huanghuacai Machixian Yin   (03.12)
黄花菜红糖饮 Huanghuacai Hongtang Yin   (34.05)
黄花菜饮 Huanghuacai Yin   (33.10)

黄豆皮饮 Huangdoupi Yin （39.05）
黄连食醋白糖山楂饮 Huanglian Shicu Baitang Shanzha Yin （28.12）
黄精茶 Huangjing Cha （05.11）

十二画

棉壳茶 Mianke Cha （13.21）
棕榈花茶 Zongluhua Cha （30.21）
棕榈槐花茶 Zonglu Huaihua Cha （24.09）
椒梅茶 Jiao Mei Cha （43.03）
款冬花茶 Kuandonghua Cha （21.47）
滋胃和中茶 Ziwei Hezhong Cha （21.51）
滑石红糖茶 Huashi Hongtang Cha （27.18）
焦大麦茶 Jiaodamai Cha （18.38）
番泻叶茶 Fanxieye Cha （39.06）
硝磺茶 Xiao Huang Cha （27.14）
紫苏叶茶 Zisuye Cha （14.12）
紫苏姜橘饮 Zisu Jiang Ju Yin （54.12）
紫草根茶 Zicaogen Cha （47.18）
腊梅绿豆饮 Lamei Ludou Yin （47.25）
萱草根茶 Xuancaogen Cha （37.14）
葛根茶 Gegen Cha （24.10）
葛根槐花茶 Gegen Huaihua Cha （23.35）
葡萄茶 Putao Cha （38.06）
葡萄须饮 Putaoxu Yin （54.13）
葫芦茶冰糖饮 Hulucha Bingtang Yin （21.53）
葱白琥珀饮 Congbai Hupo Yin （36.08）
葱姜饮Ⅰ Cong Jiang Yin Ⅰ （14.13）
葱姜饮Ⅱ Cong Jiang Yin Ⅱ （10.12）

葱豉芦根饮 Cong Chi Lugen Yin (17.13)
葱豉饮 Cong Chi Yin (14.16)
葱豉茶 I Cong Chi Cha I (14.14)
葱豉茶 II Cong Chi Cha II (14.15)
葱椒饮 Cong Jiao Yin (10.13)
葵花茶 Kuihua Cha (48.04)
葵髓茶 Kuisui Cha (41.05)
隔山消白糖饮 Geshanxiao Baitang Yin (13.22)
雄花茶 Xionghua Cha (27.15)
黑白茶 Hei Bai Cha (51.18)
黑芝麻茶 Heizhima Cha (21.49)
黑豆红花饮 Heidou Honghua Yin (51.19)

十三画

暖胃茶 Nuanwei Cha (10.11)
榆皮车前茶 Yupi Cheqian Cha (21.52)
槐叶茶 Huaiye Cha (34.08)
槐花饮 Huaihua Yin (34.07)
槐花茶 Huaihua Cha (23.36)
槐芽茶 Huaiya Cha (34.10)
槐角茶 Huaijiao Cha (34.09)
槐菊茶 Huai Ju Cha (11.06)
满天星茶 Mantianxing Cha (35.25)
粳稻根饮 Jingdaogen Yin (37.15)
蒲公英茶 Pugongying Cha (35.26)
蓄兰茶 Xu Lan Cha (37.16)
蜂蜜木瓜饮 Fengmi Mugua Yin (34.06)
蜂蜜饮 Fengmi Yin (39.08)
蜂蜜茶 I Fengmi Cha I (20.20)

蜂蜜茶Ⅱ　Fengmi Cha Ⅱ　(39.07)

十四画

嫩肤饮　Nenfu Yin　(04.03)
榕树叶茶　Rongshuye Cha　(27.19)
榧子茶　Feizi Cha　(43.04)
槟榔饮　Binglang Yin　(13.26)
蔗菊茶　Zhe Ju Cha　(18.42)
蔷薇根茶　Qiangweigen Cha　(13.25)
豨莶草茶　Xixiancao Cha　(23.38)
酸石榴饮　Suanshiliu Yin　(21.54)
酸浆草茶　Suanjiangcao Cha　(20.23)
酸梅茶　Suanmei Cha　(18.41)
鲜生地饮　Xianshengdi Yin　(47.23)
鲜萝卜饮　Xianluobo Yin　(47.24)

十五画

橄榄白萝卜茶　Ganlan Bailuobo Cha　(20.28)
橄榄冰糖饮　Ganlan Bingtang Yin　(20.27)
熟军苦丁茶　Shujun Kuding Cha　(39.09)
蝶菊茶蜜饮　Die Ju Cha Mi Yin (20.26)
醋浸生姜饮　Cuqin Shengjiang Yin　(28.13)

十六画

橘叶饮　Juye Yin　(12.13)
橘叶荔梗茶　Juye Ligeng Cha　(51.22)
橘皮竹茹茶　Jupi Zhuru Cha　(54.14)
橘皮饮　Jupi Yin　(21.57)

橘皮茶Ⅰ　Jupi Cha Ⅰ　(21.58)
橘皮茶Ⅱ　Jupi Cha Ⅱ　(24.11)
橘朴茶　Ju Pu Cha　(12.12)
橘红茯苓饮　Juhong Fuling Yin　(23.39)
橘红茶　Juhong Cha　(21.59)
橘杏丝瓜饮　Ju Xing Sigua Yin　(23.40)
橘花茶　Juhua Cha　(10.14)
橘枣饮　Ju Zao Yin　(13.23)
橙子蜂蜜饮　Chengzi Fengmi Yin　(13.24)
糖蜜红茶饮　Tang Mi Hongcha Yin　(29.03)
糖糟茶　Tangzao Cha　(10.15)
薄荷芦根饮　Bohe Lugen Yin　(15.14)
薄荷砂糖饮　Bohe Shatang Yin　(15.15)
薄荷茶Ⅰ　Bohe Cha Ⅰ　(15.12)
薄荷茶Ⅱ　Bohe Cha Ⅱ　(15.13)
薏米防风饮　Yimi Fangfeng Yin　(14.17)
薏苡仁汤　Yiyiren Tang　(36.09)
薏苡叶茶　Yiyiye Cha　(10.16)
薏苡根饮　Yiyigen Yin　(51.23)
螃蟹饮　Pangxie Yin　(27.20)

十七画

檑茶Ⅰ　Lei Cha Ⅰ　(05.13)
檑茶Ⅱ　Lei Cha Ⅱ　(05.14)
糠壳老茶　Kangkelao Cha　(35.30)

十八画

藕节茅根茶　Oujie Maogen Cha　(33.13)
藕节茶　Oujie Cha　(33.12)

藕橘饮 Ouju Yin （41.06）

十九画
藿香白蔻饮 Huoxiang Baikou Yin （14.20）
藿香芦根饮 Huoxiang Lugen Yin （17.16）
藿香苡仁饮 Huoxiang Yiren Yin （31.03）
藿香饮 Huoxiang Yin （17.15）
藿香夏枯草茶 Huoxiang Xiakucao Cha （18.49）

二十画
糯米草茶 Nuomicao Cha （26.14）
糯稻杆茶 Nuodaogan Cha （26.15）
糯稻根茶 Nuodaogen Cha （38.07）
糯稻根须饮 Nuodaogenxu Yin （35.31）

Index (Pinyin)

A

Aiye Cha　艾叶茶　(10.05)
Anshen Cha　安神茶　(07.01)

B

Badou Cha　巴豆茶　(24.01)
Baibu Siwei Yin　百部四味饮　(21.16)
Baicai Ludouya Yin　白菜绿豆芽饮　(14.06)
Baicaigen Yin　白菜根饮　(16.03)
Baiguo Dongguazi Yin　白果冬瓜子饮　(35.06)
Baihe Cha　百合茶　(08.03)
Baijie Cha　百解茶　(18.15)
Baikou Cha　白蔻茶　(13.07)
Bailiangjin Cha　百两金茶　(20.08)
Baimaogen Cha　白茅根茶　(32.04)
Baimaohua Cha　白茅花茶　(32.03)
Baitang Cha　白糖茶　(29.01)
Baitouweng Cha　白头翁茶　(47.04)
Baiyangshupi Cha　白杨树皮茶　(16.04)
Baiyaojian Cha　百药煎茶　(21.15)
Baizhuye Cha　白术叶茶　(38.03)
Baiziren Cha　柏子仁茶　(07.02)
Banbianqian Cha　半边钱茶　(35.07)
Banlangen Cha　板蓝根茶　(16.05)

Banlangenhua Cha　板蓝根花茶　(46.03)
Baqiaye Cha　菝葜叶茶　(26.12)
Baxian Cha　八仙茶　(05.01)
Bi Ou Maogen Yin　荸藕茅根饮　(46.04)
Bianbaiye Cha　扁柏叶茶　(21.33)
Biandou Shanyao Cha　扁豆山药茶　(52.02)
Biandou Yiwei Yin　扁豆益胃饮　(28.08)
Bianxu Cha　扁蓄茶　(35.24)
Binglang Yin　槟榔饮　(13.26)
Bingtang Muhudie Yin　冰糖木蝴蝶饮　(20.09)
Biqi Cha　荸荠茶　(27.13)
Biqi Maogen Cha　荸荠茅根茶　(47.15)
Biqi Neijin Yin　荸荠内金饮　(36.07)
Bohe Cha I　薄荷茶 I　(15.12)
Bohe Cha II　薄荷茶 II　(15.13)
Bohe Lugen Yin　薄荷芦根饮　(15.14)
Bohe Shatang Yin　薄荷砂糖饮　(15.15)

C

Candou Yin　蚕豆饮　(37.17)
Candouhua Bingtang Cha　蚕豆花冰糖茶　(33.14)
Candouhua Cha　蚕豆花茶　(23.47)
Candouke Cha　蚕豆壳茶　(37.18)
Cangerzi Cha　苍耳子茶　(15.11)
Cangzhu Guanzhong Cha　苍术贯仲茶　(16.10)
Canjian Cha　蚕茧茶　(26.13)
Caojueming Cha　草决明茶　(03.09)
Cebaiye Cha　侧柏叶茶　(23.25)
Cha Lan Hai Mi Yin　茶榄海蜜饮　(08.05)

Chai Gan Maogen Cha　柴甘茅根茶　(27.04)
Chai Lu Cha　柴芦茶　(47.14)
Changpu Cha　菖蒲茶　(06.06)
Chashugen Cha　茶树根茶　(44.04)
Che Xing Pipa Cha　车杏枇杷茶　(47.07)
Chencangmi Shibingshuang Cha　陈仓米柿饼霜茶　(13.18)
Chencu Cha　陈醋茶　(30.18)
Chengzi Fengmi Yin　橙子蜂蜜饮　(13.24)
Chenming Yin　陈茗饮　(13.16)
Chenpi Yin　陈皮饮　(21.45)
Cheqian Fengmi Yin　车前蜂蜜饮　(30.12)
Cheqian Haijin Yin　车前海金饮　(35.14)
Cheqiancao Cha　车前草茶　(37.09)
Cheqiangen Cha　车前根茶　(21.24)
Cheqianzi Cha　车前子茶　(17.05)
Chichengliu Cha　赤柽柳茶　(47.06)
Chixiaodou Yin　赤小豆饮　(50.02)
Chuanbei Laifu Cha　川贝莱菔茶　(21.07)
Chuanbei Xingren Yin　川贝杏仁饮　(21.08)
Chuanxiong Tang Cha　川芎糖茶　(14.02)
Cimeigen Cha　刺玫根茶　(51.09)
Ciwujia Cha　刺五加茶　(05.08)
Cong Chi Cha I　葱豉茶 I　(14.14)
Cong Chi Cha II　葱豉茶 II　(14.15)
Cong Chi Lugen Yin　葱豉芦根饮　(17.13)
Cong Chi Yin　葱豉饮　(14.16)
Cong Jiang Yin I　葱姜饮 I　(10.12)
Cong Jiang Yin II　葱姜饮 II　(14.13)
Cong Jiao Yin　葱椒饮　(10.13)

Congbai Hupo Yin 葱白琥珀饮 (36.08)
Cuqin Shengjiang Yin 醋浸生姜饮 (28.13)

D

Dahai Cha 大海茶 (20.01)
Dahai Guazi Cha 大海瓜子茶 (20.02)
Daidaihua Cha 玳玳花茶 (13.11)
Damaijie Cha 大麦秸茶 (37.02)
Danggui Buxue Yin 当归补血饮 (05.12)
Dangshen Hongzao Cha 党参红枣茶 (07.06)
Dangshen Huangmi Cha 党参黄米茶 (05.16)
Danpi Jingchang Cha 丹皮京菖茶 (11.02)
Danshen Cha 丹参茶 (25.01)
Danyan Tangshui 淡盐糖水 (18.35)
Danzhuye Dengxin Cha 淡竹叶灯心茶 (35.23)
Daodou Cha I 刀豆茶 I (10.04)
Daodou Cha II 刀豆茶 II (14.01)
Daodou Yin 刀豆饮 (10.03)
Daqingye Cha 大青叶茶 (16.01)
Dasuan Bingtang Cha 大蒜冰糖茶 (21.05)
Daxiaoji Surongyin 大小蓟速溶饮 (35.04)
Dengxin Shibing Tang 灯心柿饼汤 (35.29)
Dengxin Zhuye Cha 灯心竹叶茶 (07.05)
Dengxincao Cha 灯心草茶 (49.03)
Diandimei Cha 点地梅茶 (08.12)
Die Ju Cha Mi Yin 蝶菊茶蜜饮 (20.26)
Digupi Cha 地骨皮茶 (32.05)
Dijincao Cha 地锦草茶 (30.10)
Dingsou Dingchuan Yin 定嗽定喘饮 (21.26)

Dingxiang Cha　丁香茶　(10.02)
Dingxiang Suanmei Tang　丁香酸梅汤　(18.02)
Diyuye Cha　地榆叶茶　(18.14)
Donggua Maidong Yin　冬瓜麦冬饮　(21.14)
Dongguarang Tang　冬瓜瓤汤　(26.04)
Dongguateng Yin　冬瓜藤饮　(22.01)
Dongguaye Yin　冬瓜叶饮　(30.09)
Dongguazi Lugen Yin　冬瓜子芦根饮　(22.02)
Douchi Cha　豆豉茶　(35.11)
Duliang Cha　都梁茶　(17.12)
Duzhong Cha　杜仲茶　(23.12)

E

Ejiao Nai Yin　阿胶奶饮　(54.06)
Erchen Zhuye Cha　二陈竹叶茶　(37.01)
Ergen Cha　二根茶　(47.01)
Ergen Mai Luo Cha　二根麦萝茶　(13.01)
Erhua Cha　二花茶　(35.02)
Erhua Ju Yu Cha　二花桔萸茶　(12.02)
Erhua Shen Mai Cha　二花参麦茶　(12.01)
Erling Cha　二菱茶　(41.01)
Erlu Hehuan Cha　二绿合欢茶　(12.03)
Erlu Nuzhen Cha　二绿女贞茶　(12.04)
Erlu Yu Bing Cha　二绿玉冰茶　(08.01)
Erxian Sanhua Cha　二鲜三花饮　(18.01)
Erxian Yin　二鲜饮　(35.01)

F

Fangfeng Gancao Cha　防风甘草茶　(15.05)

Fangshu Cha　防暑茶　(18.16)
Fangxiang Huazhuo Yin　芳香化浊饮　(17.06)
Fangyi Qingyan Cha　防疫清咽茶　(20.11)
Fanxieye Cha　番泻叶茶　(39.06)
Feizi Cha　榧子茶　(43.04)
Fengmi Cha I　蜂蜜茶 I　(20.20)
Fengmi Cha II　蜂蜜茶 II　(39.07)
Fengmi Mugua Yin　蜂蜜木瓜饮　(34.06)
Fengmi Yin　蜂蜜饮　(39.08)
Fengyancao Cha　凤眼草茶　(35.27)
Fengyi Dong Mi Yin　凤衣冬蜜饮　(20.24)
Foercao Cha　佛耳草茶　(36.04)
Foshou Cha　佛手茶　(12.05)
Foshou Zao Tang　佛手枣汤　(12.06)
Fufang Guanzhong Cha　复方贯仲茶　(16.09)
Fumai Magen Cha　浮麦麻根茶　(38.05)
Fupenzi Cha　复盆子茶　(05.15)
Fuping Cha　浮萍茶　(47.13)

G

Gan Jie Surongyin　甘桔速溶饮　(20.04)
Gan Zhu Cha　甘竹茶　(35.05)
Gancao Cu Cha　甘草醋茶　(21.12)
Gancao Shengjiang Tang　甘草生姜汤　(21.13)
Ganjiang Yin　干姜饮　(10.07)
Ganlan Bailuobo Cha　橄榄白萝卜茶　(20.28)
Ganlan Bingtang Yin　橄榄冰糖饮　(20.27)
Ganlu Cha　甘露茶　(13.06)
Ganzhe Cha　甘蔗茶　(09.07)

Gaoliangye Cha　高梁叶茶　(28.09)
Gaoluye Cha　皋芦叶茶　(26.08)
Gegen Cha　葛根茶　(24.10)
Gegen Huaihua Cha　葛根槐花茶　(23.35)
Geshanxiao Baitang Yin　隔山消白糖饮　(13.22)
Gouqi Cha　枸杞茶　(03.07)
Gouqi Wuweizi Cha　枸杞五味子茶　(05.09)
Gouteng Cha　钩藤茶　(23.34)
Gualou Cha　瓜蒌茶　(22.03)
Guanzhong Banlangen Cha　贯仲板兰根茶　(45.03)
Guanzhong Cha　贯仲茶　(16.08)
Guanzhong Sigualuo Cha　贯仲丝瓜络茶　(47.21)
Gui Jiang Hongtang Cha　桂姜红糖饮　(51.16)
Guipi Shanzha Yin　桂皮山楂饮　(10.06)
Gujing Juhua Yin　谷精菊花饮　(03.04)
Gupiteng Cha　谷皮藤茶　(36.05)
Gusuibu Cha　骨碎补茶　(21.40)
Guyalu Cha　谷芽露茶　(13.08)

H

Haidai Cha　海带茶　(40.03)
Haijinshacao Cha　海金砂草茶　(37.12)
Haizao Cha　海藻茶　(40.02)
Hanliancao Cha　旱莲草茶　(35.12)
Hanliancao Hongzao Tang　旱莲草红枣汤　(34.03)
Hanqin Cheqian Cha　旱芹车前茶　(23.11)
He Yu Cha　诃玉茶　(20.19)
Hei Bai Cha　黑白茶　(51.18)
Heidou Honghua Yin　黑豆红花饮　(51.19)

Heizhima Cha　黑芝麻茶　(21.49)
Heshouwu Cha　何首乌茶　(04.01)
Heye Cha　荷叶茶　(02.06)
Heye Jianfei Cha　荷叶减肥茶　(02.07)
Heye Yin I　荷叶饮 I　(33.08)
Heye Yin II　荷叶饮 II　(54.11)
Hongchaye Cha　红茶叶茶　(54.08)
Honggaolianghua Cha　红高粱花茶　(51.11)
Hongtang Jiang Zao Cha　红糖姜枣茶　(51.12)
Hongtang Hujiao Cha　红糖胡椒茶　(55.02)
Hongzao Cha I　红枣茶 I　(05.10)
Hongzao Cha II　红枣茶 II　(49.02)
Houpuhua Cha　厚朴花茶　(12.09)
Huafen Cha　花粉茶　(09.11)
Huai Ju Cha　槐菊茶　(11.06)
Huaihua Cha　槐花茶　(23.36)
Huaihua Yin　槐花饮　(34.07)
Huaijiao Cha　槐角茶　(34.09)
Huaishanyao Cha　淮山药茶　(26.10)
Huaiya Cha　槐芽茶　(34.10)
Huaiye Cha　槐叶茶　(34.08)
Huangdoupi Yin　黄豆皮饮　(39.05)
Huangguahua Cha　黄瓜花茶　(55.08)
Huangguateng Cha　黄瓜藤茶　(23.33)
Huangguaye Surongyin　黄瓜叶速溶饮　(17.11)
Huanghuacai Hongtang Yin　黄花菜红糖饮　(34.05)
Huanghuacai Machixian Yin　黄花菜马齿苋饮　(03.12)
Huanghuacai Yin　黄花菜饮　(33.10)
Huangjing Cha　黄精茶　(05.11)

Huanglian Shicu Baitang Shanzha Yin 黄连食醋白糖山楂饮 (28.12)
Huangqin Cha 黄芩茶 (03.11)
Huajuhong Cha 化橘红茶 (21.38)
Huasheng Hongzao Cha 花生红枣茶 (06.04)
Huashengquancao Cha 花生全草茶 (23.14)
Huashi Hongtang Cha 滑石红糖茶 (27.18)
Huixiang Cha 茴香茶 (42.02)
Hulucha Bingtang Yin 葫芦茶冰糖饮 (21.53)
Huluobo Dazao Yin 胡萝卜大枣饮 (21.29)
Huluobo Yin 胡萝卜饮 (47.10)
Huluobo Yuansui Yin 胡萝卜芫荽饮 (47.11)
Huluoboying Yin 胡萝卜缨饮 (55.04)
Huoxiang Baikou Yin 藿香白蔻饮 (14.20)
Huoxiang Lugen Yin 藿香芦根饮 (17.16)
Huoxiang Xiakucao Cha 藿香夏枯草茶 (18.49)
Huoxiang Yin 藿香饮 (17.15)
Huoxiang Yiren Yin 藿香苡仁饮 (31.03)
Hutongye Cha 胡桐叶茶 (23.15)
Huzhangye Cha 虎杖叶茶 (48.02)

J

Jiajian Sanhua Yin 加减三花饮 (26.06)
Jiajian Qingzao Runfei Yin 加减清燥润肺饮 (20.07)
Jiajian Renshen Wumei Tang 加减人参乌梅汤 (28.02)
Jiajian Shigao Yin 加减石膏饮 (17.03)
Jiajian Xiangru Yin 加减香薷饮 (17.04)
Jiajian Xiaoji Yin 加减小蓟饮 (35.08)
Jianfei Cha I 减肥茶 I (02.08)
Jianfei Cha II 减肥茶 II (02.09)

Jiang Ai Hongtang Yin　姜艾红糖饮　(51.14)
Jiang Cha Surongyin　姜茶速溶饮　(30.26)
Jiang Cha Wumei Yin　姜茶乌梅饮　(30.27)
Jiang Cha Yin　姜茶饮　(30.25)
Jiang Tang Cha I　姜糖茶 I　(14.09)
Jiang Tang Cha II　姜糖茶 II　(30.24)
Jiang Tang Suye Yin　姜糖苏叶饮　(14.10)
Jiang Tang Yin I　姜糖饮 I　(14.08)
Jiang Tang Yin II　姜糖饮 II　(21.32)
Jiang Zao Yin I　姜枣饮 I　(21.31)
Jiang Zao Yin II　姜枣饮 II　(30.23)
Jiangya Cha I　降压茶 I　(23.17)
Jiangya Cha II　降压茶 II　(23.18)
Jiangzhi Cha　降脂茶　(25.04)
Jianlan Cha　建兰茶　(54.09)
Jianpi Yin　健脾饮　(30.19)
Jianqu Cha　建曲茶　(18.24)
Jianwei Cha I　健胃茶 I　(10.09)
Jianwei Cha II　健胃茶 II　(10.10)
Jianwei Cha III　健胃茶 III　(28.10)
Jianwei Cha IV　健胃茶 IV　(28.11)
Jianwei Fangai Cha　健胃防癌茶　(41.03)
Jiao Mei Cha　椒梅茶　(43.03)
Jiaodamai Cha　焦大麦茶　(18.38)
Jiawei Huaihua Yin　加味槐花饮　(34.02)
Jiawei Juhua Cha　加味菊花茶　(15.04)
Jiawei Sanqi Yin　加味三七饮　(33.06)
Jicai Cha　荠菜茶　(23.43)
Jidanhua Cha　鸡蛋花茶　(18.46)

Jidanqing Baitang Yin 鸡蛋清白糖饮 (32.06)
Jiecai Cha 芥菜茶 (15.06)
Jiegeng Gancao Cha 桔梗甘草茶 (21.39)
Jiguanhua Cha 鸡冠花茶 (52.04)
Jiguanhua Ouzhi Surongyin 鸡冠花藕汁速溶饮 (52.05)
Jigucao Cha 鸡骨草茶 (18.45)
Jin Ji Yin 金鸡饮 (27.02)
Jingdaogen Yin 粳稻根饮 (37.15)
Jinhua Mujing Cha 金花牡荆茶 (18.18)
Jinjijiaocao Cha 金鸡脚草茶 (18.19)
Jinju Cha 金橘茶 (13.10)
Jinqiancao Cha 金钱草茶 (36.06)
Jinsuo Cha 金锁茶 (20.12)
Jinyinhua Cha 金银花茶 (18.17)
Jisu Yin 鸡苏饮 (17.14)
Jixuecao Cha 积雪草茶 (18.43)
Ju Huai Lucha Yin 菊槐绿茶饮 (23.31)
Ju Jiang Cha 桔姜茶 (14.11)
Ju Pu Cha 橘朴茶 (12.12)
Ju Teng Cha 菊藤茶 (23.32)
Ju Xing Sigua Yin 橘杏丝瓜饮 (23.40)
Ju Zao Yin 橘枣饮 (13.23)
Ju Zha Jueming Yin 菊楂决明饮 (25.05)
Juanbai Cha 卷柏茶 (51.05)
Jueming Congrong Cha 决明苁蓉茶 (39.03)
Jueming Juhua Cha 决明菊花茶 (23.10)
Juemingzi Cha 决明子茶 (03.02)
Juhong Cha 橘红茶 (21.59)
Juhong Fuling Yin 橘红茯苓饮 (23.39)

Juhua Cha　菊花茶　(24.07)
Juhua Cha　橘花茶　(10.14)
Juhua Gouteng Yin I　菊花钩藤饮 I　(23.29)
Juhua Gouteng Yin II　菊花钩藤饮 II　(23.30)
Juhua Longjing Cha　菊花龙井茶　(24.08)
Juhuagen Cha　菊花根茶　(55.07)
Jupi Cha I　橘皮茶 I　(21.58)
Jupi Cha II　橘皮茶 II　(24.11)
Jupi Yin　橘皮饮　(21.57)
Jupi Zhuru Cha　橘皮竹茹茶　(54.14)
Juye Ligeng Cha　橘叶荔梗茶　(51.22)
Juye Yin　橘叶饮　(12.13)

K

Kangkelao Cha　糠壳老茶　(35.30)
Kuandonghua Cha　款冬花茶　(21.47)
Kucihua Cha　苦刺花茶　(18.22)
Kuding Cha　苦丁茶　(23.16)
Kugua Cha　苦瓜茶　(18.21)
Kuguagen Cha　苦瓜根茶　(30.14)
Kuihua Cha　葵花茶　(48.04)
Kuisui Cha　葵髓茶　(41.05)
Kuzhuye Surongyin　苦竹叶速溶饮　(09.12)

L

Laifuzi Yin　莱菔子饮　(13.17)
Lamei Ludou Yin　腊梅绿豆饮　(47.25)
Lei Cha I　擂茶 I　(05.13)
Lei Cha II　擂茶 II　(05.14)

Li Gan Cha　　荔橄茶　(42.03)
Lianhua Chaye Cha　　莲花茶叶茶　(20.25)
Lianpeng Cha　　莲蓬茶　(51.21)
Lianqiao Cha　　连翘茶　(39.04)
Lianxin Cha　　莲芯茶　(47.19)
Lingyang Juhua Cha　　羚羊菊花茶　(03.10)
Lingzhi Bohe Yin　　灵芝薄荷饮　(01.05)
Lingzhi Cha　　灵芝茶　(05.17)
Lipi Cha　　梨皮茶　(47.17)
Liuhe Cha　　六和茶　(30.06)
Liuye Cha (Ganmao Cha)　　六叶茶(感冒茶)　(15.03)
Liyan Cha　　利咽茶　(20.10)
Longyan Cha　　龙眼茶　(06.07)
Longyan Yangshen Yin　　龙眼洋参饮　(01.04)
Longyan Zaoren Yin　　龙眼枣仁饮　(06.08)
Lu He Hai Tang Cha　　绿合海糖茶　(20.22)
Lu Ju Cha　　芦菊茶　(47.27)
Lucha　　绿茶　(44.05)
Lucha Hehuan Yin　　绿茶合欢饮　(08.11)
Lucha Meihua Yin　　绿茶梅花饮　(20.21)
Lucha Mi Yin　　绿茶蜜饮　(30.22)
Ludou Caixin Yin　　绿豆菜心饮　(46.05)
Ludou Dasuan Yin　　绿豆大蒜饮　(43.05)
Ludou Fengmi Yin　　绿豆蜂蜜饮　(18.40)
Ludou Suanmei Cha　　绿豆酸梅茶　(18.39)
Ludou Yin　　绿豆饮　(28.14)
Ludouya Baipi Yin　　绿豆芽白皮饮　(34.11)
Ludouya Baitang Yin　　绿豆芽白糖饮　(35.28)
Luemei Cha　　绿萼梅茶　(12.11)

Lugen Bingtang Yin　芦根冰糖饮　(17.18)
Lugen Cha　芦根茶　(47.26)
Lugen Yin I　芦根饮 I　(13.27)
Lugen Yin II　芦根饮 II　(13.28)
Lugen Yiren Yin　芦根苡仁饮　(17.17)
Luobo Cha I　萝卜茶 I　(21.63)
Luobo Cha II　萝卜茶 II　(30.28)
Luobo Jiang Mi Cha　萝卜姜蜜茶　(30.29)
Luobo Tang Jiang Yin　萝卜糖姜饮　(20.29)
Luobo Yitang Yin　萝卜饴糖饮　(21.64)
Luoboye Cha I　萝卜叶茶 I　(13.29)
Luoboye Cha II　萝卜叶茶 II　(32.07)
Luoboye Jidan Yin　萝卜叶鸡蛋饮　(13.30)
Luobuma Jianfeicha　罗布麻减肥茶　(02.10)
Luobuma Jiangyacha　罗布麻降压茶　(23.44)
Luobuma Pingchuancha　罗布麻平喘茶　(21.61)
Luobuma Surongyin　罗布麻速溶饮　(23.45)
Luobumaye Cha　罗布麻叶茶　(23.46)
Luofumugen Cha　萝芙木根茶　(23.42)
Luohanguo Shibing Yin　罗汉果柿饼饮　(21.62)
Luohanguo Surongyin　罗汉果速溶饮　(08.13)

M

Mabiancao Cha　马鞭草茶　(27.11)
Machixian Binglang Cha　马齿苋槟榔茶　(30.16)
Machixian Hongtang Cha　马齿苋红糖茶　(35.19)
Machixian Ludou Tang　马齿苋绿豆汤　(30.15)
Machixian Yin　马齿苋饮　(35.18)
Maidong Dihuang Yin　麦冬地黄饮　(41.04)

Maidong Maogen Yin　麦冬茅根饮　(33.09)
Maidong Meizhi Cha　麦冬梅枝茶　(47.20)
Maidong Wumei Yin　麦冬乌梅饮　(26.11)
Maiya Cha　麦芽茶　(13.19)
Maiya shanzha Yin　麦芽山楂饮　(13.20)
Malan Cha　马兰茶　(52.03)
Malan Tang Yin　马兰糖饮　(48.03)
Mangchangcao Cha　盲肠草茶　(16.06)
Mantianxing Cha　满天星茶　(35.25)
Maogen Boluo Surongyin　茅根菠萝速溶饮　(37.11)
Maogen Cheqian Yin　茅根车前饮　(35.16)
Maogen Jicai Cha　茅根荠菜茶　(47.12)
Maogen Zhuzhe Yin　茅根竹蔗饮　(35.17)
Maoshancha (Xiangfengcha)　毛山茶(香风茶)　(21.10)
Maotaogan Cha　毛桃干茶　(38.02)
Meiguihua Cha　玫瑰花茶　(12.07)
Meiguihua Dengxin Cha　玫瑰花灯心茶　(35.15)
Mianke Cha　棉壳茶　(13.21)
Mingmu Cha I　明目茶 I　(03.05)
Mingmu Cha II　明目茶 II　(03.06)
Molihua Cha　茉莉花茶　(18.23)
Muer Zhima Cha　木耳芝麻茶　(34.01)
Mujinhua Surongyin　木槿花速溶饮　(30.05)

N

Nanguadi Cha　南瓜蒂茶　(54.07)
Nanguaxu Cha　南瓜须茶　(55.05)
Nanguazi Cha　南瓜籽茶　(43.01)
Naoqing Cha　脑清茶　(01.03)

Nenfu Yin　嫩肤饮　(04.03)
Niaogan Cha　尿感茶　(37.10)
Niaoliqing Cha　尿利清茶　(35.13)
Ningmeng Surongyin　柠檬速溶饮　(18.44)
Niubangye Cha　牛蒡叶茶　(53.01)
Niubangzi Cha　牛蒡子茶　(15.02)
Niubangzi Lugen Cha　牛蒡子芦根茶　(47.02)
Niujincao Cha　牛筋草茶　(45.01)
Niunai Cha　牛奶茶　(02.04)
Niuru Yin　牛乳饮　(06.03)
Nuanwei Cha　暖胃茶　(10.11)
Nuodaogan Cha　糯稻杆茶　(26.15)
Nuodaogen Cha　糯稻根茶　(38.07)
Nuodaogenxu Yin　糯稻根须饮　(35.31)
Nuomicao Cha　糯米草茶　(26.14)

O
Oujie Cha　藕节茶　(33.12)
Oujie Maogen Cha　藕节茅根茶　(33.13)
Ouju Yin　藕橘饮　(41.06)

P
Pangdahai Bingtang Cha　胖大海冰糖茶　(08.04)
Pangxie Yin　螃蟹饮　(27.20)
Pei Xiang Cha　佩香茶　(13.09)
Pinggan Qingre Cha　平肝清热茶　(11.03)
Pipa Yin　枇杷饮　(28.05)
Pugongying Cha　蒲公英茶　(35.26)
Putao Cha　葡萄茶　(38.06)

Putaoxu Yin　葡萄须饮　(54.13)
Putishugen Cha　菩提树根茶　(37.13)

Q

Qi Ju Cha　杞菊茶　(03.03)
Qiangweigen Cha　蔷薇根茶　(13.25)
Qincai Daji Yin　芹菜大戟饮　(51.06)
Qincaigen Cha　芹菜根茶　(23.13)
Qincaigen Chenpi Cha　芹菜根陈皮茶　(21.25)
Qingcijian Cha　青刺尖茶　(44.03)
Qinggan Lihuang Cha　清肝利黄茶　(27.12)
Qingguo Lugen Cha　青果芦根茶　(47.08)
Qingguo Shiliu Cha　青果石榴茶　(42.01)
Qinghao Danpi Cha　青蒿丹皮茶　(51.08)
Qinghou Cha　清喉茶　(08.07)
Qinglin Cha　清淋茶　(35.21)
Qingluo Yin　清络饮　(18.28)
Qingming Liuye Surongyin　清明柳叶速溶饮　(35.22)
Qingpi Maiya Yin　青皮麦芽饮　(12.08)
Qingre Liqi Cha　清热理气茶　(23.27)
Qingshu Cha I　清暑茶 I　(18.29)
Qingshu Cha II　清暑茶 II　(18.30)
Qingshu Cha III　清暑茶 III　(18.31)
Qingshu Jiedu Cha　清暑解毒茶　(18.33)
Qingshu Mingmu Cha　清暑明目茶　(18.32)
Qingshu Yiqi Yin　清暑益气饮　(18.34)
Qingxiangzi Surongyin　青葙子速溶饮　(24.05)
Qingxin Zhisou Cha　清心止嗽茶　(21.41)
Qingxin Zhixue Yin　清心止血饮　(51.17)

Qingxuan Yin　清眩饮　(31.02)
Qingyan Siwei Cha　清咽四味茶　(20.17)
Qingyan Yin I　清咽饮 I　(08.06)
Qingyan Yin II　清咽饮 II　(20.16)
Qingzao Runfei Yin I　清燥润肺饮 I　(21.42)
Qingzao Runfei Yin II　清燥润肺饮 II　(21.43)
Qiuli Chungenpi Cha　秋梨椿根皮茶　(34.04)
Qixian Cha　七鲜茶　(18.04)
Qixian Tang　七鲜汤　(18.03)
Qiye Changshou Cha　杞叶长寿茶　(05.06)
Qiye Lugen Yin　七叶芦根饮　(18.05)
Qugouchong Cha　祛钩虫茶　(43.06)
Qushu Qingxin Cha　祛暑清心茶　(18.26)

R

Rendong Xiakucao Cha　忍冬夏枯草茶　(46.02)
Rendongteng Cha　忍冬藤茶　(19.01)
Renshen Cha　人参茶　(01.01)
Renshen Dazao Cha　人参大枣茶　(01.02)
Renshen Gouqi Yin　人参枸杞饮　(11.01)
Renshen Hetao Yin　人参核桃饮　(05.02)
Renshen Shuanghua Cha　人参双花茶　(21.01)
Renshen Tang　人参汤　(06.01)
Renshen Wumei Cha　人参乌梅茶　(09.01)
Renshen Zaoren Tang　人参枣仁汤　(06.02)
Renzicao Cha　人字草茶　(35.03)
Rongshuye Cha　榕树叶茶　(27.19)
Runfei Zhike Cha　润肺止咳茶　(21.56)

S

Sanbai Cha 三白茶 (21.04)
Sanbao Cha 三宝茶 (23.02)
Sanfen Cha 三分茶 (21.03)
Sang Bo Hua Mi Yin 桑薄花蜜饮 (17.10)
Sang Ju Bo Zhu Yin 桑菊薄竹饮 (15.10)
Sang Ju Cha I 桑菊茶 I (15.08)
Sang Ju Cha II 桑菊茶 II (54.10)
Sang Ju Douchi Yin 桑菊豆豉饮 (15.09)
Sang Ju Gouqi Yin 桑菊枸杞饮 (23.22)
Sang Ju Xiangchi Lipi Yin 桑菊香豉梨皮饮 (17.09)
Sang Ju Xingren Cha 桑菊杏仁饮 (21.37)
Sang Mi Cha 桑蜜茶 (18.25)
Sang Xing Douchi Yin 桑杏豆豉饮 (21.36)
Sang Xing Yin 桑杏饮 (21.35)
Sang Yin Cha 桑银茶 (03.08)
Sanggenbaipi Cha 桑根白皮茶 (23.21)
Sangshugen Cha 桑树根茶 (23.20)
Sangye Cha 桑叶茶 (15.07)
Sangye Kuding Cha 桑叶苦丁茶 (51.15)
Sangye Pipa Cha 桑叶枇杷茶 (21.34)
Sangzhi Cha 桑枝茶 (02.05)
Sanhua Jianfei Cha 三花减肥茶 (02.01)
Sanjin Cha 三金茶 (36.01)
Sanqihua Cha 三七花茶 (23.03)
Sanxian Cha I 三鲜茶 I (09.03) (18.07)
Sanxian Cha II 三鲜茶 II (15.01)
Sanxian Cha III 三鲜茶 III (17.01)
Sanxian Yin 三鲜饮 (32.01)

Sanye Cha 三叶茶 (18.06)
Sanzhi Yin 三汁饮 (09.02)
Sanzi Cha 三子茶 (23.01)
Sanzi Yin 三子饮 (21.02)
Sha Mu Ercao Cha 沙母二草茶 (18.20)
Shanbiandoucao Cha 山扁豆草茶 (37.03)
Shanyao Cha 山药茶 (26.01)
Shanzha Cha 山楂茶 (13.02)
Shanzha Hetao Cha 山楂核桃茶 (05.03)
Shanzha Heye Cha 山楂荷叶茶 (18.08)
Shanzha Hongbaitang Cha 山楂红白糖茶 (30.02)
Shanzha Jueming Cha 山楂决明茶 (23.05)
Shanzha Jupi Cha 山楂橘皮茶 (13.03)
Shanzha Maiya Cha 山楂麦芽茶 (50.01)
Shanzha Shenqu Tang 山楂神曲汤 (13.04)
Shanzha Xiangrikui Yin 山楂向日葵饮 (51.01)
Shanzha Yin Ju Cha 山楂银菊茶 (02.03)
Shanzhagen Cha 山楂根茶 (02.02)
Shanzhaye(hua) Cha 山楂叶(花)茶 (23.04)
Sharen Gancao Cha 砂仁甘草茶 (13.12)
Shashen Baihe Yin 沙参百合饮 (21.21)
Shashen Lipi Yin 沙参梨皮饮 (21.22)
Shashen Maidong Yin 沙参麦冬饮 (21.23)
Shashen Zhezhi Yin 沙参蔗汁饮 (38.04)
Shayuanzi Cha 沙苑子茶 (05.07)
Shen Qi Jing 参芪精 (06.05)
Shen Wei Cha 参味茶 (07.03)
Shengdi Qingguo Cha 生地青果茶 (47.03)
Shengdi Shigao Cha 生地石膏茶 (26.05)

Shengjiang Cha　生姜茶　(16.02)
Shengjiang Kouren Tang　生姜蔻仁汤　(31.01)
Shengjin Cha　生津茶　(09.10)
Shengjun Cha　生军茶　(39.01)
Shengmai Yin　生脉饮　(18.13)
Shengshigao Biqi Tang　生石膏荸荠汤　(45.02)
Shenqu Yin　神曲饮　(13.15)
Shenxu Jingchang Cha　参须京菖茶　(11.04)
Shenye Qingguo Cha　参叶青果茶　(08.08)
Shidi Cha　柿蒂茶　(21.28)
Shihu Bingtang Cha　石斛冰糖茶　(09.08)
Shihu Cha　石斛茶　(28.01)
Shihu Ganzhe Yin　石斛甘蔗饮　(09.09)
Shihua Cha　石花茶　(27.01)
Shiliupi Cha　石榴皮茶　(30.08)
Shiliuye Cha　石榴叶茶　(30.07)
Shishuang Sangshen Yin　柿霜桑椹饮　(51.10)
Shiwei Cheqian Cha　石苇车前茶　(36.03)
Shiye Jiangzhi Cha　柿叶降脂茶　(25.03)
Shuanghe Tang　双荷汤　(33.11)
Shuanghe Yin　双核饮　(42.04)
Shuanghua Xing Mi Yin　双花杏蜜饮　(21.60)
Shuanghua Yin　双花饮　(09.14)
Shuangpi Cha　双皮茶　(18.47)
Shuiwenghua Cha　水翁花茶　(17.02)
Shuiwugong Cha　水蜈蚣茶　(48.01)
Shujun Kuding Cha　熟军苦丁茶　(39.09)
Sigua Cha　丝瓜茶　(09.13)
Sigua Surongyin　丝瓜速溶饮　(20.18)

Sigua Yin I　丝瓜饮I　(07.04)
Sigua Yin II　丝瓜饮II　(08.09)
Sigua Zhima Hetao Yin　丝瓜芝麻核桃饮　(50.03)
Siguahua Mi Yin　丝瓜花蜜饮　(21.48)
Sihua Yin　四花饮　(33.05)
Siru Yin　四乳饮　(55.01)
Sitan Zhilou Cha　四炭止漏茶　(51.03)
Siwei Cha　四味茶　(18.12)
Songshupi Cha　松树皮茶　(51.07)
Su Lian Cha　苏连茶　(49.04)
Su Qiang Cha　苏羌茶　(14.19)
Su Xing Tang　苏杏汤　(14.18)
Suanjiangcao Cha　酸浆草茶　(20.23)
Suanmei Cha　酸梅茶　(18.41)
Suanshiliu Yin　酸石榴饮　(21.54)
Suye Bohe Cha　苏叶薄荷茶　(18.50)
Suye Cha　苏叶茶　(08.14)
Suye Shengjiang Cha　苏叶生姜茶　(54.15)

T

Taizi Wumei Yin　太子乌梅饮　(18.11)
Taizinai Yin　太子奶饮　(05.04)
Tang Mi Hongcha Yin　糖蜜红茶饮　(29.03)
Tangzao Cha　糖糟茶　(10.15)
Tiancai Cha　甜菜茶　(47.16)
Tianluo Cha　田螺茶　(26.03)
Tianma Juhua Yin　天麻菊花饮　(23.06)
Tianzhong Cha　天中茶　(14.03)
Tuihuang Yin　退黄饮　(27.10)

Tuniuxi Cha　土牛膝茶　(20.03)
Tusicao Cha　菟丝草茶　(27.17)
Tusizi Cha　菟丝子茶　(11.05)

W

Wangjiangnan Cha　望江南茶　(23.28)
Weikuiyang Cha　胃溃疡茶　(29.02)
Weile Cha　胃乐茶　(12.10)
Weilingxian Cha　威灵仙茶　(20.13)
Wuhuaguo Cha　无花果茶　(21.50)
Wuhuaguo Tang Yin　无花果糖饮　(30.20)
Wuhuaguoye Cha　无花果叶茶　(27.16)
Wujunzi Yin　五君子饮　(33.02)
Wumei Qingshu Yin　乌梅清暑饮　(18.27)
Wumei Yin　乌梅饮　(43.02)
Wupi Yin　五皮饮　(37.04)
Wushen Tang　五神汤　(14.04)
Wushi Cha　午时茶　(14.05)
Wutong Cha　梧桐茶　(23.26)
Wuwei Gouqi Yin　五味枸杞饮　(18.09)
Wuweizi Yin　五味子饮　(09.04)
Wuxian Cha　五鲜茶　(40.01)
Wuye Lugen Cha　五叶芦根茶　(18.10)

X

Xia Ju Cha　夏菊茶　(16.07)
Xiaku Gualuo Yin　夏枯瓜络饮　(12.14)
Xiakucao Cha　夏枯草茶　(23.23)
Xiakucao Heye Cha　夏枯草荷叶茶　(23.24)

Xiancai Cha　苋菜茶　(30.17)
Xiangfu Cha　香附茶　(51.13)
Xiangfu Chuanxiong Cha　香附川芎茶　(24.06)
Xiangjiaogen Cha　香蕉根茶　(23.19)
Xiangrikuigen Cha　向日葵根茶　(35.10)
Xiangrikuihua Cha　向日葵花茶　(37.08)
Xiangrikuijing Yin　向日葵茎饮　(52.01)
Xiangrikuiye Yin　向日葵叶饮　(23.09)
Xiangru Yin　香薷饮　(17.08)
Xiangyuan Cha　香橼茶　(28.07)
Xianhecao Cha　仙鹤草茶　(33.07)
Xianluobo Yin　鲜萝卜饮　(47.24)
Xianshengdi Yin　鲜生地饮　(47.23)
Xiaoer Qixing Cha　小儿七星茶　(13.05)
Xiaohuang Cha　消黄茶　(27.03)
Xiao Huang Cha　硝磺茶　(27.14)
Xiaojigen Cha　小蓟根茶　(33.01)
Xiaoke Cha　消渴茶　(26.07)
Xiaomai Dazao Yin　小麦大枣饮　(21.06)
Xiaoshi Cha　消食茶　(13.14)
Xiaoyan Cha　消炎茶　(20.15)
Xiaozhi Cha　消滞茶　(13.13)
Xigua Jueming Cha　西瓜决明茶　(23.07)
Xiguacuiyi Cha　西瓜翠衣茶　(23.08)
Xiheliu Yin　西河柳饮　(47.05)
Xing Ju Yin I　杏菊饮 I　(24.02)
Xing Ju Yin II　杏菊饮 II　(24.03)
Xing Li Yin　杏梨饮　(21.17)
Xingren Bingtang Yin　杏仁冰糖饮　(21.18)

Xingren Maidong Yin　杏仁麦冬饮　(47.09)
Xingren Nai Cha　杏仁奶茶　(21.19)
Xinyihua Cha　辛夷花茶　(24.04)
Xionghua Cha　雄花茶　(27.15)
Xiqingguo Cha　西青果茶　(08.02)
Xixiancao Cha　豨莶草茶　(23.38)
Xiyangshen Cha　西洋参茶　(05.05)
Xu Lan Cha　蓄兰茶　(37.16)
Xuancaogen Cha　萱草根茶　(37.14)
Xuanfei Yin　宣肺饮　(21.30)
Xuanmai Gan Jie Tang　玄麦甘桔汤　(20.06)
Xuanshen Qingguo Cha　玄参青果茶　(20.05)
Xuanshen Sanhua Yin　玄参三花饮　(46.01)
Xuegeng Tang　雪羹汤　(21.44)
Xueli Yin　雪梨饮　(18.37)
Xunshen Maidong Cha　玄参麦冬茶　(41.02)

Y

Yan Cha　盐茶　(17.20)
Yan Mei Cha　盐梅茶　(47.28)
Yan Ningmeng Cha　盐柠檬茶　(17.19)
Yangru Yin　羊乳饮　(28.04)
Yangtao Surongyin　杨桃速溶饮　(48.05)
Yanhou Cha　咽喉茶　(20.14)
Yaowangcha　药王茶　(18.48)
Yejuhua Cha　野菊花茶　(53.02)
Yeshugen Cha　野秫根茶　(18.36)
Yimi Fangfeng Yin　薏米防风饮　(14.17)
Yimu Tang Cha　益母糖茶　(55.06)

Yin Chan Yin　银蝉饮　(47.22)
Yin Di Cha　茵地茶　(35.20)
Yin Ju Cha　银菊茶　(23.37)
Yin Mai Gan Jie Yin　银麦甘桔饮　(08.10)
Yinchen Cha　茵陈茶　(27.05)
Yinchen Chenpi Cha　茵陈陈皮茶　(27.07)
Yinchen Hongtang Yin　茵陈红糖饮　(27.08)
Yinchen Xiang Lu Cha　茵陈香芦茶　(27.06)
Yinchen Yinhua Yin　茵陈银花饮　(27.09)
Yinhua Bo Huang Yin　银花薄黄饮　(46.06)
Yinhua Diding Cha　银花地丁茶　(53.03)
Yinhua Gancao Cha　银花甘草茶　(45.04)
Yinhua Ludou Cha　银花绿豆茶　(19.03)
Yinhua Lugen Cha　银花芦根饮　(21.55)
Yinhua Shishuang Yin　银花柿霜饮　(44.06)
Yinhualu Cha　银花露茶　(19.02)
Yinxingye Cha　银杏叶茶　(25.06)
Yiren Zhuye Yin　苡仁竹叶饮　(17.07)
Yiwei Cha I　益胃茶 I　(10.08)
Yiwei Cha II　益胃茶 II　(26.09)
Yiwei Shengjiang Yin　一味生姜饮　(10.01)
Yiwei Shuyu Yin　一味薯蓣饮　(30.01)
Yiyigen Yin　薏苡根饮　(51.23)
Yiyiren Tang　薏苡仁汤　(36.09)
Yiyiye Cha　薏苡叶茶　(10.16)
Youpi Cha I　柚皮茶 I　(30.13)
Youpi Cha II　柚皮茶 II　(55.03)
Youzi Jidan Yin　柚子鸡蛋饮　(28.06)
Youzike Heye Yin　柚子壳荷叶饮　(21.27)

Yuansui Cha　芫荽茶　(14.07)
Yuejihua Tang　月季花汤　(51.02)
Yumigenye Cha　玉米根叶茶　(36.02)
Yumihua Cha　玉米花茶　(32.02)
Yuminenyi Cha　玉米嫩衣茶　(54.02)
Yumixin Cha　玉米芯茶　(37.05)
Yumixu Bingtang Cha　玉米须冰糖茶　(33.04)
Yumixu Cha　玉米须茶　(37.06)
Yumixu Chixiaodou Yin　玉米须赤小豆饮　(54.03)
Yumixu Jupi Cha　玉米须桔皮茶　(21.11)
Yumixu Surongyin　玉米须速溶饮　(37.07)
Yupi Cheqian Cha　榆皮车前茶　(21.52)
Yuxingcao Yin　鱼腥草饮　(21.46)
Yuzhu Bohe Yin　玉竹薄荷饮　(03.01)
Yuzhu Cha　玉竹茶　(09.05)
Yuzhu Surongyin　玉竹速溶饮　(25.02)
Yuzhu Wumei Yin　玉竹乌梅饮　(09.06)

Z

Zaojiaya Cha　皂荚芽茶　(21.20)
Zaoshugenpi Cha　枣树根皮茶　(51.20)
Zaoxintu Cha　灶心土茶　(54.05)
Zaoxintu Zhuye Cha　灶心土竹叶茶　(44.02)
Zhe Ju Cha　蔗菊茶　(18.42)
Zhihan Yin　止汗饮　(38.01)
Zhike Cha　止咳茶　(21.09)
Zhima Cha　芝麻茶　(30.11)
Zhima Gouqi Yin　芝麻枸杞饮　(04.02)
Zhima Hetao Cha　芝麻核桃茶　(39.02)

Zhiou Cha　止呕茶　(54.01)
Zhixiaoke Surongyin　止消渴速溶饮　(26.02)
Zhixie Cha I　止泻茶 I　(30.03)
Zhixie Cha II　止泻茶 II　(30.04)
Zhixue Cha　止血茶　(33.03)
Zhu Mao Yin　竹茅饮　(35.09)
Zhuli Cha　竹沥茶　(54.04)
Zhumagen Yin　苎麻根饮　(51.04)
Zhumaocai Cha　猪毛菜茶　(23.41)
Zhuru Lugen Cha　竹茹芦根茶　(28.03)
Zhuye Cha I　竹叶茶 I　(44.01)
Zhuye Cha II　竹叶茶 II　(49.01)
Zicaogen Cha　紫草根茶　(47.18)
Zisu Jiang Ju Yin　紫苏姜橘饮　(54.12)
Zisuye Cha　紫苏叶茶　(14.12)
Ziwei Hezhong Cha　滋胃和中茶　(21.51)
Zonglu Huaihua Cha　棕榈槐花茶　(24.09)
Zongluhua Cha　棕榈花茶　(30.21)

图书在版编目（CIP）数据

中国保健茶饮/党毅主编.-北京：新世界出版社，1999
ISBN 7-80005-554-X
I.中...II.党...III.①茶叶-保键-中国　②茶叶-饮食疗法-中国
IV.R247.1

中国版本图书馆CIP数据核字（1999）第44077号

中 国 保 健 茶 饮

主　　编：党　毅
责任编辑：任玲娟
封面设计：贺玉婷
版式设计：方　维
出版发行：新世界出版社
社　　址：北京阜城门外百万庄路24号
邮政编码：100037
电　　话：0086-10-68994118
传　　真：0086-10-68326679
经　　销：中国国际图书贸易总公司发行
印　　刷：北京晨光印刷厂
开　　本：850 × 1168　1/32
字　　数：150千
印　　张：11.875
版　　次：1999年10月（英）第1版第1次印刷
书　　号：ISBN 7-80005-554-X/G · 187
定　　价：£20.00

17E-3357P